DIVINE
RENOVATION

Beyond
the
Parish

Fr. James Mallon

the WORD
among us®
press

Published by The Word Among Us Press
7115 Guilford Drive, Suite 100
Frederick, Maryland 21704
wau.org

24 23 22 21 20   1 2 3 4 5

ISBN: 978-1-59325-143-7
eISBN: 978-1-59325-162-8

Nihil obstat: +Brian Joseph Dunn
Coadjutor Archbishop of Halifax-Yarmouth
March 4, 2020

Imprimatur: +Brian Joseph Dunn
Coadjutor Archbishop of Halifax-Yarmouth
March 4, 2020

Cover design by Suzanne Earl

Made and printed in the United States of America

Library of Congress Control Number: 2020905014

Praise for *Divine Renovation Beyond the Parish*

"Fr. Mallon provides his usual unsparing and brilliantly honest analysis of the very grave situation we are facing as the Church in the West declines in virtually every measurable area. At the same time, he vigorously presents the case for hope and our ability to do something about our current crisis if we utilize the wisdom that is available, of which this book is abundantly supplied."
—**Ralph Martin, S.T.D.**, president of Renewal Ministries and director of graduate theology programs in the New Evangelization at Sacred Heart Major Seminary

"In this book, Fr. James not only bolsters his reputation as a genuinely visionary leader in global Catholicism, but he bequeaths to us a genuinely viable model for the renewal of the church as transformative mission agency, as well as some really practical tools that will enable leaders to implement real and lasting change."
—**Alan Hirsch**, author of award-winning books, including *5Q*, and founder of the Forge Missional Training Network, 100 Movements, and The 5Q Collective

"Fr. James Mallon's new book, while filled with passion and zeal for the mission of the Church, is also incredibly practical and helpful for laypeople, priests, and bishops seeking new and better ways of bringing Jesus Christ to others. I have seen for myself the transformation of priests and parishes on the Divine Renovation Network and am confident that this book will lead to even more abundant fruit in the lives and ministry of all who read it."
—**+Wilfrid Cardinal Napier O.F.M.**, archbishop of Durban, South Africa

"Theory is one thing, and making fresh approaches work in the real world is quite another. I am so excited for this latest book by Fr. James Mallon because he takes parish renewal further than he ever has before, showing you exactly how to make renovation work in the parish and diocese. Perhaps the only danger in reading this book is that it will remove all your excuses for change and renewal in the name of Jesus, which is exactly what the Church and the world need."
—**Carey Nieuwhof**, founding pastor of Connexus Church and bestselling author

"Fr. Mallon's new book raises challenging questions that, if taken seriously, will explode complacent attitudes, outdated paradigms, and dysfunctional structures. It is the strong medicine we need to follow the Church's call for a "missionary conversion"—a radical evangelical turn outward, in fidelity to Jesus Christ. This book is not for the faint of heart. It is for those who long to see parishes and dioceses flourish as places of vibrant spiritual life and missionary dynamism."
—**Dr. Mary Healy**, professor of Scripture at Sacred Heart Major Seminary

"Perhaps no one has a better perspective on the structural and systematic obstacles that prevent the Church from fulfilling its mission of making disciples as Fr. James Mallon. Read this book for a better understanding of those problems and to discover practical ways to solve them no matter where and how you serve the Church."
—**Fr. Michael White and Tom Corcoran,** coauthors of *Rebuilt* and *Churchmoney*

"Strategies and structures which served the Church well in the past are no longer working. *Beyond the Parish* provides a combination of vision and tactics which can change culture. Any parish or diocese would benefit from what Fr. James Mallon offers here—his diagnosis of the problem and his proposal of a way forward. It is a timely word also to the universal Church."
—**+Mark Coleridge,** archbishop of Brisbane and president of the Australian Catholic Bishops' Conference

"In *Beyond the Parish*, Fr. James Mallon weaves biblical theology, Church teaching, leadership principles, and reflections from his own pastoral experience into a challenging narrative that offers hope for the renewal of the Church. Priests, bishops, and laity eager on becoming and forming missionary disciples will find in it material that is richly rewarding. Highly recommended!"
—**+Terrence Prendergast, SJ,** archbishop of Ottawa

"This exciting book is the fruit of relentless hard work and scientific research based on extensive factual data and grounded on Scripture and theology. I am very happy to recommend it to all my brother bishops."
—**Oswald Cardinal Gracias,** archbishop of Bombay and president of the Catholic Bishops' Conference in India

"Fr. James knows how to portray the present situation of the Church not only as a storm at sea, but he also shows, with great sensitivity, how this divine 'why' can also motivate us today to bring hope into this storm. For all those who dream of a living community of faith, this book will help to make that dream a reality."
—**Urban Federer,** abbot of the Territorial Abbey of Einsiedeln and member of the Swiss Bishops' Conference

"Fr. Mallon understands what it takes to transform a mediocre parish into a dynamic, missionary one, and he understands that parishes need diocesan leadership to transform the Church as a whole."
—**Patrick Lencioni,** cofounder of The Amazing Parish and author of *The Five Dysfunctions of a Team*

What impairs our sight are habits of seeing as well as the mental concomitants of seeing. Our sight is suffused with knowing, instead of feeling painfully the lack of knowing what we see. The principle to be kept in mind is to know what we see rather than to see what we know.

—Abraham Heschel, *The Prophets*[1]

To my father, Ronnie Mallon (1946–2019),
who never settled for the status quo.

Table of Contents

Preface

"Why?"

That word rang out in the small room in the center of Paris, amplified by just a tinge of frustration. My companion, a fellow priest from the south of France, had been telling me about the state of his parish. Clearly, he loved his people, and they loved him. More importantly, however, he was *effective*—at creating a vision, as well as structures and processes that were starting to bring people to life in Jesus Christ. All of that could change though, for as he had just informed me, he was getting ready to wrap things up at that parish and head to his new assignment.

Thus, my question.

Why?

"Why do you have to leave?" I pressed on.

He looked at me with mixture of surprise and confusion. "Because my assignment at this parish is coming to an end, and I have to move on to my next assignment."

"But why?" I asked again.

More confusion—and then some hesitation.

"Because that's what the bishop wants," he replied at last.

I asked once more, "Why?"

"Because that's the policy in my diocese."

My brother priest looked back at me blankly, as if he did not even understand what I was asking. That blank look was not caused by a lack of intellectual firepower. The man sitting with me was intelligent, articulate, and exceptionally accomplished. He was, however, partially blinded by the current model that his bishop (and the diocese) were working from. His diocesan culture, and the structures of governance which flow from that culture, made it almost impossible for him to consider any other alternative than for a pastor who is bearing fruit in a parish to leave that parish because his assigned time was up.

And that kind of cultural blindness is present throughout the Church.

Universal Principles for a Universal Church

Perhaps you have come to *Divine Renovation Beyond the Parish* after reading my book *Divine Renovation* or some of the other material published by our Divine Renovation ministry. Maybe you have listened to a few of our podcasts, watched some YouTube videos, or heard one of the Divine Renovation ministry team members speak at an event. Some of you may have attended an open house sponsored by a parish that we coach; or maybe you belong to a coached parish or subscribe to our Divine Renovation Network.

As important as parish renewal is in this present time, we recognize that the parish does not exist by itself. Catholics do not have a Congregationalist ecclesiology. In other words, we are not independent community churches governed solely by local leaders. In fact, for Catholics the Church in a local area is not the parish, but rather the diocese. If the Apostle Paul could somehow write a letter to those of us at Saint Benedict Parish in my home community, he would begin it like this: "Paul, an apostle of Christ, to the Church in Halifax—Yarmouth" and not like this: "Paul, an Apostle of Christ, to the Church of Saint Benedict Parish."

This is so because a church is gathered around a bishop who is the chief Shepherd. This is why the *cathedra* (or chair) of a bishop is the symbol of his authority and why the bishop's cathedral holds primacy of place within a diocese. Parishes, then, are communities of faith that are gathered in union with their bishop. In the years since the publication of *Divine Renovation*, as we have been blessed to accompany and work with so many ordained and lay leaders throughout the world, we have been convicted of one thing—*the success and long-term fruitfulness of a parish as it moves into a missionary posture is absolutely dependent on diocesan leadership.* The Achilles' heel of a missionary parish is a maintenance-minded diocese, and the Achilles' heel of a missionary diocese is a maintenance-minded apostolic nuncio (no offense to any apostolic nuncio who may be reading this). In truth, this principle goes even further, encompassing structures beyond the diocese—not just the nuncio, but even conferences of bishops and Vatican congregations.

Remember my priest friend from the beginning of this chapter? He was not necessarily looking forward to this change of assignment.

Priest changes can be disruptive both for the priest and the parish. The incoming pastor often has a different (or worse, no) vision. The parishioners watch as all that they had invested in begins to atrophy and, eventually, die, and the outgoing pastor sees the fruits of his leadership wither and disappear. It is difficult to build across generations when we move our pastors every six to eight years—just about the time it takes for real, lasting fruit to start emerging from a renewal effort. We are basically training both our people and our pastors not to bother thinking missionally. Why invest in a vision when in six to eight years, someone else will come along and everything gets knocked down?

Here is the tragedy: this same dynamic is present at the episcopal level as well. If parish priests are sometimes moved around every half a dozen or so years, many bishops are moved around as frequently, or sometimes every ten to twelve years. Just as a diocese is beginning to mobilize and do something, the bishop may be removed and replaced with someone who may have no buy-in to the diocese's current vision. Perhaps this new bishop arrives and lets everything fall apart or actually dismantles it because he has a very different vision. Or perhaps he is a different kind of leader than the previous man and is simply unable to work with the leadership culture in place. Just as at the parish level, we soon find ourselves back at maintenance.

Sixty years ago, this would not have been much of a problem. In the world of Christendom, maintenance sufficed. Today, however, Christendom is gone. Like the early Church, we find ourselves living in an Apostolic age, a time period that requires a missionary mindset. If we do not make this turn from maintenance to mission—not just at the parish or the diocesan level, but universally—our very future will be at stake again.

That is why we have created *Divine Renovation Beyond the Parish*—to take what we have learned over the past several years at Divine Renovation ministry and through my role over the last three years working at the diocesan level in the Archdiocese of Halifax-Yarmouth, and place it at the service of the Universal Church. We want to help you navigate the delicate balance between helping parishes become healthy and maintaining our Catholic identity as a communion of parishes gathered around the person of the bishop. We also want to be a resource for the global Church as together we ask the question: what does it mean for us to be a missionary Church in our various places while remaining a communion of Churches who are, in turn, living in communion with the successor of Peter?

Just as the original *Divine Renovation* book struck a nerve and helped transform a conversation at the parish level, our hope is that *Divine Renovation Beyond the Parish* will join with so many other voices from great leaders, prophets, and teachers in wonderful ministries throughout the world to transform the conversation at a diocesan, international, and global level.

The world is hungering for the fruit of a Church that has embraced her missionary identity—and so am I.

Uncovering the Framework

God is richly blessing many ministries and leaders who are working for the sake of parish renewal today with many ways to communicate with one another about what is being discovered. With that blessing comes the opportunity to create a common language around transformation and renewal. The central purpose of these efforts is to equip the Church, in its varied organizational expressions, to move from maintenance to mission. What do we mean by these terms?

Maintenance and Mission: A Deeper Dive

When people speak of maintenance, they are often referring primarily to structures, processes, systems, and practices. To a certain degree, that makes a lot of sense based on the experience of the Church in many areas of the world. Over the years, however, as we have traveled and connected with leaders of parishes, we have witnessed firsthand that the major struggle of dioceses and parishes is not with maintenance but with decline—decline in membership, finances, buildings, cultural influence, and so forth. When caught in a spiral of decline, it is natural for communities to clutch on to administrative realities that have worked in the past, in hopes of stemming the tide.

Maintenance has a dimension that is essential and positive. Authentic maintenance is fundamentally about people—about maintaining the flock. This is Peter's message to the Church in his first letter: "Tend the flock of God in your midst, [overseeing] not by constraint but willingly, as God would have it, not for shameful profit but eagerly" (1 Peter 5:2).

This quote recalls Jesus' conversation with Peter chronicled in the Gospel of John. Three times Jesus asks Peter, "Do you love me?" Three times Peter responds, "Lord, you know that I love you." In reply Jesus offers a gentle command to Peter: "Feed my lambs;" "Tend my sheep;" "Feed my sheep" (John 21:15-17).

Maintaining the flock that God has entrusted to us means feeding the sheep. According to Jesus and his apostles, feeding the sheep occupies a high pastoral priority; it is something that we *must* do.

And it is not easy work.

If you are seeing some success in maintaining the flock, then congratulations. We live in a decidedly anti-faith culture. Wolves are circling the flock, and people are being picked off left, right, and center. Keeping the flock together in any way is a real accomplishment.

While maintenance focuses on feeding the sheep we do have, mission focuses on reaching those outside the flock. A mission-focused Church is concerned with the needs, hopes, sorrows, joys, and eternal destiny of all men and women—especially those furthest from Christ and his Church. The posture of a mission-focused Church is fundamentally outward, toward the world.

Integrity and the Church's Identity

Though we have contrasted maintenance and mission in order to better understand their respective emphases, we cannot pit one against the other—both are essential if the Church is to live out her identity in Christ. There is great danger, however, in focusing primarily on maintaining the flock. Even if you do that perfectly, the sheep will eventually get older until they start to die off—and then you will be left with no flock at all.

Think about a few of the other images Jesus used in speaking of the Church's mission: harvesting crops, for example, and catching fish. Among several references to the harvest, he said, "The harvest is abundant but the laborers are few; so ask the master of the harvest to send out laborers for his harvest" (Matthew 9:37-38). Jesus also said, "Come after me, and I will make you fishers of men" (Matthew 4:19). To catch fish is to live out the Great Commission that we find in the Gospel of Matthew: "Go, therefore, and make disciples of all nations, baptizing them in the name of the Father, and of the Son, and of the holy Spirit, teaching them to observe all that I have commanded you" (Matthew 28:19-20).

We must maintain the flock, but we must also "harvest" and "fish," expanding the flock by going out to encounter and accompany those outside the boundaries of the parish.

Jesus uses another powerful image to speak of the Church's life: bearing fruit. "I am the vine, you are the branches. Whoever remains in me and I in him will bear much fruit" (John 15:5). In working with parishes, speaking to priests, and at Saint Benedict Parish itself, we have learned that a community's fundamental posture—maintenance or mission—greatly impacts its ability to bear that fruit.

In other words, when parishes or dioceses see their primary purpose as feeding the sheep, most never quite get around to the evangelizing mission of the Church—to reach those on the outside—even if they know this mission is central to the Church's identity. Pope Paul VI reminded us of this in his ground-breaking 1975 apostolic exhortation *Evangelii Nuntiandi* (On Evangelization in the Modern World) when he boldly stated that "Evangelizing is in fact the grace and vocation proper to the Church, her deepest identity" (14). The demands of the flock are unending and consuming. These parishes and dioceses never find enough time to do what they know they are called to do—go on mission.

On the other hand, communities often do a pretty good job of both caring for the sheep *and* evangelizing their broader communities when they act as if their *primary* purpose consists of reaching the people *they do not have*. Through the grace of God, their outward-focused posture generates new believers who are passionately in love with the Lord, his Church, and the Church's mission. In short, these mission-oriented communities bear fruit; they make disciples. Pastoral leaders harvest their gifts, channeling them both into the parish community and out-ward, beyond the parish, as they send out these new disciples.

In this way, the fruits of the kingdom multiply and spread.

Bearing Fruit That Remains

We all want our parishes to bear fruit.

Jesus said, "By this is my Father glorified, that you bear much fruit and become my disciples" (John 15:8). Sometimes, however, we desire fruit so much that we rush and try to make things happen right away. That is what happened to me as a leader working toward parish renewal. I was not particularly interested in changing structures, systems, or cultures; I did not know anything about that. I just wanted fruit.

I will never forget the first Mass I celebrated in my new parish when I became a pastor for the first time. My heart sank. As I processed in, it became apparent that I was the only person in the church singing the hymn. The only person. As we continued with the Mass, people looked miserable. There seemed to be no joy in the place. The congregation barely responded to the prayers, and at the end of Mass, when I said, "Go, the Mass has ended," you would have thought I pulled a fire alarm. They bolted. No one seemed to want to be there.

In addition, the parish had no adult faith formation, no discussion of discipleship, no study, no evangelization, and very little ministry. Maybe 2 percent of parishioners were involved in something. For the most part, the parish felt dead—and with good reason.

I remember having such pain in my heart. I wanted to see fruit, not in order to boast or point out what a great priest I was. I did not want something *from* people; I wanted something *for* them. I wanted them to experience the fruit that comes from a relationship with Jesus and his Church: the fruit of transformation, healing, wholeness, restored identity, forgiveness, intimacy with God, a growing capacity to love others unconditionally, and so much more. Jesus came to transform lives, and he still wants to do so today. That is what I wanted for my parish.

Over the years, as we have been living through this renewal at Saint Benedict and working with parishes and leaders throughout the world, we have focused on fruit in two major areas—holiness and mission. Parishes and dioceses that experience authentic renewal grow in holiness and mission. If pastoral leaders can feed the sheep well, the community grows in holiness, and if pastoral leaders attend to the missionary priority and focus on those outside the parish walls, others will come to know Jesus and join his Church. The beautiful thing about these movements of maintenance and mission in the Church's life is that if we get it right, they can be mutually reinforcing: the better we feed the sheep, the greater desire the community will have to go out on mission.

As we labor for these fruits of holiness and mission, we might try to rush things—searching for silver bullets, loopholes, programmatic shortcuts, and the latest trend in ministry that will leapfrog us to where we want to be. That is what I tried to do in my first parish, and I learned the hard way that there are no shortcuts. Humanity is, in some sense, difficult "soil" in which to cultivate fruit. By the grace of God, however, over the last few years we have uncovered several foundational elements that build on one another. These elements must be present and functioning well in order to produce fruitfulness in its fullest sense at the parish level.

Not a Pyramid Scheme

As the Divine Renovation team identified these foundational elements and their relationship to one another, we created a simple pyramid schematic to show the elements in the proper order. These elements must be present and applied *within* a parish in order to produce fruit. The pyramid's true power, however, lies in using it *beyond the parish*. That is how we will use it throughout this book. In fact, the structure of this book mirrors the structure of the pyramid, allowing us to demonstrate the interrelation between the parish, the diocese, and the universal Church.

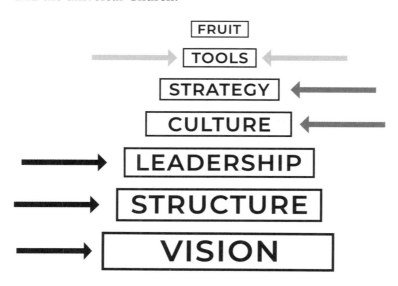

The three dark arrows toward the bottom of the pyramid have everything to do with leadership at the (arch)diocesan level—and even beyond that, since so much of what a diocese can or cannot do comes from the reality of living within a global Catholic structure.

We begin with vision. What is the vision of a diocese? What is the vision of the bishop? Does he have a vision for his church to become a missionary people?

Then comes the critical question of structure. Beyond even the canonical regulations as to what structures a parish must have in place, bishops and their curia, over time, create particular structures within dioceses that need to be examined in light of mission.[2] These structures either facilitate or hamper the essential task of leadership of pastors within their parishes.

Finally, the diocese can truly hamper the exercise of leadership, not only through structure, but also through policy and procedures. These diocesan decisions will impact whether pastors and leaders within the diocese will truly be able to function in a missionary mode or not.

The middle arrows represent collaboration between the diocese and the parish. By unleashing their own leadership and structural resources in conjunction with an overarching vision, dioceses can come alongside parish leadership to help parishes transform their cultures and develop strategies.

Finally, the arrows at the top of the pyramid call for the implementation of concrete tools at the parish level, so that fruit can ultimately emerge.

As we have worked through this essential pyramid across the world, we have seen this blending of diocesan and parish responsibility, and it has strengthened our conviction that we cannot multiply the number of missionary parishes unless we can also multiply the number of missionary bishops and dioceses. Again, that is what we hope to do with this book and with the work of Divine Renovation ministry.

So let us attend to the journey at the most critical of places: the beginning.

PART 1

VISION

CHAPTER 1

The Essence of Hope

Pope Francis has given us one of the most significant magisterial statements in recent years in his encyclical *Evangelii Gaudium* [The Joy of the Gospel]:

> I dream of a "missionary option," that is, a missionary impulse capable of transforming everything, so that the Church's customs, ways of doing things, times and schedules, language and structures can be suitably channeled[3] for the evangelization of today's world rather than for her self-preservation.[4]

This statement is significant because it captures Pope Francis' dream—and dreams are what inspire. In 1963, when Martin Luther King Jr. stood before the Lincoln Memorial to address those who had come to participate in the March on Washington for Jobs and Freedom, he did not say, "I have an idea," or, "I have a plan," or even, "I have a to-do list." He said, "I have a dream!"

Whenever we talk about dreams, we are speaking the language of vision, and vision is essential. A powerful vision does not just inspire; it also points in a direction: Here's what we can achieve! Here's what we can become! It encourages, enlivens, and often makes us feel good.

When I speak to audiences and use this statement from Pope Francis, I ask, "Who likes this quote?" Often two-thirds of those present raise their hands. I always point out that the people who did not put up their hands are probably being more honest than those who did.

If we listen closely to Pope Francis' dream, we will see that it is absolutely revolutionary and therefore demanding. When he talks about a "missionary impulse capable of transforming everything," he is not just talking about theories of parish life. Rather he is talking about how we live and how we do things concretely.

Our parishes have customs and schedules—and we generally do not want anyone to change those familiar patterns and structures. Ever. Have you pastors tried changing a Mass time, for example? I mean, you almost get death threats. The truth is that we talk about our parishes being communities of missionary disciples, but often they are simply collections of religious consumers. These Catholic-lite consumers have preferences—and you do not mess with those preferences!

This attitude is one of the greatest challenges we face in terms of the renewal and transformation of parishes and dioceses: We are fixated on and attached to our preferences and our ways of doing things. We like our times and schedules. We like our structures. We like our languages. And if you look at what we do as parishes and dioceses, you could conclude that these things are much more important to us than the evangelization of today's world. It does not matter what our mission statements, websites, and social media pages *say*. If you look at what we *do*, our values are quite clear.

Ultimately—if we are truly committed to renovation, transformation, and renewal— vision lies at the heart of what we do. Vision taps into passion; it galvanizes the leadership of a community at the level of the parish, the diocese, or the universal Church. Vision enables us to move in a new direction; it creates a picture of a dynamic future. The passion that vision arouses, however, rests on something even more foundational—namely, hope.

Hope is one of the three theological virtues, the other two being faith and love. When there is a deficit of hope, we lose our passion. We become cynical, disillusioned, tired, and depressed. Hope is critical to the Christian life. As St. Paul writes to the church in Rome: "May the God of hope fill you with all joy and peace in believing, so that you may abound in hope by the power of the holy Spirit" (Romans 15:13).

If we are going to push forward in this task of mission and renewal, we need to begin with the supernatural reality of hope. Christian hope is rooted in the God who raised Jesus Christ from the dead; it allows us to stand at the cross on Good Friday and yearn for Easter Sunday.

In the face of death and defeat, our hope remains undimmed, because the One who brings forth rivers of water from the desert can also bring forth streams of life from our heart. He is the God of hope, and it is through the power of the Holy Spirit that we receive this hope, which brings with it the capacity for passion and the capacity to dream.

I am not talking about optimism here. Optimism tends to censor the data, put on rose-colored glasses, and selectively filter reality. Optimism says, "I will only look at certain parts of the truth and ignore anything that conflicts with the picture that I am trying to paint." Hope, on the other hand, has the strength to look at the whole picture, to look at reality as it currently exists, both its good and bad components. The virtue of hope throws off the shackles of denial to stare reality in the face, sure that God is going to do something new, even though what he might do is not readily discernible.

Hope in the Face of Statistics

With that in mind, I want to look at some recent statistics about the Church, mostly in the Western world. I know that where statistics are concerned, it is easy to become overwhelmed. It seems everywhere you turn nowadays some organization is publishing statistics about the Church—and most of these numbers are not hopeful. This is not just true for the Catholic Church but for all Christian churches to a greater or lesser degree. I am convinced, however, that if we accept the reality that statistics reveal and if we approach the situation in hope, then we can find the energy and conviction to embrace new models of church life. We can shift our culture. So here we go!

We will speak later in this book about the kind of things we measure. Certainly some measurements are more helpful than others. A most common starting point is to seek numbers around Church attendance. This is not the most critical measurement, but it is a starting point. The struggle, however, is that different surveys frame the question in different ways. There is the issue of frequency of church attendance and the relative nature of these numbers.

The easiest numbers to use in order to compare the relative health of the Church in different countries is the percentage of Catholics who attend weekly Mass. This does not just serve utility; it also starts us with a minimum expectation of what it means to be a faithful

Catholic. Secondly, any percentage of attenders that we may find in online reports is always relative to something. For Catholics there are two starting points that can yield very different numbers: the percentage of self-identifying Catholics who go to weekly Mass and the percentage of cradle Catholics who go to weekly Mass. If we are measuring to answer the question "How are we doing?" I think we need to make the broadest measurement.

Finally, surveys vary based on when the data was gathered. This is significant today, as the landscape is changing rapidly in many countries.

For example, in their 2018 report entitled "Contemporary Catholicism in England and Wales," the Catholic Research Forum, based in St. Mary's University in Twickenham, London, used data from 2012 through 2014 and concluded that 27.5 percent of self-identifying Catholics attend weekly Mass. I remember being pleasantly surprised when I saw that number, but then I read another data point that said 44.2 percent of cradle Catholics no longer identify as Catholic. This means that only about 14 percent of people raised in the Catholic faith go to Mass every week. As bad as this sounds, the Catholic Church in England and Wales has the strongest retention rate of the main Christian denominations in those countries. The Catholic Church there is also doing better than the Catholic Church in most other European nations.

In the United States, research done by Gallup and published in the April 9, 2018, article "Catholics' Church Attendance Resumes Downward Slide" states that 35 percent of self-identifying Catholics go to weekly Mass.[5] Again, this does not sound too grave, until we consider that 41 percent of cradle Catholics have left the Church and no longer identify as Catholic.[6] This means that fewer than 20 percent of people raised in the Catholic faith attend Mass each week, as 6 percent of self-identifying Catholics are adult converts.[7]

In Canada 15 percent of self-identifying Catholics attend Mass each week, according to research by Canadian sociologist Reginald Bibby.[8] A closer look at his data shows that Mass attendance in English-speaking Canada was 22 percent, compared to 8 percent in Quebec. There is no readily available data about the percentage of cradle Catholics who have left the Church. We also have to remember that in urban centers throughout Canada, those numbers are boosted by a significant immigrant population, which can mask the fact that the Church is hemorrhaging its members.

The statistics are even worse in France, the "oldest daughter of the Church." According to a Harvard Divinity School report, "Catholicism in France," which examines a 2010 study by a French institute, only 4.5 percent of Catholics go to Mass each week.[9] The scary thing is that this study used data from 2006.

In Germany in 2016, only 10 percent of the 23.6 million registered Catholics attended Mass. Again, these numbers cast light on the number of self-identifying Catholics who are choosing to remove themselves from the life of the Church. They do not mention those who no longer identify as Catholics, and in the case of Germany, have formally left the Church by opting out of the state-sponsored church tax. "From 2010 to 2015, an average of 167,000 Catholics left the Church in Germany each year."[10]

This snapshot of church attendance throughout the Western world should trouble us, but it is only a snapshot without context. The more relevant issue is the long-term trajectory. The same Gallup Survey that reported that 35 percent of US Catholics go to Mass each week reports that this is down from 75 percent in 1955. It also tells us that only 25 percent of US Catholics aged twenty-one through twenty-nine go weekly.

Let us look more closely at the decline in the US Church. I am focusing on the US as it is arguably the most robust expression of Catholicism in the global Church. In an article on its archdiocesan website, the Archdiocese of Philadelphia cites a 48 percent decline in Mass attendance over twenty-eight years.[11] This decline was shown to be steady from 1990 to 2018 but likely has been taking place much longer.

Certainly such a rate of decline is not ubiquitous in the US, but decline is decline. I was recently speaking in a major US diocese that, on the surface, has a lot of life. There are very large parishes with full churches every Sunday. However, according to their own statistics, from 1995 to 2017, weekly Mass attendance has dropped from 28 percent to 17 percent of Catholics, an average of 0.5 percent each year.[12] If that trajectory continues, this diocese, which appears to be full of life, has approximately thirty-four years until it is dead.

This decline is occurring even within traditionally Catholic cultures and countries, such as Poland and Ireland. I was startled by what I learned when I was in Ireland for a speaking engagement in November of 2017. The preliminary report from the 2016 Irish census revealed that the number of people identifying as Catholic had decreased from 84.4 percent to 78.3 percent, compared to the 2011 census numbers. That is a drop of 5.9 percent in five short years. Even more startling, nearly half a million people identified as having no religious affiliation (becoming what some call Nones). That is a 73.6 percent growth since the 2011 census—and 45 percent of these newly identified Nones are between the ages of twenty and thirty-nine. Those are stunning changes!

Within my own Archdiocese of Halifax-Yarmouth, Archbishop Mancini has spoken about our situation as a moment of crisis. In 2001 we took a diocesan-wide count of Mass attendance. There were twenty-seven thousand Catholics at Mass on a particular Sunday. In 2016, just fifteen years later, another diocesan-wide count revealed that only seventeen thousand Catholics were at Mass. This is worse than it sounds, because in between the two counts, the Archdiocese of Halifax reunited with the neighboring Diocese of Yarmouth, so the 2016 numbers for Mass attendance include participation by Catholics in two dioceses. While we do not have the 2001 numbers for Yarmouth, I conservatively believe that we have experienced a 50 percent drop in Mass attendance in fifteen years.

I do not know if this downward direction has reversed in the last three or four years. In fact, if you look at attendance statistics from 2017 and compare them to census statistics from 2015, only about 8.2 percent of Catholics in the archdiocese attend Mass. In addition, comparing diocesan data with the census, 75 percent of churchgoing Catholics in the archdiocese are now over the age of fifty-five.

I mentioned that the struggle with decline is not just a Catholic issue. Several months ago, I received a copy of a report that was written for the House of Bishops of the Anglican Church of Canada.[13] The report was an analysis of data from 2017. Its conclusion was stark and shocking: "Projections from our data indicate that there will be no members, attenders or givers in the Anglican Church of Canada by approximately 2040." This claim was based on the premise that their present trajectory will not be altered as the pattern of decline has been consistent for sixty years, in spite of repeated warnings in the past. The report included very significant statistics on key metrics. Among them was the fact that between 1961 and 2017 the number of confirmations had decreased by 94 percent, while the number of ordinations had actually increased, by a whopping 47 percent.

At this point, you might be wondering when we will get to the hopeful part. As a priest of an archdiocese like Halifax-Yarmouth, I do have hope—in fact, I have a great deal of hope. Why? Because I trust in the living God, and because our archdiocese has actually developed a plan in the face of this reality.

We cannot avoid the truth. Unless Christian hope suffuses our vision, planning, and hard work, the statistics point to a grim destiny. Seen through the eyes of hope, however, these numbers become an opportunity, a clarion call for the Church to live out her evangelizing and missionary identity.

Battling the Demons of Defeatism

Christian hope is rooted in the reality of God's grace that conquered the grave, destroyed the power of sin, and raised Jesus from the dead. This Jesus now offers that divine life to the world through the Church. Therefore we have hope, a thoroughly Christian hope. Our God is a God of victory! Pope Francis highlights this truth in *Evangelii Gaudium*:

> One of the more serious temptations which stifles boldness and zeal is a defeatism which turns us into querulous and disillusioned pessimists, "sourpusses." Nobody can go off to battle unless he is fully convinced of victory beforehand.[14]

I know this: if we are apathetic, if we lose hope and fall victim to a defeatist attitude, then the future indeed is dire. There are indeed many reasons to lose hope; the pain we experience when we try to lead others is one of the most common. If you have ever stuck your neck out and tried to lead something or do something new, you know what opposition is. People come against you. Our natural wiring tells us to avoid this painful experience.

Exhaustion can also lead us to lose hope. We can be so worn down by the demands of parish life that we end up overwhelmed and wondering if we can make a difference. Everyone who steps into some kind of ministry wants to bear fruit. When we see our hard work and grueling schedules bearing fruit, then we retire at the end of each day in a kind of joyful exhaustion.

Parish life, however, often becomes a voracious machine. When everything we do centers around the structure and mechanics of maintaining parish life, when maintenance becomes the end game and we (often inadvertently) sacrifice mission, then the parish becomes a kind of ecclesial vampire. We give and give and give, and it takes and takes and takes. That kind of exhaustion is soul numbing. It produces burnout and depression, and it strips us of hope for the future.

Disillusionment is another enemy of hope. From an etymological perspective, the word means, essentially, to be free of illusion, and so it would seem to be a good thing to become disillusioned: you want to be a realist. In contemporary usage, however, it means being stripped of your capacity to dream. In other words, the disillusioned become so firmly rooted in reality as they are experiencing it that they cannot see beyond that reality. Unable to conceive of something that could move them in a different direction, they lose hope,

Cynicism is another enemy of hope. I have thought about this one a lot because I have struggled with it in my own life, and I see many church leaders—deacons, priests, and bishops—struggle with it in their ministries. Ultimately cynicism is a kind of wisdom stripped of hope. Cynicism focuses attention on the strength of the problem and not on the possibility of a solution. In cynicism's grip, you will never mobilize.

Here is the tricky thing about cynicism: it not only tries to cripple the hope in your own heart, but it also tries to destroy hope everywhere. It has a broad mission. Cynicism can detect the presence of hope in others and will try to strangle that hope when it finds it. Cynicism is a real and prevalent disease in the Church, especially among clergy. I have had the opportunity to speak to deacons, priests, and bishops across the world, and there is always a small group of clerics in any group who, because they are forced to go to a meeting, let their cynicism out publicly. They might challenge the speaker, cross their arms, lean back in their chairs, and whisper to one another about why whatever we are discussing will never work. They are quick to find other clergy who are more open to the message and stamp out any burgeoning hope they find in them.

The final enemy of hope that I want to highlight is a strange one: contentment. Contentment looks at the reality of our current situation and says, "I am not bothered by the decline and all these statistics. I am okay with doing palliative care, not just with parishioners but with my parish or diocese. I am quite content. You know, I get three square meals, a paycheck, four weeks off a year; I have a pretty good life. I'll just keep doing what I'm doing; it doesn't bother me."

Often the desire to see parishes come alive begins with dissatisfaction with the current state. It is hard to experience that dissatisfaction if your heart is overcome by contentment. Contentment with the present state of affairs in our Church is by far the biggest threat to hope for the future, and if we do not have hope, we likely do not have a future.

Living Proof

If we can serve our Church and her people with an attitude of hope, if we trust in what God wants for his body, then we will have started on the path to renovation—a path that can lead to real and lasting change. As Paul writes, "Hope does not disappoint, because the love of God has been poured out into our hearts through the holy Spirit that has been given to us" (Romans 5:5).

I have been blessed to witness the renewal of a parish. Actually I have seen renewal happen in various places throughout the world. I am thinking of a parish in Brisbane, Australia, a parish outside of Lisbon, Portugal, and a parish in East London, one of the poorest boroughs of the UK. I think of a parish in Montreal, a city considered by many to be one of the most secular on the face of the earth. I think of parishes across the United States and around the globe, parishes that are very different from my own parish of Saint Benedict in Halifax, with leaders very different from me or the current pastor of Saint Benedict Parish, Fr. Simon Lobo.

These parishes are experiencing incredible transformation. Transformed lives yield a growing army of missionary disciples. These parishes celebrate stories of transformation; they see people step into ministry; authentic Christian communities are forming; worship and sacraments are coming to life. These parishes are even seeing dramatic increases in giving.

I have lived through renewal myself, making lots of mistakes along the way. I know that transformation is possible—not just theologically, not just in theory, but in real settings with real (and very fallible) people. If God can do it with broken, foolish people in a small town like Halifax, God can do it anywhere. But first we need to take hold of hope, dream big, and call our people to a vision that moves them.

CHAPTER 2

Anatomy of Decline

Have you ever heard the phrase "May you live in interesting times"?

It is an old expression, apocryphally believed to be an ancient Chinese curse. Why a curse? Because living in interesting times often means living in a time of change—and change brings with it uncertainty, anxiety, disruption, and the passing away of the familiar.

As we have demonstrated from the sociological data, and as many of us experience firsthand in our parishes, the Church in the twenty-first century is living in interesting times. We can see the decline, not only in numbers but also in missionary vitality. For those who are serving on the front lines, so to speak, it has become clear that our methods no longer work. We are struggling; and amid that struggle, we can easily experience the burden of failure and the uncompromising weight of shame.

The truth, however, is that our difficulties go far beyond our own parish, our own diocese, and our own geographic area of the world. Global cultural shifts are occurring at an unprecedented rate. Pope Francis, in remarks made at a national conference of the Italian Church in 2015, highlighted this reality. "We are not living an era of change," he said, "but a change of era."[15]

The tectonic plates of history have been shifting over these last sixty years, and I believe these are some of the most significant shifts in fifteen centuries. We happen to be the lucky ones who find ourselves in the middle of this shift. I think of the words spoken by Gandalf in *The Lord of the Rings*, in response to Frodo's "I wish it need not have happened in my time." "So do I," said Gandalf, "and so do all who live to see such times. But that is not for them to decide. All we have to decide is what to do with the time that is given us."[16]

There was a time in history, from about the late fourth century until the 1960s, when popular culture generally aligned with Church culture. This, of course, is a generalization, but one that was generally true. If you went with the flow of culture during that extensive period, you would eventually find yourself in the Church. Now, of course, the results are quite different. If you follow the flow of popular culture, you will end up far from the Church. This is an enormous change, a break with a vast expanse of our history.

We use lots of fancy names to talk about this new age we live in—post-Christian, post-modern, post-Christendom. Whatever we call it, we live in a time when the alignment of popular culture and Church culture has ended, and the pace of change continues to accelerate.

So how can we view our current reality through the eyes of hope?

Feeling Loopy

About two years ago, during a Divine Renovation ministry staff meeting, our president, Dan O'Rourke, went up to the whiteboard and shared with us a model for understanding the dynamics of change that he had learned while working for the government. He called this model the Two Loop Theory and attributed it to the Berkana Institute, a secular nonprofit enterprise that studies the dynamics of change and works with communities to apply those dynamics to specific problems.

As I looked at this simple diagram, I had a light-bulb moment. This Two Loop concept perfectly described my experience of working fruitfully for renewal within parishes. It also perfectly described my experience of seeing something new emerge within a diocese, and it gave a hopeful context for what I saw happening in the global Church. It is such an important tool for making our way forward that I want to share it with you:

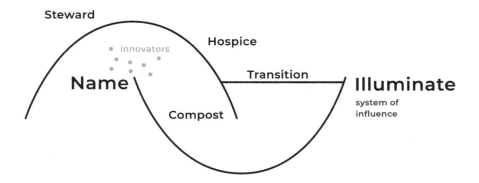

We will explore more of this diagram in chapter four, but for now, I want to focus on the rising momentum of the first loop. When applied to the dynamics of an organization, this initial movement upward represents the burst of energy and excitement that follows the genesis of a fruitful movement. There is vision, commitment, alignment—and as a result, growth occurs quickly. That growth often generates more excitement, galvanizing the organization and its members. Overall it is a wonderful, life-giving experience.

At some point in this model, however, things start to stabilize: they level out. As that happens, members experience a growing awareness that there is a problem. Usually the perception of problems occurs well after those problems begin, and so what follows, in the midst of the alarm bells ringing, is a period of rapid decline. Leaders transition from serving as stewards to becoming hospice workers, tending a dying organization. We can see this progression from genesis and growth to decline everywhere we work, and therefore I would like to focus on those dynamics for a moment.

The best way to understand them is to highlight the essential differences between a movement and a museum. Generally speaking, a movement is constantly looking ahead to its future; it is blazing a trail. Museums, on the other hand, are principally about preserving the past. The problem is that movements can quickly become museums. Why? Because it is exciting to be part of a movement, and individuals within growing organizations are proud that their actions have worked well to secure growth. Therefore they want to enshrine their methods. In effect, they put them in a glass cabinet and write up a history so people can visit and learn about them.

Those organizations then lose focus, shifting away from their forward-thinking mission, fixating on preserving their past, and transforming into museums. In relation to twenty-first-century culture, many dioceses and parishes have become museums—sometimes literally, in places like North America and Europe. Museums eventually can become mausoleums, and I have been to several churches that are such.

Six Stages of a Dying Church

We have seen that over time, as an organization stabilizes, grows, and prospers, leaders go from a pioneering, or mission-focused, mindset to a maintenance or museum mindset. These maintainers categorize, classify, and curate the museum artifacts. In North America, for example, as our immigrant-founded parishes began to grow, and as Catholics integrated into the surrounding secular culture, pioneering leaders became experts at maintenance. Maintenance progresses inevitably to palliative care, however, and yields leaders who function like hospice workers, managing the dying process of parishes and dioceses. That is mostly what is going on today in terms of leadership.

It is a hard thing to consider many of our parishes in this light—as dying communities of faith. But as we will see, not staring reality in the face simply hastens the process. Thom Rainer, an Evangelical Protestant who studies church health, wrote an article on the six stages of a dying church. His insights, though written in an Evangelical context, have a great deal to teach us about our current situation.[17]

Denial
The first stage Rainer identifies in the death of a faith community is *denial*. In this initial stage, a parish might experience numerical decline, but no one seems too concerned. Remember the statistics from the last chapter? What is so alarming about those numbers is that they show a continuous trend that has been going on for twenty, thirty, or fifty years! The decline we are experiencing is not a new phenomenon, yet even ten years ago no one really seemed to be all that concerned, because we did not necessarily feel it.

In 2018 I was at a conference in the Philippines, speaking to priests and to lay leaders. In preparation I did some research on the Church in the Philippines, and I discovered something fascinating: on average over the last twenty-three years, there have been 750,000 fewer people going to church in the Philippines *each year*! Yet if you go to Sunday Mass there, it is standing room only. It is standing room only even at some weekday Masses.

There is still a lot of faith in the Philippines. Since the churches are packed, it is difficult to be concerned about the very real numerical decline occurring under the surface. In a situation like this, Church leaders struggle to meet the needs of the current churchgoing population. There is much to do, and they cannot keep up.

This is not an uncommon situation. In many places throughout the world, our church buildings are not big enough, and yet paradoxically we are hemorrhaging people. If that keeps happening, guess how the story ends?

For those who have eyes to see, we need to ring the fire alarm at this point. Too often, however, Church leaders are firmly in the denial phase; no one really cares. It is essentially business as usual, and the folks who try to raise an alarm are viewed as an inconvenience, distraction, or threat.

In this stage, the parish or diocese has become focused on itself, functioning somewhat like a club that exists to meet the needs of its members. This is the essence of a maintenance parish, whose primary purpose is to serve the needs of parishioners and not the salvation and transformation of the world beyond the parish.

I am haunted by a question I heard years ago: If your parish closed tomorrow, would anyone who isn't a member care? Would they feel the difference? Or has your parish become self-serving, with negligible impact on the community? Sadly, many Catholic churches in the Western world are experiencing decline, and the response from Church leaders is primarily denial.

Recalibration

The second stage that Rainer highlights is *recalibration*. In this stage, an organization admits that something is wrong and tries to fix the issue with one of two approaches, neither of which offers a comprehensive plan of change.

The first approach is to double down on a losing strategy. Rather than break new ground, parish leaders continue their current strategy and throw more money, personnel, and resources at it. The thought process goes like this: "Remember that thing we were doing that doesn't work? We are going to do it again, but this time, we'll try *harder!*"

The second approach parish leaders take in this stage is to do an old thing in a new way. Instead of changing the fundamental model, they make tweaks and minor course corrections to the current model, but nothing substantive changes. This approach is obsessed with finding the silver bullet—the one program or event that will save the parish or diocese.

Parishes and dioceses in this stage put on a workshop, bring in a popular speaker, or find an effective program, like Alpha, and then wait for the fruit to emerge. The problem is that there really is not a silver bullet. We cannot simply stream a talk or pop a DVD into a DVD player, and then sit back as everything gets fixed. Programs, workshops, speakers, and events must flow from a clear vision, an intentional culture, and a leadership committed to deep change. The issues we face are systemic, and they require systemic responses.

What both these recalibration responses have in common is that they are not undergirded by a real desire for change. The sense instead is that the community simply needs an adjustment. We have come up against this attitude among parish leaders, but we have actually found it to be more prevalent at the diocesan level. Bishops and their staff may not say this to us explicitly, but they communicate the following: You come in and work with our priests and get *them* to do something different; tell *them* to change. *We're* not going to change. We're not going to change *our* leadership style or leadership model or try to transform *our* culture. No, no, no, no. Tell *them* to do it!

Over the years, we have had to be bold in working with those who invite us to come to various dioceses. We ask them, "Are you serious about this, or are you just looking for a quick fix? Because unless you are serious about deep change, we don't have the time or the energy." Church renewal, at every level, is fundamentally about deep change.

Finding a heart for deep change, as opposed to quick fixes, is a major issue in the Church today. I have long thought, for example, that for all the talk in recent years about the new evangelization, what we have in many parishes is neither new nor evangelization. Often it is simply the old catechesis model reheated with different verbiage. This is a very human response: to continue to do what we have always done. Of course, it is also a famous definition of insanity: to continue to do the same thing over and over, expecting different results, as if our earnestness alone would make the difference.

Many of our leaders are earnest and sincere, but it does not matter how hard working or wonderful you are, or even, dare I say it, how much you pray. If what you do does not work, it does not work. It is time to find the courage to discern and follow through on the fundamental changes that have become critical.

Anger

The next stage Rainer talks about is *anger*. Parishes move into this stage when they begin to realize that doubling down on the losing strategy is not working, or they discover that the magic bullet really does not have any magic at all. The problem in this stage is that parish leaders do not take responsibility for their lack of fruit. They get angry and choose to consciously or unconsciously deflect the blame to some other group or person(s).

Parishioners blame the pastor, and often the pastor blames the bishop, and the Lord knows whom bishops blame. People get angry at all the young people who are not coming to church. Some people point the finger at those who have fallen away, at those men and women who come and take their pews twice a year, at Christmas and Easter. If they would just show up regularly, the thinking goes, all our problems would be solved. Still others blame the culture—postmodernism, consumerism, hedonism, materialism, relativism, and all of the other "isms."

These can all serve as targets for anger; the one thing they have in common is that they focus the blame somewhere else. Leaders in the anger stage blame other people and often play the victim. They refuse to accept responsibility. Instead of trying to console ourselves by blaming other forces, people, influences, or conspiracies, we need to ask ourselves what we have done to live as a missionary people, meeting and connecting with the world.

Even in blaming ourselves, however, we must be careful. We certainly bear some responsibility as a Church for our failure to do what Scripture and Vatican II have asked us to do—namely, to read the signs of the times and respond adequately. We have missed these opportunities. Realistically though, how could we have anticipated the magnitude of change that we have experienced in our lifetimes?

Exodus

The fourth stage is Exodus. After years of gradual loss, the outflow increases. Remember the statistics from my diocese about the 50 percent decline in fifteen years? Even those who do not leave attend less frequently. When I was a teenager, the churches I went to were filled to the brim; sometimes dividers in the back would have to be opened, and these sections too would be packed to capacity. Now those very same churches have a fraction of the people attending. Churches can be desolate on Sundays. And this change occurred in half a lifetime.

Sunday Mass can be even more dispiriting because many parishes have the same Mass schedule that they had when a thousand people attended, even though they might see only 250 people all weekend. Why do we Catholics do this? Often it is because we value convenience and stability, so we do not mess around with Mass schedules. Now we get sixty people in a church that seats six hundred, and in the Catholic version of Boyle's law—which states that gas molecules expand to fill an available space—we have people sitting as far away as possible from each other, with mathematical precision!

My good friend Carey Nieuwhof said about the unchurched, "They don't feel any more guilty about not being in church on Sunday than you feel guilty about not being in synagogue on Saturdays. How many Saturdays do you feel badly about missing synagogue? That's how many Sundays they feel badly about missing church."[18]

Guilt as a motivator no longer has much authority. Our parishes truly are declining. It is important to acknowledge the anger we feel about this, because this anger can lead to something else—namely demoralization, and demoralization chips away at the foundation of hope.

Desperation

The next stage of dying that Rainer mentions is *desperation*. In this moment of the dying process, remaining community members finally open themselves up to the possibility of change—largely because there does not seem to be any other available option. Someone once put it like this: The Church is like an addict. She will only be open to change when the pain of remaining as she is would be greater than the pain of change.

Looking at it from the outside, this desperation does not seem too bad, because it at least forces leaders to be open to some kind of change.

In this stage of dying, however, openness to change is grounded not in conviction but in self-preservation.

If we are not careful, this instinct of self-preservation can morph into a kind of spiritual vampirism. I know that phrase might sound a little crazy, but think about it for a few moments. A community that has been in decline and not noticed it (or not cared to notice it), a community that has shown little interest in an outward, mission-focused stance but instead has spent all of its energy and resources catering to current membership, suddenly realizes that it needs other people—not primarily for what it might have to share with them but simply because it needs new blood to live.

Often the attitude of Church leaders in this stage is that we should bring people into our parishes so we can extend our lifespan. That is vampirism. The motivation is primarily about what we want *from* people rather than what we want *for* them.

Desperation is indeed a critical period in the dying of a church; the handwriting is on the wall. Of course, the Church is not simply about parishes and dioceses. The Church also contains religious orders, movements, and institutions (hospitals and universities, for example). Yet the parochial and diocesan system currently makes up the heart of the Church, and this system has been in a period of precipitous decline. We need to address this situation forthrightly and with real vision and commitment.

In this time of desperation, we have a window of opportunity. Perhaps this experience of desperation can lead us to our knees, so that we can plead with the Lord to change our hearts and to renew the Church. This conversion will allow us to move from desperation to a dynamic commitment to change, not simply because we want to live but because we long to bear God's fruit in the world. Thus we turn away from a calculating, survivalist practicality and embrace a heart for mission, sharing the Father's love in Jesus Christ with others.

Death

If this does not happen, we will move to Rainer's sixth and final stage: *death*. In this stage, our parish or diocese becomes a sad and tragic statistic—tragic because that death did not need to happen. I do not think that we can ever say it is the will of God for any parish to close. Sometimes closing a parish might be necessary in the larger action of diocesan renewal. It can never be seen as a victory, however, no matter how much we try to spin it. That death probably has little to do with the Lord and everything to do with how the people have lived as a parish.

CHAPTER 3

A Case for Hope

Someone once asked me, "James, where is your hope? God would never let this [the death of a particular church] happen." I thought about that and came to the conclusion that, since "this" really has been happening over the last thirty or forty years in the West, God doesn't seem to be doing a very good job.

The thing is, I believe those of us in the Church expect God to do a new thing, while we seem unwilling to embrace anything that is new. Jesus' promise that he would be with us until the end of time is a promise to the universal Church and not to a particular church. We just need to look at the churches of the New Testament, the great churches to whom St. Paul wrote letters, the churches spoken about in the Book of Revelation, the great historical founding churches of Christianity—in Alexandria and Carthage—to see that. Where is the church of Hippo today? The church of Ephesus? They no longer exist, yet the universal Church goes on.

I bring this up not as a way of chipping away at your hope but as a way of bolstering it. One morning during a council of priests, someone made a reference to this idea about the death of dioceses. At the same time, I saw that an auxiliary bishop somewhere in the world had retweeted something that I had posted on Twitter. As I checked out his profile, it struck me: Every auxiliary bishop serves a particular diocese in support of the ordinary (the bishop) for that diocese. In addition, every auxiliary bishop is made an ordinary of some other diocese, because bishops must be connected to a local church. The dioceses that are given

41

to auxiliary bishops are called titular dioceses, and they all have one thing in common: *they no longer exist, except on paper*. Most are dead.

So I turned to my brother priests at the meeting and said, "I'll be darned if one day the Archdiocese of Halifax-Yarmouth becomes the titular diocese of some auxiliary bishop! No way. We're going to fight against that!"

God has called each of us—he has called the universal Church—to fruitfulness and new life. I have experienced this call in my priesthood. Will this fight be easy? No. Can local churches and dioceses die? Yes. But they do not have to.

Carey Nieuwhof frequently says that "when the rate of change outside an organization becomes greater than the rate of change within that organization, the organization will become irrelevant." It might not become unimportant, but it can become irrelevant. This is critical to understanding our current situation.

I mean, there is no greater message of import than the gospel message. There is nothing more important than the person of Jesus Christ, his mission, his kingdom, and his Church. Yet for many people, even those raised within the Church, the Church no longer plays a significant (or any) role in their life and decision-making.

Scripture tells us to "taste and see that the LORD is good" (Psalm 34:9), but many of our own (Catholics) and those in our society have tasted and seen, and they have decided that the Lord is not good. This is our painful reality—and it has nothing to do with the Lord and everything to do with how we have lived out our common baptismal vocation as sons and daughters of God gathered in parishes and dioceses. Irrelevancy is a very painful thing to live through, and yet that is our present reality.

Three Strategies for Church Interaction with the World

Now, I want to be clear that when I talk about the "rate of change," I am not speaking about changing the Church's teaching or the demands of the moral life that come to us through Scripture and Tradition. Rather, I am talking about the ways in which the Church interacts with the world. Historically, in different times and places, the Church has taken three fundamental approaches to interacting with the world: accommodation, engagement, and isolation.

What do I mean by *accommodation*? Accommodation says that for the Church to be relevant, for the Church to fulfill her mission, we need to embody and reflect the key values of the culture we are trying to reach. Often this is expressed as "The Church has to get with the times." Today this primarily means that the Church needs to "get with" contemporary thinking regarding human sexuality. In other words, we need to capitulate and embrace all the teachings out there in the world about human sexuality, including current thinking about issues such as abortion and transgenderism. If we just give in on those things, we will be okay.

A number of years ago, when Pope Benedict XVI resigned, a local radio talk show asked me to join them for a live call-in session. After the show, I spoke with the host, who was a fallen-away Catholic. He had been an altar boy when he was a kid, but he now considered himself an agnostic or an atheist. He certainly was not a practicing Catholic, and he was going on and on and on about how the Church needed to change.

Finally, I asked this man whether he would go back to church if the Church changed her stance on the issues he had just identified as essential. He paused in silence for a few moments, and then he smiled and said, "No."

The journalist Peter Seewald conducted a series of interviews with Cardinal Ratzinger many years ago, well before the cardinal became Pope Benedict XVI. These interviews were collected into a book, *Salt of the Earth*. Seewald asked Ratzinger about this attitude of accommodation, and the future pope said that this experiment had already taken place. There are many churches and ecclesial communities in the Western world and, indeed, throughout the ages, that have taken the accommodation approach. In many places in the world, including Canada and the United States, churches and communities that have embraced accommodation are actually declining at a greater rate than the Catholic Church is.

If accommodation had been the primary strategy of the Church, I believe she would have ceased to exist by the eighth century. Archbishop Fulton Sheen put it this way: "He who weds himself to the present age will find himself a widower in the next."[19] Accommodation does not lead to fruitfulness. While the temptation to accommodation will always exist, and while there will always be elements of the Church that will succumb to it, it does not work as an overarching approach to culture.

Why? Because the spirit of the world will always be at enmity with the spirit of truth. St. Paul reminds us of this in his Letter to the Romans: "Do not conform yourselves to this age but be transformed by the renewal of your mind, that you may discern what is the will of God, what is good and pleasing and perfect" (Romans 12:2). Accommodation is not a viable long-term strategy for renewal.

Isolation is another strategy for how the Church might interact with the world. Imagine, if you will, a small community of people living on an island. That community has explicit instructions to reach out and share their way of life with another people, who live across the water. However, the journey across the water might be risky, and those other people might endanger their way of life. So the island inhabitants refuse to spend their energy or risk themselves by traveling across the water, via boat or bridge. Instead they build fortifications and retreat behind their walls. They invent passwords, secret codes, impenetrable rituals, and a unique language, which prevent outsiders from understanding them and gaining access to their community. The islanders welcome new people into their group only if they are willing to learn their language and completely conform to their way of life.

I think that the Church today is sometimes tempted to live in similar isolation. We see the decline around and within our communities, and we are afraid to venture out and take risks. Instead we pull up the drawbridge and become an isolationist church. Pope Francis called this impulse toward isolationism a form of Gnosticism.[20] It sees the Church as an inward-focused club, leading to a lack of vitality and health as well as an increase in paranoia.

Communities that have a stake in this approach not only pull up the drawbridge and put guards at the door; they also post snipers on the battlements. This paranoia can become so intense that any kind of movement toward those on the outside is perceived as accommodation.

I do not see how we can reconcile these images of the Church in isolation with the images of the kingdom of God about which Jesus speaks in the Gospels. Jesus did not sit in isolation; he went out and engaged with people. He was known as a friend of tax collectors and sinners. He scandalized people who thought that the community of Israel should be small and only for the pure ones.

This brings us to the third approach: *engagement*. I believe that engagement is the stance most proper to the Church. We could expand this concept to speak about *missionary engagement* or even *incarnational missionary engagement*. What do I mean by this?

Well, let us return for a second to our island metaphor. In that scenario, engagement would involve building a bridge to cross the water, not simply so that people can find their way to the island but primarily so that the islanders can send people out across the water to meet with the folks they should be trying to reach. Notice that word "send." That is the language of mission. That is what it means to be apostolic—the word "apostle" comes from the Greek word *apostellein*, meaning "to send."

When we say that the Church is apostolic, this is the primary reality that we acknowledge. To be an apostolic Church is to be a *sent* Church, to be a Church on mission.[21] Scripture acknowledges that "God so loved the world that he gave his only Son" (John 3:16). Jesus takes this reality one step further when he tells his followers, "As the Father has sent me, so I send you" (John 20:21).

When the Church begins to live more intentionally her apostolic identity, when she embraces mission, she more faithfully reflects the heart of God, because Jesus is a sent savior. He "made his dwelling among us," literally *pitched his tent* (John 1:14). When we cross the bridge, we do likewise; we imitate the one who dwells among us by living and dwelling among those he loves—especially those far from him. That is incarnational mission.

Jesus did not just incarnate in the sense that he emptied himself and took on our human nature (see Philippians 2:6-11). His incarnation included the human life that he lived among us, spending his first thirty years, for the most part, in seclusion and anonymity, working as a carpenter. He lived among us, and then he lived his mission from there. That is incarnational mission.

That too is what the Church is called to do. We worship a missionary God who sent a missionary Jesus who sends a missionary Church.[22] Another way to think about this is that Jesus is the sacrament of God, and the Church is the sacrament of Jesus. What does a sacrament do but make an invisible reality—that is, the love of God—visible? In other words, Jesus makes the Father's love visible through his life, death, and resurrection, and the Church is sent out to make the life of Jesus visible and available to all people That means we need to build the bridge and cross it; it is not enough for us to stay on the island.

Let me give you an example. Imagine that we are back on our metaphorical island, and we meet the people across the water. We discover that those people speak French, and in order for our missionaries to be able to preach the gospel to our target community, they have to learn French. Hundreds of years go by, and our missionaries are doing really well. Unfortunately, we discover that the people across the water, for a variety of reasons, no longer speak French; they now speak Spanish.

The problem is that we have fallen in love with French. We have been speaking French for hundreds of years. Sending French-speaking missionaries is what we do; it is who we are. So we decide that our target community's inability to understand is not our problem; it is their problem. Therefore we will continue to send French-speaking missionaries, as is our custom.

Guess what will soon happen? We will become irrelevant to our target community. We may carry within us the greatest message known to the universe, but that is irrelevant because we cannot connect with the people we are sent to reach.

The disposition of incarnational missionary engagement, on the other hand, spurs us to change our methodologies so that we can best accompany and engage the people God has called us to serve. This is the manner of God himself. This, I believe, is what the Church is called to do in the twenty-first century.

To do this requires two things: The first is a commitment to live our apostolic identity. That is, we need to understand that evangelization is not something that the Church simply does; it is who she is. Every member of the Church, no matter his or her vocation, state in life, or office, shares in this apostolic and missionary identity (see *Catechism* 863).

Second, it requires us to have a strong foundation, so that when we engage with other cultures and worldviews, we can remain rooted in the one who is Truth and resist being seduced by those other entities. We need a healthy place where we can be formed, renewed, and reformed as we engage in our mission. This is a real and necessary balance to find. The danger is that this strong center—what we could call a culture focused on holiness—can be seen as an end in itself, thereby obscuring our missionary identity.

Living in Balance: Holiness and Mission

It might seem strange to talk about holiness in an almost negative way, but that is not my intention. I am not saying that holiness is "bad," dangerous, or somehow secondary in the life of a Christian. Living as a disciple of Jesus Christ means embracing fullness, what theologians call the "both/and" of Catholicism. Holiness *and* mission are *both* essential to the Christian life. One of the reasons we have three different approaches to the relationship between the Church and the world is that we have not always understood and lived this balance between holiness and mission.

So what is holiness? The core meaning of the Hebrew word for holiness is "set apart." Holiness is a reflection of the essence of God, who is set apart from his creatures. He is wholly *other*. The Scriptures are clear about this. God did not create out of necessity but out of free choice. Likewise, creation is not an emanation or an intrinsic part of God; that is a pantheistic understanding. God existed before creation, and he created everything out of nothing. Thus God is holy, and because God is holy, the people God has called for himself are holy. That is, they are set apart for the worship of God and for his purposes.

This is also true of the things associated with God. Think of liturgical objects. They are holy because they are set apart for a holy purpose. We respect that purpose.

When I worked with teenagers, as I used to often do, I would ask them what they would think if they saw me with my feet up, watching a football game and drinking beer out of a chalice. Would that be OK? They all knew that this would be a profane use of a holy object—even if they did not use that language. They had an instinctual sense that the chalice is set apart for use in the celebration of the Eucharist.

We often think of holiness as intimacy with God, and of a holy person as someone who possesses an intense, mature spiritual life characterized by moral perfection. In other words, we reduce holiness to the idea of being a saint. Of course, the saints have progressed, in cooperation with the grace of God, to profound levels of subjective holiness, but we must not lose sight of the objective meaning of holiness: to be set apart. The Church has been set apart by God and is, therefore, objectively holy—even if not all its members live saintly lives. All of the baptized, in this sense, are holy, regardless of how far along the spiritual path they have progressed.

Mission, on the other hand, means to be sent. The word "mission" comes from the Latin root *miss* (from the verb *mittere*), which literally means "to be sent." To say that we are a missionary Church means that we are a "sent" Church. To say that we are missionary disciples means that we are disciples Jesus sends into the world.

Now, whether we choose to go or to ignore our mission is entirely subjective. Just as we can say that the Church is objectively holy even if all its members are not subjectively living saintly lives, we can say that the Church is objectively missionary even if a majority of the Church is not living out its mission. Thus, our missionary call as Church is not about what we might do, or should do, or could do. Rather, it is our identity. It is who we are.

If we are to live out that identity, it has to be translated into a "posture." To live as missionary parishes or dioceses means to live with an outward-focused posture, oriented toward the world. We must, in turn, translate that posture into a culture, meaning that our outward-focused priorities become the standard or norm. Just as you could say that your parish has a culture of holiness because it is normative for your people to seek after a deeper holiness, you can say that you have a missionary culture in your parish when it becomes normative for parishioners to answer the call to mission.

One of the many radical truths highlighted during the Second Vatican Council is the reality of this universal call to holiness and mission. For many centuries, holiness and mission were seen primarily as the purview of priests and religious. This was evident, for example, even in lay-led initiatives such as the Catholic Action movement of the nineteenth and twentieth centuries. Catholic Action members worked to spread the gospel in word and deed and to promote social justice, but the Church saw their work as a participation in the apostolic office of their bishop.

Vatican II, however, definitively located the call to holiness and mission not in the Sacrament of Holy Orders or religious profession but rather in the Sacrament of Baptism. Christ calls *every* baptized Christian to both holiness and mission. In other words, we are objectively holy and called to grow in holiness because of our Baptism. Likewise, our Baptism gives us an objective missionary identity and calls us to subjectively live as missionary disciples.

A disciple is one who is committed to a lifelong, disciplined process of learning and growing toward maturity in Christ. If you are an authentic disciple, you will pursue holiness and experience a desire for mission. In fact, growth in holiness ought to impel us toward mission. As we become more like Christ, we experience a greater interior freedom and a growing desire to give our lives for others. Therefore, disciples will contemporaneously live out the call to holiness and the call to mission.

The challenge is not to allow the two calls (mission and holiness) to become disconnected. I am reminded of the call of the bishops of Latin America to pastoral conversion, in what is known as the Aparecida Document. In the section that outlines aspects of the formation process of missionary disciples, the bishops state, "Mission is inseparable from discipleship, and hence it must not be understood as a stage subsequent to formation."[23]

There are those in the Church today who put up a kind of artificial barrier between holiness and mission. They say that the first task of the Church is to help others encounter Jesus and become disciples. These disciples must be formed and must grow in holiness before they can be sent out on mission. In other words, missionary discipleship becomes a task of only a subset of God's people. However, I do not think this squares with experience.

Think of St. Paul. He had an encounter with Jesus on the road to Damascus, and within a few days, he was baptized. "At once," Scripture tells us, he went out to tell people about Jesus (Acts 9:20). St. Paul was immature as a Christian and had lots to learn. That does not change the fact that he was objectively called to be a missionary disciple and subjectively lived like one, right from the start.

In our work at Saint Benedict, and throughout the world with Divine Renovation ministry, we find that the best missionary disciples are not necessarily those who have spent their life in the Church, possibly even pursuing a life of discipleship. Rather, the most energetic and fruitful missionary disciples are often the people who met Jesus the week before! They possess an enthusiasm and ardor that is contagious, and they have no problem inviting family and friends to come to the parish and experience an evangelizing process like the Alpha Course.

Back when I was a teenager, I was forced to go on a "stupid" retreat weekend. I really was not too excited about any of it, but I encountered Jesus Christ and his Spirit in a life-changing way on that weekend. In that moment, I knew two things: I wanted to go deeper, and I wanted to tell others about what I had experienced. I wanted to live as a disciple and grow in holiness—even though I did not know what any of that was called. I also wanted to share God's love with my friends, family, and those I met.

My conversion experience was barely thirty minutes old, and I was a missionary disciple. Truthfully, I was not very good at it, but I was a missionary disciple.

Sometimes, as we grow in holiness, we become disconnected from mission. We focus too much on our own spirituality or on the riches of our Tradition, neglecting our call to be missionary. We spend our time with the rest of the Catholic Club, talking about exceptionally Catholic things. We do not realize how non-Catholics or non-Christians see us, that they have no clue what we are talking about.

Furthermore, we sometimes treat people who are not in the "club" as "less than" we are. Even if not intending to, we can project an attitude of moral superiority. Consider how movies and TV shows portray Christians—typically as miserable, closed-minded, judgmental people. Sure, there are folks like that in the Church, but certainly not the majority of us. Yet that is how others perceive us.

Even if we do not come across as weird or judgmental, we might seem totally irrelevant to the many people who have come to see the Church—and by extension, Jesus—as having nothing to offer. That sense of irrelevance is largely because we, the baptized, called to bear Jesus into the world, have chosen not to do so, whether intentionally or unintentionally. Furthermore, many of the folks we need to reach with the gospel are not outside the Church; they are sitting in our pews. Since we have lost our missionary edge, we even fail to reach the people who actually go to church but who increasingly find their experience of faith irrelevant to their lives.

When a parish loses a missionary focus, intolerance sets in. We saw this at Saint Benedict. Some of our folks—even those who three or four years before had not been churchgoers or believers—became Super Catholics and lost their missionary edge. From that point on, they began to view someone seeking the Lord, even a new believer, as a threat—someone from whom you could catch spiritual germs. They wanted to spend their time hanging out with individuals who were as spiritually mature and deeply rooted in the Catholic faith as they were. Spending time with those seeking God or who were beginning to develop a relationship with him was definitely not their preference or priority. This retreat into the Catholic Club—the world of the Super Catholic—is a major temptation for long-time and new Christians alike, when holiness and mission become unbalanced.

Jesus told his disciples, "Come after me, and I will make you fishers of men" (Matthew 4:19). Well, have you ever gone fishing? When you catch a fish, it does not come out of the water on a plate, cleaned, gutted, breaded, and cooked with a piece of lemon on the side. It is slimy, and it wriggles all over the place. You have to deal with that before you can produce the finished dish. Somehow in our parishes, however, we have developed an intolerance toward people who are fresh out of the water, so to speak—who are not spiritually mature, who cannot speak the language, who do not have their life all together. If we want to live out missionary engagement, we need to embrace all of the messiness in the lives of others.

In *Divine Renovation*, I spent time exploring the model of Belong, Believe, Behave. This model says that if people belong to a life-giving church community and come to believe in and have a relationship with Jesus, they will ultimately behave according to Christian principles. The model is based on the premise that, in the twenty-first century, it is difficult for people to come to belief in Jesus without first experiencing the sense of acceptance and love that comes with belonging to a community rooted in Jesus.

In the past, we operated out of a Behave, Believe, Belong paradigm. In other words, if you behaved and believed the right way, you could then belong to a community of faith. Back then society had clear norms regarding behavior, as well as a more clearly defined social structure. If you knew what broad social tribe you belonged to, you could easily see how you should behave and what you should believe.

In many Canadian rural towns, for example, the Catholics lived on one side of the tracks, and the Anglicans lived on the other side. You knew where the division lay, and you knew how to behave and what to believe. In that world, if you behaved the right way and believed the right things, you could belong to a particular faith community.

If we want to live as missionaries in the world today, however, we have to begin with belonging. We need to help people experience the love and acceptance of a community of faith—even if they do not quite believe the same things that we do. That is part of the missionary act.

Of course, we are not talking about watering down the Church's teaching or welcoming and approving of sinful behavior. That often is the first objection Catholics raise when we talk about meeting people where they are, creating a space for them within community life, and loving them. These Catholics seem to fear that we are trying to change Church teaching. Perhaps that immediate reflex is a sign that many of us have not yet mastered this balance between holiness and mission— that perhaps our embrace of mission lags behind our quest for holiness.

Creating an experience of belonging for people does mean that we must be willing to share life with those who may be different from us. We would do well to remember our own journey of faith. No one comes in contact with the Church and suddenly lives the Christian life perfectly. None of us do, including me and you.

When our focus on holiness overwhelms our missionary sensitivity, we become intolerant and unwelcoming of people who are at different stages of the faith journey. This is a serious problem in many of our parishes. We see it often in Alpha Courses, when nonchurchgoers are put in small groups with a bunch of "churchy" people. It takes all of three minutes for the nonchurchgoers to recognize that they do not belong there.

In many ways, parishes and dioceses can be like families where all the adult children live at home. There is a rhythm and pattern to that life. Imagine that same family when a newborn infant shows up. Now the rhythm of life is interrupted by this addition to the household who requires attention. The baby's presence is inconvenient; it disturbs family members, some of whom can easily come to resent the child. That is what can happen in a parish community if the commitment to holiness grows faster than the desire for mission.

Parishes also find themselves in trouble when their desire to an-swer the call to mission is not equally rooted in a desire for holiness. When that happens, mission is reduced to ideology, and ministries can become simple ego trips. In these situations, it can be difficult to distinguish the parish from any other charity or nongovernmental organization (NGO).

Think about how often faith becomes entwined with politics and political issues. Of course, the principled application of Church teaching to particular social and political issues is part of the responsibility of missionary disciples. However, if a parish's social engagement is not rooted in Christ, politics can co-opt faith. We are called to see our politics through the lens of our faith, but when the desire for mission is not balanced with holiness, we end up seeing faith through the lens of politics.

On an individual level, when our desire for mission is not connected to our search for holiness, ministry becomes less about God's will and more about our own agenda. It becomes ego driven, a tool for human ambition. We start doing things for God whether or not he is actually calling us to do them. If our activism is not absolutely grounded in the person of Jesus, it can go off the rails.

Ultimately, holiness and mission are linked realities. Remember that holiness means to be set apart for God's purposes, and Scripture and Tradition clearly reveal that God's purposes are missionary. He sent his Son, Jesus, into the world to seek out those who were lost and help them return home. We receive the life of Christ, become daughters and sons of God, and thereby share in the missionary work of Jesus. Everything we do is through him, with him, and in him in the unity of the Holy Spirit; otherwise it ceases to be Christian mission.

Fundamentally then, mission cannot be separated from holiness. We see this unity manifested perfectly in the life of Jesus Christ.

CHAPTER 4

Living Jesus' Model

In Paul's Letter to the Colossians, he writes that Jesus is "the image of the invisible God" (1:15). In Greek, the word used for "image" is *eikon*, or "icon."

The Jews understood that God's holiness, his other-ness, was infinite, and they forbade the making of any images to represent God. The incarnation of Jesus, however, reveals to humanity the face of God, rendering visible what was unseen. What we see when we look upon Jesus can be shocking! Why? The One who was the image of the invisible God consistently sought out and befriended the lost and outcast.

I heard someone say that if Jesus carried a business card, it would read: Jesus of Nazareth—Friend of Tax Collectors and Sinners. Jesus perfectly embodies the mission that the Church is called to live. Yet at the same time, he is the perfection of holiness. There was no one holier or more missionary than Jesus. His life is the model for how we should live as Church.

Remember our discussion of the Church's three possible stances in relation to the world? This may be a bit of an oversimplification, but mission without holiness can be *accommodation*. Likewise, holiness without mission tends toward *isolation*. Finally, holiness balanced with mission fosters *missionary engagement*, which as I have said, is the proper stance of the Church.

Missionary Engagement

Looking at the life of Jesus, we see that he came to seek and to save the lost. He did not just hang out, open an office, book appointments, and wait for people to come to him. He went out. Jesus' ministry followed a consistent pattern of encounter—encountering others in the midst of their pain, suffering, and brokenness. Jesus was *the* missionary; he was a missionary *par excellence*.[24] He was sent by the Father, and after his resurrection, this sent One sends his own followers. Before he releases them into the world, however, he commands them to "stay in the city until you are clothed with power from on high" (Luke 24:49).

Jesus sends the Church on mission and bestows on the Church power to accomplish that mission through the gift of the Holy Spirit, given at Pentecost. The Church truly begins on that amazing day when the Holy Spirit descended upon the disciples of Jesus with tongues of fire. If we want to live out the reality of missionary engagement fruitfully—as individuals, parishes, and dioceses—we *must* actively invite and cooperate with the presence, person, and power of the Holy Spirit.

We need to experience a new Pentecost in our lives. In John's Gospel, we read that Jesus breathes upon the disciples, bestowing on them the Holy Spirit. He says to them (and by extension, to us), "As the Father has sent me, so I send you" (John 20:21).

I love the words of Pope St. Paul VI in *Evangelii Nuntiandi*: "It is the Holy Spirit who, today just as at the beginning of the Church, acts in every evangelizer who allows himself to be possessed and led by him."[25]

When we were baptized, we received the Holy Spirit, who "breathed upon us" new life in Jesus Christ. As Jesus pitched his tent among us, we the Church must pitch our tent among those we are called to reach. By the power of the Holy Spirit, we can do this, becoming the Father's incarnate love for others as we break open our lives and walk with people wherever they are.

As we do this, we must proclaim the whole truth: the entirety of the gospel and the richness of life in Christ that comes to us through the apostles and their teaching. The real question though is, how should we proclaim that whole truth to a world that no longer understands our worldview, that no longer thinks in the theological and philosophical categories of the Church? How do we translate it so that the world can hear and experience the freedom to receive or reject the gospel?

It is quite possible that the vast majority of people who reject Christianity do not understand it because we have failed to present the gospel message and Christian Tradition in a way they can receive. We have not translated properly for those we are trying to reach.

There is an old Italian phrase, *Tradutorre, traditore,* which simply means "to translate is to betray." In other words, whenever we translate something, we run the risk of losing some meaning in the translation. However, it is possible to translate properly and not lose anything. How best to translate unchanging truths into a different language is one of the most pressing questions in the Church today.

This translation effort is made more difficult by the presence of factions within the Church. As we have seen, accommodationists, under the guise of translation, want to undermine and surrender parts of the Tradition. Isolationists, on the other hand, often perceive any attempt to translate as betrayal and a source of ambiguity and confusion. The isolationist will only tolerate "insider" language. Remember, however, the words of Pope Francis and his "dream of . . . a missionary impulse capable of transforming everything [including language] . . . for the evangelization of today's world."[26]

The missionary impulse will change our vocabulary, our language, and how we communicate the gospel. It can do so while maintaining the unchanging dimension of our Tradition as found in the great creedal statements of the faith and in the *Catechism of the Catholic Church.* However, if we want to live as missionaries and engage the people we meet where they are, we will have to commit to and persevere in this translation, even if isolationists believe, incorrectly, that this will introduce impurities into the faith.

Again I wish to quote Pope Paul VI and his foundational reflection on evangelization in the modern world, written in 1975, ten years after the close of the Second Vatican Council. In this document he recognizes the necessity for and the risk of such a translation:

Evangelization loses much of its force and effectiveness if it does not take into consideration the actual people to whom it is addressed, if it does not use their language, their signs and symbols, if it does not answer the questions they ask, and if it does not have an impact on their concrete life. But on the other hand, evangelization risks losing its power and disappearing altogether if one empties or adulterates its content under the pretext of translating it.[27]

The isolationist worldview has been with us from the earliest moments of Christianity. Think for a second of the incarnation itself. The Word became flesh. This is not only a kind of translation, but the ultimate translation. The earliest Christological heresies were not denials of the divinity of Jesus; those came later. Rather the first heresies about Christ were denials about his *humanity*. Those obsessed with purity found the idea that God would take on flesh repulsive, offensive, and scandalous. John writes in the fourth chapter of his first letter that the spirit of the antichrist is the one who denies that Jesus has come in the flesh (see 1 John 4:2-4).

Why would God take on human nature, after all? Why would the perfect and holy choose to become one of us and live among the impure and broken? Fundamentally the incarnation is a scandalous translation. The stance of those with rigid isolationist views, who see missionary engagement as a threat and translation as betrayal, can reflect the spirit of the antichrist.

Yet Jesus is the model of missionary engagement. Think of the great hymn of emptying that Paul includes in the second chapter of his Letter to the Philippians (see 2:5-11). This is one of the earliest texts of the New Testament, and it actually predates Paul's letter. Scholars tell us that this hymn was used a great deal in the early Church. St. Paul uses it to implore the Philippians (and us) to have the same mind that was in Christ.

What does the mind of Christ reveal? It reveals the integral connection between holiness and mission. Jesus was fully holy and fully missionary without compromise. Philippians 2:6 begins by telling us that "though he was in the form of God," this did not prevent him from emptying himself.

Many translations do not quite capture the nuance of this text. St. Paul used a present participle, which carries the connotation of "while being the whole time in the form of God." This may be an over translation but not a betrayal. Jesus never stopped being divine, but he did not regard equality with God as something to be exploited. He emptied himself, taking the form of a slave (see Philippians 2:6-7). The incarnation did not violate his integrity. It did not violate his holiness. The Word of God took on flesh to become fully incarnate in order that he might reach those for whom he had been sent. The Word of God was translated, but there was no betrayal.

Jesus is our model for living out the Church's mission. So we see in this great hymn an acknowledgment that, like Jesus, the Church can empty itself and take the form of a slave without compromising integrity or the truths of the faith.

Thus both the accommodationist and isolationist positions are errors that we must carefully discern and deal with so that they do not influence parish and diocesan life and culture. Sometimes the errors are so apparent that it does not take much discernment to uncover them.

For example, I first encountered the isolationist mindset in a conversation with another priest. He told me that his priestly vocation was primarily to protect the Eucharist from people! Why? Because sometimes people receive the Eucharist who should not.

Perhaps these people are not spiritually prepared or in a state of grace; they may not even be Catholic. This often happens in parishes, particularly at weddings and funerals. It is a challenging situation. We want people to feel welcomed, but we want to uphold the Church's teaching around the Eucharist. We fail to adequately explain this teaching, however, and rather than helping people understand the nature of the sacrament, the isolationist attempts to protect God from people.

If that was God's stance, we would not have the incarnation or Christianity, let alone the Eucharist. God's stance is one of missionary engagement. It is risky. It opens itself up for possible abuses and errors, but in the light of the incarnation it must be so.

Missionary engagement also challenges our disposition. We are never going to reach people we do not love. We will not be effective channels of God's love to the world if we are angry at the world.

I remember waiting for a meeting to start and listening to people share what had been happening in their lives and where they were in their faith. One person started talking about all the people in his life who did not have any faith—and none of what he said was positive. Basically his message was that these folks lived pathetic, messed-up lives without Jesus. I almost lost it.

I started to think about my own life. I have a relationship with Jesus, and I am still kind of messed up! Imagine where I would be without him at all. How easy it is to forget this. Instead of looking on people with understanding, we can sometimes look down our noses at them. We can be like the pharisee coming to the synagogue and saying, "O God, I thank you that I am not like the rest of humanity" (Luke 18:11).

Jesus had a radically different approach. We see it in Matthew's Gospel. When Jesus looked upon the crowds or met individuals, he was moved with compassion. He was not disgusted by them. He loved them. If we do not share that same compassion, we might as well retreat into our fortress, man the towers, and protect our perfect club from the impurities of outsiders.

Jesus, of course, modeled that sometimes we must speak challenging truths, but this must always be "the truth in love" (Ephesians 4:15). Compassionate love must be the foundation of the Church's missionary efforts, or we will not bear fruit. Today many Catholics, particularly in North America, exhibit anger—not at individuals necessarily but at the culture. We used to have a powerful Christian culture in the West that produced stirring works of art, architectural marvels, beautiful music, and our modern rule of law. For a host of reasons, that Christian culture has fractured and all but disappeared. We now live in a post-Christian culture, and plenty of Christians are angry about that. They seem to feel that secular culture has hijacked and deliberately destroyed Christian culture.

If you hold that worldview, how could you not be mad at the world and those secular voices and entities? Think of the language that we use when we talk about the "culture wars." It is hard to share the love of God with a culture if you see yourself at war with it. This is not to deny that we must do battle with particular insidious ideas or ideologies. We cannot be naïve, but we must also take great care that in our battle fervor we do not begin to see people as just an enemy to be opposed rather than one to be loved.

Scripture does not say that "God so hated the world that he sent his only Son to sit in judgment over all humanity." The One who is perfectly holy and just has the right to sit in that kind of judgment, but instead we read that "God so loved the world that he gave his only Son, so that everyone who believes in him might not perish but might have eternal life" (John 3:16).

This is our call: to love the world as God does and to pour ourselves out so that others might live in the fullness of God's kingdom. The ultimate goal of parish renewal is not simply to have an amazing parish but to have an amazing world, a world renewed by the grace of God. The key to this lies in fruitful missionary engagement.

Model or Mission?

To ensure that we are living in a spirit of incarnational missionary engagement, we must wrestle with a fundamental question: Are we more attached to our model or to our mission? This is the most important question we can ask at all levels of Church life—parish, diocesan, and universal. What is most important to us? Our model—that is, our customs, structures, habits, methodologies, and schedules—or our mission, the salvation of the world? If we want to bear fruit, we must become a Church that is willing to change its model in order to dwell fruitfully with those to whom we have been sent.

Whenever I use this language of change, I can sense the resistance. The way we have lived out our common baptismal vocation within parochial structures may have worked well at one time, but everything has shifted around us, and it is time to examine our models so that we can fruitfully impact individuals, culture, and society through the power of the gospel. Otherwise we risk becoming irrelevant.

Perhaps two examples from recent history will illustrate my point:

When I give a talk, I will often ask those wearing watches to look at them closely. Then I ask if anyone has a watch that says "Made in Switzerland" on the dial. The last time I did this, there were four hundred people in the audience, and only a couple of people raised their hands. If I were giving a talk fifty years ago, probably 50 percent of the people would raise their hands. So what on earth happened to the famous Swiss watch industry? (I was recently in Switzerland, speaking to 350 people, and only about twenty had Swiss watches!)

The answer is found with the development of the digital wristwatch, powered by quartz technology. The first quartz-powered wristwatch debuted from Seiko in 1969 and caused what is known as the Quartz Crisis in horological history, with a massive shift in market share going to this cheaper and more accurate new technology.

The curious thing is that a Swiss company created one of the foundations for the first quartz wristwatch in 1966: namely, a quartz pocket watch. The response to this new tech was moderate at best, and the leadership of the Swiss watch industry doubled down on their mechanical approach to watchmaking. Essentially they believed that they were known for the intense and time-tested craftsmanship of mechanical watchmaking—the gears, levers, escape wheels, and balance springs. That was who they were, and so they kept going down their traditional path and largely ignored quartz technology.

Within roughly ten years, the watch industry shifted. By 1978 the industry produced and sold more quartz watches than mechanical ones. Today mechanical Swiss watches have become the purview of a very small group of wealthy collectors, and the supreme beauty of their gears and levers have become totally irrelevant to most people.

The Kodak film company offers another example of the fruit of resisting change. While some readers will have to google this, others may remember a time when you had to buy a canister of film and place it in a camera in order to take pictures. You only had enough film for twelve or perhaps twenty-four pictures per canister. What is more, you could not preview your shots. When you reached the end of your film, you had to take it out and bring it somewhere to be developed. Sometimes you had to wait days before you got back the photographs and negatives of the film. Then you could call the family around you and gaze at the pictures—only to find that ten of them consisted of close-ups of the photographer's thumb!

Back in the day, Kodak cameras and their film were ubiquitous. Whenever I see the Kodak logo, it brings back warm and fuzzy feelings associated with family vacations. All the clunky aspects of the picture-taking process only added to the experience.

In 1976 Kodak held 90 percent of all film sales and 85 percent of camera sales in the United States. Then, in 1994, digital cameras rose in popularity. Now you could take pictures, preview them instantly, and share them quickly. Analog, film-based cameras quickly became a thing of the past.

Surprisingly, it was a Kodak engineer by the name of Steven Sasson who developed the first digital camera. Kodak leadership decided not to move forward with a line of digital cameras because they feared, rightly so, that it might destroy its film business. They pronounced the digital camera a dead end and told themselves it would never catch on. On January 19, 2012, Kodak filed for Chapter 11 bankruptcy protection and passed into irrelevancy, though it still exists as a company.

A Cause for Hope

We must all wrestle with this reality: any organization that places greater value on its model rather than its mission will ultimately die. Strangely, though, I think this is another reason why I have hope. As difficult as it is to answer the model vs. mission question, *if* we answer it properly, *if* we actually choose to let go of our fruitless, outdated models and focus on our mission, cooperating at all times with the Holy Spirit, something new *will* emerge.

Amazing things are going to happen because the gospel has lost none of its potency. Jesus Christ *is* the Lord of the universe. He is *still* alive, and he is *still* changing lives. The Holy Spirit is *still* poured into the hearts of believers, and God is *still* capable of doing infinitely more than we can ask or imagine.

Yet God continues to ask the ancient question we see throughout Scripture: "Whom shall I send?" and he looks for men and women who will say, "Here I am; send me—in spite of my weaknesses and limitations. Send me!" (see Isaiah 6:8).

Why is God constantly on the lookout for such disciples? Because the life, death, and renewal that we experience in the Church is cyclical: it echoes throughout Scripture and Church history. The people of God struggle; they are in dire straits. They cry out to God, and God comes to the rescue. Things get better, but because of these improvements, people become complacent. They once again grow distant from God; and because they are distant, things go badly. So they cry out to God, and he shows up—and it goes on, and on, and on in this manner.

The growth of the monastic system provides an example. St. Benedict, who lived from about A.D. 480 to 547, is generally credited as the founder of Western monasticism. As a young student, Benedict went to Rome, where he was appalled by the decadence of this supposedly Christian city. No longer outlawed, Christianity was the accepted religion of the empire and of the upwardly mobile. Only a short time before, martyrdom was the price you could pay for your faith, but devotion was now at a low ebb.

Benedict was appalled by the pagan behavior of his supposedly Christian classmates. He left Rome and headed to Mount Subiaco, where he became a hermit. Others soon joined him, and he created a rule of life that ushered in a way of living as a Christian in community.

This way of life was spiritually austere and attractive to the serious Christians who were fleeing the increasingly corrupt cities. These monastic communities spread throughout Europe. But as they grew in influence, the members became complacent, and monasticism declined.

As it did, however, a new movement emerged from the Abbey of Cluny in the early 900s. This Cluniac reform focused on reclaiming the traditional elements of Benedictine monastic life. New Cluniac monasteries spread around Europe and became influential—and then this movement too lost its vitality and declined.

That is when God raised up St. Bernard of Clairvaux, who entered the abbey of Cîteaux, an abbey established in 1098 as a reform of the Benedictine order. Bernard was sent out to found the abbey of Clairvaux in eastern France, to further the aims of that reform. From there the Cistercian movement (from the word *Cîteaux*) flowed out to renew the stagnating Benedictine order.

Later still the life of the Cistercian movement faltered, only to be renewed by the efforts of the monks at the abbey of La Trappe. Thus Trappist monasteries grew throughout Europe, until that movement also began to decline.

The point of this trip through monastic history is to highlight a pattern we see in both secular and Church history: new systems begin to emerge as the dominant system levels off and starts to decline. Decline, renewal, and new life do not happen in a strict chronological order. It's not that something dies and then something new is born. Renewal and new life happen simultaneously alongside stagnation and decline. As the dominant system dies, something new *is already* emerging.

This is what the Berkana Two Loop diagram, which we looked at in chapter two, captures. Even as most leaders in a dying organization focus on palliative care, there are always a few who see the seeds of new life and work as midwives to ensure that this renewal is birthed. This dynamic also applies to parishes, dioceses, and the global Church: the new emerges from within the old. How, then, do we bring this renewal to birth?

Many parishes and dioceses face immediate problems related to the issues surrounding mission over infrastructure. Why is this important? Recall the pyramid framework from the introduction. The right structure is essential to mission; it helps or hinders leadership in the creation of cultures that support effective mission strategies, which in turn allow parishes to use tools effectively in order to bear the most fruit.

Recognizing this, parish and diocesan leaders all over the world are asking the same question: "How do we change our infrastructure?" This book will offer some help in that area, but as we said in chapter 1, those who successfully give birth to the new reality, illustrated in the two-loop renewal process, start with a compelling vision.

It begins with vision.

In my first book, I wrote about a vision of the Church that inspires me. I used the image of a photocopier, not in the sense of making everyone the same but rather in terms of the process of photocopying. A good photocopier brings something in from the outside, processes it, and then sends it out, possibly to change the world. Bringing something in from the outside is like evangelization: we bring people into the life of the Church, and we offer the sacraments of initiation. Then comes the processing: printing, sorting, hole punching, and stapling. Those are like the processes we have for discipling people: bringing them into a deeper relationship with the Lord and helping them grow spiritually: to identify and develop gifts, discern their unique call, and then go out to be ambassadors for Christ to the world.

This is what a well-functioning Church should do. Yet the Church is often like a broken-down photocopier. It has a jam in the entry, and it is jammed on the inside, and the out tray is not functioning either. Instead it is overheating, and smoke is coming out, and everyone is angry and upset. Life in the Church is often like this.

In the midst of these malfunctions, however, the Lord is doing something new. He is bringing forth new life, a new kind of movement capable of transforming parishes and the life of the Church beyond the parish.

The Necessity of *Titanic* Change

Most people are familiar with the tragic tale of the *Titanic*—a British passenger ship built in the early part of the twentieth century and considered unsinkable. On its maiden voyage in 1912, it narrowly avoided an exposed section of iceberg, only to run into that iceberg's submerged mass. As the ship started to take on water, crew members attempted to usher passengers into lifeboats. Incredibly, most of the passengers ignored these attempts.

In James Cameron's 1997 movie about this tragedy, the *Titanic* passengers' belief in the invulnerability of the ship kept them from even considering the need for a lifeboat. Without that sense of reality, guests felt it was too cold and noisy on the ship's deck to bother heading there. Instead they enjoyed cocktails and music while the ship headed to its doom. The "unsinkable" *Titanic* ultimately went down, and many lives were lost.

What most people do not know is that the salvage operation for the *Titanic* launched from Halifax, my hometown, and the recovery ship brought the bodies of many victims back there. Unclaimed bodies were buried in a cemetery close to where I live. So the history of the *Titanic* is visceral and very real for me.

There are many ways in which the image of the *Titanic* describes the situation of the Church today. I want to be clear that I am not saying the Church *is* the Titanic; I do not believe that for a second. The Church will live on; it is bigger than the parochial system. I do not even believe that parish-diocesan expression, in and of itself, is the *Titanic*. I do, however, believe that the model we have for parishes in many places—and by model, I mean everything we take for granted about how parishes currently function, as well as the whole network of parishes that make up a diocese—is dying.

It is sinking.

I think we have a choice. Either we cling to the established structure and go down, or we salvage what we can and launch the life boats, so we can cooperate with the Holy Spirit in building something new. Many Catholics today, however, are like those *Titanic* passengers, so assured of the unsinkability of our ship that they find the reality of change too cold and noisy. They would rather stay inside, drink brandy, and enjoy their meals while the ship continues to take on water.

People say, "Put your trust in God," but often they use that sentiment to justify clinging to the current model, as if God himself will somehow swoop in and change everything. Looking at the geography of the interior life and the history of salvation, I see the call of faith focused not on clinging to something but on letting go of something. Surrender requires great faith, but not the kind of faith by which we cling with white knuckles to what is going down in the hope that God is going to work a miracle. The invitation for us now, in this historic moment, is to let go and return to our identity as a pilgrim people of God, ready to trust boldly where God is leading us. We need to let go with hope as we head to the lifeboats and build a new reality.

The real question for us is "How badly do we want new life?" In talking with many Catholics, I have witnessed an interesting dynamic. Given an explicit choice between dying and changing, many Catholics literally pause and think about that choice, sometimes at great length. Sadly, many say, "Hmm, I'll take death, please—as long as it dies after I'm gone."

I would like to think that this reaction is rooted in a deep misunderstanding about the nature and mission of the Church, but sometimes it comes out of an intense selfishness. We have been given an incredible mission by the Lord, and yet we have made it all about us. Too many parishes are willing to cling to the sinking structure, even if it means cannibalizing the resources that would help build a new reality.

How badly do we, as parish and diocesan leaders, want new life? Are we willing to embrace a new vision for parish life, which may call us to stop doing some things that were once "successful" or are beloved by core members of the community? Change means letting go of what we have known in terms of our model and venturing forth to cooperate with the Lord. The Israelites had to make a similar choice when God called them to leave Egypt—a place of bondage but also a place of some comfort and safety—and move into the desert to search for the Promised Land. Change takes great faith; it is not a comfortable path.

I'm reminded of a cartoon in which a man asked a group of people, "Who wants change?" All the hands went up. Then he asked, "Who wants to change?" And not a single hand was raised.

In the Church, we often want the fruit of change without the pain of change. If you ask a group of Catholics if they want a parish that would be relevant to their sons, daughters, grandsons, and granddaughters; a parish that possessed dynamic worship and fostered the growth and transformation of its people; a parish that would have great missionary outreach, helping people come to know Jesus; a parish that went to the existential peripheries to work with the poor and the broken—they would generally say, "Of course!" Everyone wants that kind of church. Then you change a Mass time to try to build that kind of parish, and there is a revolt!

Letting go of the model and cooperating with the Holy Spirit means that we need to lead change. This kind of authentic leadership is difficult. John Ortberg, an evangelical pastor and speaker, defines leadership as "the art of disappointing people at a rate they can accept."[28]

This is often the essence of leadership. Why? When we lead change, we move away from people's preferences to embrace a higher purpose or vision. It requires sacrifice from all of us: leaving what is familiar and comfortable, what may have defined us and our experience of being Catholic. We need to mobilize for the vision and create an infrastructure that supports and nurtures it.

That means we will experience pushback. If you are a leader, you will suffer, because no matter what you do, once you set a course in the direction of a new vision, you will be opposed. No matter what you do, you will be criticized. No matter what you do, you will be attacked. Since that is the case, strive to suffer for the right thing rather than for the wrong thing.

Grading on the Curve

The Rogers Innovation Adoption Curve might help you make this vision-oriented journey as a leader. It is a secular change-management tool that looks at the distribution of change acceptance across a general population.

It is very easy, when we are in the middle of "leading the charge," to become overwhelmed by the resistance. In many cases, the passion and volume of the resistors can amplify our perception of the actual size of this oppositional cohort and obscure the strength and depth of the supportive cohort that embraces the change. Examining the Rogers framework can help put our leadership efforts in perspective:

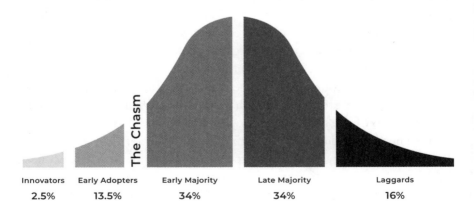

ROGER'S INNOVATION ADOPTION CURVE

The Chasm

Innovators	Early Adopters	Early Majority	Late Majority	Laggards
2.5%	13.5%	34%	34%	16%

This chart shows that, among every group of people, about 2.5 percent are what we would call Innovators. Despite the presence of problems, these folks will try new things to solve issues. They are hardwired to push forward, and they are less averse to risk than the average population. While they do not love the thought of failing, they do not see failure as a negative. Rather, failure is simply part and parcel of the drive toward a solution.

The next group in the Rogers diagram is the Early Adopters, which makes up about 13.5 percent of the general population. These folks watch the Innovators and, if nothing explodes in their faces, will get on board with the new approaches coming from the Innovators. That means that in any organization, you can count on roughly 16 percent of the population to lead change within that system.

If you look carefully at the Rogers Innovation Adoption Curve, you will likely see a delay between the Early Adopters and the 34 percent of the population who will become the Early Majority. This part of the curve is called the chasm, because the Early Majority will wait a while to see if there are positive results from the work of Innovators and Early Adopters. If strong evidence exists that new approaches are working, and if these approaches seem sustainable and reproducible, the Early Majority will, over time, embrace the new reality. Once the Early Majority does this, the Late Majority, another 34 percent of the population, will follow suit.

The final group in the Rogers Curve is called Laggards, and they make up the remaining 16 percent of the population. In general, the Laggards resist all change and will never adopt the new reality. Often they manifest as CAVE (Consistently Against Virtually Everything) Dwellers. They exist in every community and every organization, and they will often be the most vocal group.

Laggards complain constantly and generate such noise that their presence is felt disproportionately to their actual numbers. They are the ones who write anonymous letters in which they claim to represent five thousand like-minded people, who think that your idea is stupid and definitely not going to work. They send angry e-mails and make angry phone calls. Sadly, in church settings, these folks often cause leadership to question their direction and contemplate stopping.

Years ago, after a particular weekend at Saint Benedict, a staff member told me that there were lots of unhappy people and that he had received a number of complaints. I thought to myself, "Oh, that's not good." So I asked exactly how many complaints we had received. When I heard the answer, I was shocked. There were three complaints. We had fourteen hundred people at Mass over the weekend, and there were only three complaints. I was ecstatic.

Yet, three complainers can sound quite loud, especially when they claim to represent a larger contingent. Our human instinct tells us to pay attention to that, and we can become overwhelmed. All too often in the Church, therefore, we hit the pause button. Priests and bishops do this all the time. Of course, there are times when people have legitimate, critical feedback for us, but we need to discern how to handle it.

Here is a quick process of discernment you can use when trying to determine what to do with feedback.[29] The first question you should ask is whether the feedback is anonymous. If it is anonymous, then simply ignore it. Feedback that does not come from a thoughtful, real-life person willing to engage in dialogue is worthless.

If it is not anonymous, the next question is whether this person is on board with the vision. In other words, is he or she committed to where we are going? If you are trying to row to the north shore of a lake, for example, and this person wants to go to the south shore, then a disagreement about *how* you are rowing does not really matter. What the person disagrees with is your direction, and that is not negotiable.

If the person is supportive of the vision, the next question centers on the reason for the feedback. Is the person giving a theologically grounded critique, or does the disagreement rest on a question of preference? In my experience, the vast majority of the negative feedback we receive comes from a place of unsettled preferences. We are messing with the personal inclinations, habits, and proclivities of people who do not like to be unsettled. We are messing with their favorite Mass time, favorite style of music, preferred way of doing things, and so on.

Everyone has preferences; that is part of being human. In today's consumer society, however, our preferences can become enmeshed with a sense of entitlement, and that can lead to a sense of the primacy of one's preferences. Missionary disciples too have preferences, but they will surrender any preference for the sake of the mission of the Church.

So if there is a solid theological reason for the critique and the person is on board with the vision, then we have to pay attention to that feedback. But if the objection is about preferences, we cannot be distracted by it. The grumblings and machinations of the Laggards, who make up only 16 percent of our communities, cannot determine our direction, even if we risk losing these people.

The task of parish renewal and transformation can seem almost herculean. But there is really good news when we look at the Rogers Innovation Adoption Curve. We do not need to immediately convince the entire organization to leap into change; we only need to capture the hearts of 16 percent (the Innovators and Early Adopters) in our parishes and dioceses.

Many pastoral plans, at the diocesan and parish levels, fail because they do not move on that premise. Too often Church leaders listen to the Laggards, then exhaust themselves trying to lift everything and everyone up at the same time. It cannot be done. And when leaders follow this pattern and repeatedly see lack of fruit, they give up.

If you want to see authentic and sustainable transformation, identify the 16 percent (the Innovators and Early Adopters) among the clergy and laity, with whom you can work. Who are the 16 percent of people in your diocese who have the vision, the passion, and the willingness to risk doing something new? Identify them, come around them, and work with them to lead the change, knowing that eventually others will get on board—though perhaps not the Laggards, who believe every new idea is useless. We will talk more about this later in the book.

This reality is such good news for us. Many priests and bishops are burdened by the fact that not everyone is on board, but we do not need to have everyone on board; we can work in phases. Instead of one strategic plan for the renewal of a diocese, we need to have at least three strategic plans: one for the 16 percent willing to do something new; one that is a kind of holding pattern plan for the Early and Late Majority, who will wait; and a plan of action for how to handle the Laggards who would write a letter of complaint if Jesus himself showed up at the parish as a pastor invested in change.

What's in a Name?

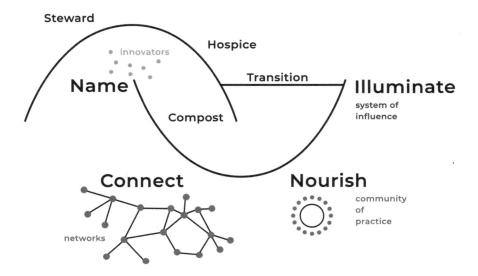

Returning to the Berkana Two Loop Theory we discussed in chapter two, we can see in the image above that, as the dominant system levels out and starts to decline, a new system begins to emerge. This is where the Innovators show up to start something fresh.

In order to start something fresh, however, the Innovators need to name the problems that they see. When a dominant and powerful system begins to decline, its leaders and proponents do not take kindly to individuals who start calling out issues. The prophetic Innovators are often seen as mosquitos or other pests; they are often not welcome.

In fact, the dominant system often sees Innovators as a threat, because the leaders of that system get their identity, security, and paycheck from that system; it is their livelihood. Within the Church, that means that those invested in the declining system raise all sorts of theological, cultural, and canonical roadblocks against the work of Innovators. As the dominant system slides into hospice mode, the Innovators will begin to connect with one another and form networks of innovation.

This is exactly what happened at the parish level at Saint Benedict. As Christ transformed people's lives through Alpha, these new disciples began to form networks. Whether they were cradle Catholics or previously had little connection to any church, they found each other.

Something new began to emerge, in spite of the dominant system that was still present.

Something new is emerging in the global Church as well. The Holy Spirit is raising up people and inspiring them to name the issues and provide fruitful solutions. People are coming together, sharing insights, praying together, supporting one another—and very slowly, as the dominant system continues to decline, these connections are becoming communities of practice.

Currently the goal of Divine Renovation Ministry is to move beyond networking and into establishing and nourishing intentional communities of practice. Other apostolates, ministries, and organizations are coming alongside parishes and dioceses to work toward the same goal. I have seen this happening at the parish level, and I am seeing it happen at the diocesan and global levels.

Finally, as we look to the Berkana Two Loop diagram, we can see three important words present as the dominant system dies: *illuminate, transition,* and *compost.*

A choice between the old and the new is *illuminated* as the old system fails and the new one begins to emerge. When the *Titanic* first struck the ice, and even when it became evident that the ship was in danger, there was some sense of alarm, but it was nothing compared to the alarm when the whole ship began to rapidly sink. The choice was much easier to make at that point. Within the Church, the worse things get within the dominant system and the more fruit emerges from the new system, the clearer the choice will be. Moving from the old system into the new, then, requires an experience of *transition.*

The third term, *compost,* reflects our call to salvage as much of our patrimony as makes sense for the new system—and here I am talking about a patrimony of buildings and the land upon which they are built. We have inherited these from past generations, and we must be good stewards, using them in cooperation with the Holy Spirit to create something new. They are not meant to be a means of sustaining our dying process.

As we have seen, there will be some people, both laity and clergy, who will not be able to let go of the dying system. Not everyone is going to be able to make the jump, which means that some people will be called to remain behind and to shepherd and care for the people who cannot transition. This will be a legitimate calling. We will need to be very careful to avoid labeling people as for or against change, because some of them will be called to remain, not out of opposition but out of obedience to the Lord.

This is undoubtedly a painful time in our Church, because we are going through a dying process. I think of the words of St. Paul, that we should be "always carrying about in the body the dying of Jesus, so that the life of Jesus may also be manifested in our body" (2 Corinthians 4:10). Jesus himself talked about how a seed must fall to the ground and die in order to bear fruit (see John 12:24).

Today we participate in the paschal mystery: the life, death, and resurrection of Jesus. This has always been central to the life of the Church, but we happen to be caught up in this mystery in a particular way as God calls us to lead during this historic moment.

I want to conclude with the words of Martin Luther King Jr.:

> Cowardice asks the question, is it safe? Expediency asks the question, is it politic? Vanity asks the question, is it popular? But conscience asks the question, is it right? And there comes a time when one must take a position that is neither safe, nor politic, nor popular but one must take it because one's conscience tells him it is right.[30]

I believe that in this time, the Lord is calling us forward, to be people of conscience and a people of loving consciousness—of the mission of the Church and the delight in which the Lord holds all people, especially those who are far from him. The Lord offered all of himself for the redemption of every human soul. Should we do any less?

CHAPTER 5

The Father's Heart

No, this is not a misplaced chapter or a nice spiritual detour in an otherwise organizationally minded book.

So far we have explored a framework for renewal both within and beyond the parish, and we established that this renewal must be grounded in a compelling vision. We have seen, however, that in order to create a dynamic vision, we must understand and confront the reality of our current situation, be founded on a solid theology of incarnational missionary engagement, and articulate a dream for the future.

In previous chapters, we examined the truth of the Church's current reality. Now it is time to articulate a dream for the future.

Consider the question we posed earlier: Is our desire for renewal rooted in what we want *from* people or what we want *for* people? What we want *from* people is about using people. What we want *for* people is about love, and only when the Church acts out of love will we reveal the heart of the Father to the people to whom we have been sent.

It is Jesus who—in his person, in his ministry, and in his teachings—most perfectly reveals the Father to us. As he said to the apostle Philip, "Whoever has seen me has seen the Father" (John 14:9). I believe that the Father's love is most powerfully revealed to us in the parable of the prodigal son, an extremely familiar Scripture passage for most of us. In this parable, Jesus gives us insight into the heart of God the Father, a heart for the lost. Parables, of course, are not allegories. The reflection that follows is meant to soften our hearts and remind us that all missionary our efforts should be formed and informed by what is revealed in this parable.

The challenge in breaking open an overly familiar passage of Scripture is that often we have already drawn our conclusions and are unconsciously closed to new insights. So try to erase everything you think you know about God, and come to the parable with a blank slate. Imagine, for example, that you have never heard of the God of Abraham and Isaac and Jacob, and you have never heard of the Gospels. All you have is this parable.

Ready to begin?

The Path of the Prodigal

Then he said, "A man had two sons, and the younger son said to his father, 'Father, give me the share of your estate that should come to me.' So the father divided the property between them. After a few days, the younger son collected all his belongings and set off to a distant country where he squandered his inheritance on a life of dissipation. When he had freely spent everything, a severe famine struck that country, and he found himself in dire need. So he hired himself out to one of the local citizens who sent him to his farm to tend the swine. And he longed to eat his fill of the pods on which the swine fed, but nobody gave him any. Coming to his senses he thought, 'How many of my father's hired workers have more than enough food to eat, but here am I, dying from hunger. I shall get up and go to my father and I shall say to him, "Father, I have sinned against heaven and against you. I no longer deserve to be called your son; treat me as you would treat one of your hired workers."' So he got up and went back to his father. While he was still a long way off, his father caught sight of him, and was filled with compassion. He ran to his son, embraced him and kissed him. His son said to him, 'Father, I have sinned against heaven and against you; I no longer deserve to be called your son.' But his father ordered his servants, 'Quickly bring the finest robe and put it on him; put a ring on his finger and sandals on his feet. Take the fattened calf and slaughter it. Then let us celebrate with a feast, because this son of mine was dead, and has come to life again; he was lost, and has been found.' Then the celebration began. Now the older son had been out in the field and, on his way back, as he neared the house, he heard the sound of music and dancing. He called one of the servants and asked what this might mean. The servant said to him, 'Your brother has returned and your father has slaughtered the fattened calf because he has him back safe and sound.' He became angry, and when he refused to enter the house, his father came out and pleaded with him. He said to his father in reply, 'Look, all these years I served you and not once did I disobey your orders; yet you never gave me even a young goat to feast on with my friends. But when your son returns who swallowed up your property with prostitutes, for him you slaughter the fattened calf.' He said to him, 'My son, you are here with me always; everything I have is yours. But now we must celebrate and rejoice, because your brother was dead and has come to life again; he was lost and has been found.'" (Luke 15:11-32)

As you begin to reflect on this parable, think about how those listening to Jesus would have received it. These listeners were part of Jesus' culture and were attuned to certain cultural realities that today's readers often miss. They would have immediately recognized, for example, that Jesus stacked the deck against this young man. He set up the story in such a way that his audience would be disgusted, not only by the actions of the younger son but also by the younger son himself. Jesus' listeners would have zero sympathy for this ungrateful man.

As the story opens, the younger son asks his father to give him his inheritance. Instantly the son is on thin ice with Jesus' listeners. Generally, only the older brother would receive an inheritance, not the younger, and only after the father died. By asking his father this question, the younger son basically declared that his father was as good as dead to him. Imagine how transgressive such a request would appear in a culture where respect for parents was written in the Mosaic law and where lack of respect was punishable by death.

Anyone hearing this story would have been shocked by the behavior of the younger son, but even more, they would have been surprised by the father's reaction. Instead of sending his son into exile, imprisoning him, or even putting him to death, the father allows the son to leave with half his property.

Scandalizing as these facts are, Jesus ups the ante. The younger son does not simply disrespect and shame his father; he also disrespects his family and the land of Israel, which was deeply connected to Jewish identity. He chooses to leave the country and live among Gentiles. He has essentially rejected his identity as an Israelite. Furthermore, the younger son lives an immoral lifestyle in the foreign land where he settles, further alienating himself from God and bringing shame on himself.

As if that is not enough, when famine hits, the younger son hires himself out to feed pigs. At this point, we can imagine that the Jews listening to this parable would have been beside themselves. Mosaic law regarded pigs as unclean animals, and yet the son not only tends the swine but also contemplates eating their food. The only reason he does not, according to the story, is that no one offers him any.

There is almost nothing redeeming about this young man—except, perhaps, the fact that he eventually decides to repent. A careful reading of the story, though, reveals that his "conversion" was not particularly authentic. Exhausted, tired, and hungry, the young man thinks back to his father's house and recalls that even the servants there had enough food. In other words, his repentance is motivated by self-interest.

He is truly a wretch!

Ten Revelations about the Father

Yet something powerful happens when the young man decides to return to his father. As we proceed with the story, we find that Jesus makes points about the father that give us a glimpse of the heart of his Father and, in turn, offer us a vision for his Church.

He Is Outward Looking

We hear in the parable that "While he was still a long way off, his father caught sight of him" (Luke 15:20). The father was facing outward toward the world; he had positioned himself to see his son as he approached. He was not turned inward, focused solely on the concerns of his household.

In the same way, the fundamental orientation of the Church must be outward. According to this parable of Jesus, the orientation of God the Father is outward; this is the orientation of love. We discussed this already in the introduction, when we distinguished between maintenance and mission.

Of course, we must maintain the flock, but when we deny this outward orientation as a Church, when we focus our resources primarily on our inner life, we become sick. We experience the symptoms of this sickness today. Earlier we used a malfunctioning photocopier, jammed and overheated, as an image of parishes that are turned in on themselves. This pull to be insider focused is normal and powerful. If we are not constantly intentional about maintaining a missionary posture, so many internal issues compete for our attention as leaders that we become exhausted and have nothing left for the outsider.

This inward focus is too often the norm in our Church. I recently went through my Twitter feed and came across a tweet from a relatively well-known Catholic. He wrote that he just wanted to be friends with people on "Catholic Twitter" so that we could pray for each other and help each other become saints. Does that not sound laudable and holy? It is good to be friends, to pray for one another, and to encourage each other to greater holiness. Who could argue with that sentiment?

At the same time, think about the implications of labeling this communication tool "Catholic Twitter," as if it is a club for Catholic insiders. Twitter is not a private chat room; it is a public forum. It is a tool for social engagement. Holiness is good, but it is not enough. We are called to holiness *and* to mission, not to one or the other. We must live out these two truths at the same time.

I yearn for a time when we will say that "Catholic Twitter" should disappear, and we should see ourselves as Catholics on Twitter, no longer an insider's club but heralds of the gospel to an increasingly digitized world. Social media—whether on Twitter or other platforms—is increasingly a very self-referential place, impenetrable to people on the outside, similar in a way to many of our parishes.

This way of thinking is problematic and symbolic of an inward focus. When Christians are inward focused rather than outward focused, our concerns and conversations become unhealthy. It is no surprise that when people on the outside of the Catholic world look in on Catholic social media, they are unlikely to find it an attractive place, burdened as it is by criticism, judgment, and infighting.

It does not have to be that way. Changing direction means changing from an inward to an outward focus.

He Is Vigilant

Not only did the father see the son, but he caught sight of him from a long way off. In other words, the father was not simply oriented outward; he was also scanning the horizon. This was not passive gazing. The father was attentive: he was awake and keeping watch. I can imagine him climbing up on the roof of his house every day and looking longingly down the road, finally catching sight of his son as soon as he came into view.

Are we focused on looking for men and women who are returning to God? Are we vigilant? Are we looking at all?

Ultimately this point about vigilance is a challenge for us as parishes and dioceses. Even when we do look outward, sometimes the farthest we get is the front door or the parking lot. The father's gaze, however, sees his son when he is *a long way off*. What does that mean for us as a Church as we reflect on the call to be missionary?

He Is Moved

Scripture tells us that when the father caught sight of his son, he "was filled with compassion" (Luke 15:20). The word that St. Luke uses here is derived from the Greek noun *splankna* (σπλάγχνα), which essentially means the bowels, intestines, or the innards. It is a visceral, *feeling* word in the Scriptures, referring to something that happens not in the heart but deep inside the guts. It is a difficult word to translate but one that Luke also uses to describe the movement of the heart of God in the *Benedictus*, the Song of Zachariah:

> In the tender compassion (*splankna*) of our God,
> the dawn from on high shall break upon us. (Luke 1:78, Liturgy of the Hours)[31]

Luke uses this word again to describe the compassion of the good Samaritan in that parable (see Luke 10:33). A variation of the word describes what Jesus experiences when he sees the crowds who are like sheep without a shepherd (see Matthew 9:36). And when he encountered the widow of Nain, *esplanknisthe* (ἐσπλαγχνίσθη)—"he was moved" (Luke 7:13). What was true of the compassion of Jesus in his ministry is a reflection of the heart of God the Father.

In light of this, we must ask ourselves as a Church—as dioceses and parishes—do we care? Is that care visceral? Are we moved by the plight of people who are lost?

I know that we are sometimes uncomfortable using the word "lost" to describe people who are not connected with Jesus or the Church. It sounds as if we are passing judgment on them. I want to be clear that it is beyond our pay grade, so to speak, to pass judgement on others, grade their relationship with God, or forecast their eternal destiny.

However, we do know that knowing Jesus makes a difference in this world and the next.

Foundationally, we are created by love, in love, and for love. Our hearts are fashioned to fit within the Father's heart. Jesus is the icon of the Father, and because we come to the Father through him, all humanity is lost unless we come "home" to the Father's love. In Jesus we discover our deepest identity, our truest purpose, and our ultimate destiny. Outside of Jesus, we live disconnected from those things and will never be able to fulfill our deepest longing for peace, perfect love, forgiveness—all the realities found in the home of the Father.

The use of "lost" reflects the language of Jesus himself: "For the Son of Man has come to seek and to save what was lost" (Luke 19:10). I encourage you to pray with the Scriptures, to come before the Father and ask him to help you be at peace with this language that describes the essence of Jesus' mission.

Many years ago, in the parish I pastored before Saint Benedict, we were holding an Alpha session one night in the parish hall. Sixty or so guests were attending, half of whom were disconnected from the Church, did not go to Mass, and did not go to any other church. They were coming in from the outside.

We asked a particular ministry that was meeting on the same night to use the basement of the church. Before we had started Alpha in the parish, this ministry had had a near monopoly on the use of parish facilities. They went down to the basement very reluctantly.

When the time came for the Alpha session to break into small groups, we sent two or three of the groups downstairs to some small meeting rooms. In order to get there, the people had to walk through the meeting space of the ministry we had consigned to the basement, temporarily interrupting that gathering. The woman who was in charge of this ministry group came upstairs immediately and confronted me. She was very angry.

I listened to the woman, trying my best to be patient. When I could get a word in, I asked her to think about it this way: The people who are here for Alpha often don't go to any church, and some of them don't even believe in God. Yet they are here, and they are our guests. So many of these folks are young, I remarked, and they are here to learn about Jesus and his Church. Isn't that incredible?

It took the woman only a second to respond. She rose up in my face and screamed, *"I don't care!"*

In that moment, I realized something: this woman really did not care. Maybe in the heat of the moment, her anger got the best of her, but at face value, she did not care. She was not moved by the thing that moves God the most.

That was a profound experience for me. I had been concerned for a long time about what this woman thought of me and my decisions, and now I felt a freedom I had never felt before. She did not care, and now I did not have to worry about her approval.

As a Church, we must care about—be moved by—the fact that so many people are far from God and not yet established in the Father's house.

He Goes to the Son

As we read in the story, the father did not simply wait for his son to knock on the door, nor did he just go to the son; he ran to him. This was a rather undignified action for the head of a household in ancient times, especially because the son was a complete wretch.

Do we as a Church run out to those headed toward us, or are we satisfied to merely open the doors of the Church and hope those on the outside drift in? So often the best of our parishes do the latter, failing to realize that the obstacles preventing people from coming into our parishes are bigger than they have ever been. We are basically saying to the world, "We're not going to you; you can come to us."

It is almost as if we expect nonchurchgoers and nonbelievers to be the missionaries, rather than the Church. "Leave your comfort zone, and come to us," we say in effect to those on the outside. "We're not going to leave our comfort zones and go to you."

Rather than saying to those on the outside, come in, what we as Church need to do is throw open the doors and say to the people *on the inside*, get out! Indeed, is that not what we do at the end of every Mass? That is the *missa*!

The words of sending—*ite, missa est*—used to be the very last words of Mass. That is where we find the root of the word "Mass" (*missio*). At the end of every single celebration of the Eucharist, we essentially say to the Church of God, "Get out and go to people. Serve them in love, care for them, befriend them. And when people ask you for the reason for your hope, reply, 'Come and see,' and invite them to return home."

I think of the analogy of a fishing boat, something very real to me because, in Nova Scotia, we have lots of fishing communities. Imagine that the Church, called by Jesus to be fishers of men and women, is a fleet of fishing boats. One of our primary purposes is to set out to catch people, just as the first followers of Jesus caught fish on the Sea of Galilee. Rather than going out into the deep and putting down our nets for a catch, however, we are tied up in the harbor. If we do manage to catch a fish, it is because that fish has swum into the harbor and jumped into the boat, causing us to say, "Oh, my goodness, what the heck is that?"

Frankly, we do not know what to do with that kind of fish other than flick it into the RCIA program or a similar ministry. The Church resembles a fishing fleet that never goes out to sea!

This is a major problem, but we are seeing change in a positive direction.

A number of years ago, for example, Christ the King parish in Ann Arbor, Michigan, joined our coaching network. It is a wonderful parish that has produced more vocations to the priesthood and religious life than perhaps any other parish in the United States in the last twenty or thirty years. It probably has one of the highest proportions of committed disciples of any parish in the United States. It is a community of holy people.

But the parish realized that, although many members were doing some form of evangelization, as a parish they had become self-referential. As a body, they had forgotten about mission. Their parish purpose statement underscored this reality: it was to be a parish for committed Catholics. By inference, therefore, the not so committed would have to go somewhere else. As a result, the parish was perceived as irrelevant to people on the outside and even a bit judgmental.

Christ the King joined our coaching network, and it has become a parish that is not only holy but also mission oriented. Instead of locking themselves in a holy huddle, parish members are increasingly able to reflect the heart of the Father and go to those on the outside.

He Does Not Focus on the Son's Repentance
Remember that the son's repentance was inauthentic, based on his need rather than contrition. When the father goes to him and embraces him, the son rattles off his repentance—perhaps he has even rehearsed it.

When he does this, it is as if the father is not even listening. He cuts the son off and tells his servants to get the finest robes for his son and rings for his fingers.

These were symbols of familial status. The father was clothing the young man once again in his dignity as son and heir. He restored the son to the family without making reference to his repentance or making the son squirm in any way.

Without a doubt, I have had some amazing encounters as a priest celebrating the Sacrament of Reconciliation. I have been privy to moments of unspeakable anguish and breathtaking beauty. Sometimes though, when people make an act of contrition and dwell with grizzly detail on how they really deserve to be punished by God, I wonder what this says about their image of God. Many seem to think of God as vindictive and angry. This is not the God revealed in the parable of the prodigal son.

Once, when I was a young priest, I made my confession, and the priest chastised me for not using a version of the Act of Contrition that he thought was the proper one. I was humiliated. Perhaps there are people who can identify with that experience. As I pray through the fifteenth chapter of Luke, I am struck again by the reality that the father is not even paying attention to the son's contrition. I am unsure how to process that theologically. We know that Jesus does demand repentance, but I think we need to process it spiritually and emotionally. The father did not humiliate the son. He did not make him squirm. He did not focus on the repentance, let alone on the sin.

What does that say to us when it comes to the kind of Church God is calling us to be? It does not mean that we disregard the reality of sin or move into moral relativism. However, it does invite us to be as gentle with others in their sin and brokenness as God has been to us, and to reflect on how well we, as parishes and dioceses, reflect the heart of the Father to others.

He Makes No Reproach

If I was the father in this parable, I probably would have gone down to the basement to watch Netflix or something as soon as I caught sight of my son. When the young man came in, I would have made a sarcastic comment. Something like "Oh, you're back? I told you so."

That is not the father that Jesus reveals in the story. There simply is no reproach in the heart of the father.

Looking back on my own ministry, when I was perhaps less wise, I want to cringe. I reproached people a lot, not actively but often in a passive-aggressive manner. For example, priests face an emotional struggle twice a year—at Christmas and Easter—when our churches fill up with people. At those times, I made lots of lighthearted but pointed comments about how we do this every week and not just twice a year, or how we decorate our sanctuary with more than just Easter lilies and poinsettias. These comments were reproaches disguised as good-natured humor.

I have since repented of this attitude, and now I try to better deal with that movement in my heart. I have realized that in those moments, I was taking things personally, as if people were rejecting me. In a sense, I took offense. Authentic and divinely rooted love, on the other hand, takes no offense (see 1 Corinthians 13:5). The heart of the Father is pure love.

This reality can challenge our image of God the Father, especially if we were raised with an understanding that when we sin, we offend God. In an ontological sense, we can say that sin is always an offense to God, who is all holy and all loving. Many people today, however, lack the philosophical and theological context that would help them understand the nuances behind the concept of what it means to offend God. For most people, the word "offend" will be placed in the context of personal relationships. When we "offend" somebody, we really put them off; we do something that makes them angry with us.

In this personal and relational sense, God is not offended by our sin; there is no reproach. If therefore we as a Church are going to reflect the Father's heart to the world, then we have to wrestle with the vision of being a Church that does not reproach the sinner in search of forgiveness—even if we feel they have not expressed contrition in the way we think is most appropriate.

He Has a Sense of Urgency

When the father commands his servants to put a robe on his son and rings on his son's fingers, he says to do so "quickly." There is no time to be lost. Quickly put sandals on his feet. Quickly, quickly, quickly.

We see in this urgency a reminder that the father ran to the son and a larger reminder that reconciliation, restoration, and celebration are urgent tasks of the Church. St. Paul says that we are "ambassadors for Christ, as if God were appealing through us" (2 Corinthians 5:20).

How it grieves my heart when even parishes that we work with in our ministry say that they will get to that evangelization thing at some point—maybe in a year, maybe in two. Where is the sense of urgency? It is the most important thing that we can do. Please do not put it off.

Make it one of the first things you do—and not just for the folks within the walls of your parish. I know that some parishes embrace a strategy that says, "Let's reach the people on the inside first." We cannot, however, simply put off the mission to those on the outside. We must reflect the heart of the Father, becoming the kind of Church we are called to be.

I heard a story about someone who went to his bishop to speak about the future of Alpha in the diocese. The bishop said that because they did not have any plans for what to do with people after Alpha, they should not start any new ones—just keep the ones that were presently going. I was perplexed by this. It is as if you are in a lifeboat and decide not to rescue any more people because there are not enough blankets and supplies to care for them.

No, you go and rescue the drowning people! Rescue people first, and then figure out the rest. We need to call on the Holy Spirit to restore in the Church—in us—a deep sense of urgency that flows from the Father's fierce love for his children.

He Kills the Fatted Calf

The killing of the fatted calf signified the start of a celebration, and celebration—specifically, what we celebrate—shapes the culture of any organization, including our parishes and dioceses. When we celebrate a person, event, process, or milestone, we communicate its value to us. In other words, celebration is a form of reward, so we should strive to be intentional about celebrating the right things.

In this parable, Jesus tells us what God celebrates: the return of the lost. For God it is the most important thing. How does that compare to our priorities as Church? What do we celebrate?

Often we celebrate whoever has been around the longest: "This person has been here for twenty-five years; let's give him a medal. This other person has been here forty years; let's give her two medals." The people who have returned to the Church do not even get a mention. This is not what God celebrates.

Look at the whole of Luke, chapter fifteen. Jesus offers three parables: the parables of the lost sheep, lost coin, and prodigal son. These parables have several things in common: something has been lost, something has been found, and there is a party.

The woman in the parable of the lost coin invites her neighbors to come and have a party when she finds the lost coin. Here is the great irony: the woman finds one coin, and she likely spends two coins to throw a party because she found the one coin. This is the economy of the kingdom of God; it is how God operates.

The question remains: how do we as a parish, as a diocese, and beyond celebrate what God celebrates and not just celebrate ourselves? How do we celebrate when we reach people who are on the outside?

We have done this over the years at Saint Benedict Parish through testimonies—written testimonies in our monthly magazine and in our annual financial report, testimonies delivered at special events such as prayer breakfasts, and even testimonies given after the homily at Mass several times a year, especially as we launch a new season of Alpha. The most important thing for us as a parish is helping people encounter Jesus Christ in a life-changing way and returning, or coming for the first time, to the Church and the sacraments. That's what we celebrate.

When we first started doing this, we experienced a lot of pushback. People were uncomfortable with it; they said, "We're Catholic, we don't do this. This is not what we celebrate." Other people were upset that we were celebrating the return of the lost and not the presence of the perennially faithful. In spite of this, we kept doing it.

And over the years, the attitude has changed. The celebration of people's return to Jesus is now an integral part of parish life at Saint Benedict.

He Has a Heart for the Older Brother

Throughout most of my ministry as a pastor, I have struggled with the "older brother" type, the one who starts to complain when the focus of the parish shifts outward and the community starts to celebrate the return of the prodigals. I found it difficult to be compassionate, loving, and patient with these older brothers. I would be frustrated by their anger and seeming blindness to the importance of the prodigal's return.

About two years ago, I was praying through the text of this parable, and it struck me: the father has the same heart for the older brother as he does for the prodigal! I came to see that if the father had a deep love for them, then so should I.

The reality is that our parishes are filled with older brothers. You might not notice it until your parish starts to focus on mission. Once a community adopts a sense of urgency, raises its focus beyond the walls of the parish, and starts to bear fruit, the older brothers will emerge, and they tend to not be happy. The idea that leaders would choose not to focus all their attention on the nurturing, celebration, and safety of the current community, and instead invest time, money, and resources into mission, is foreign to them.

Yet Jesus himself said, "What man among you having a hundred sheep and losing one of them would not leave the ninety-nine in the desert and go after the lost one until he finds it?" (Luke 15:4). I often imagine Jesus sharing this parable and those listening bursting into laughter. For right-thinking shepherds, it is a preposterous proposition. The answer to Jesus' question is quite simple: no one would leave their entire flock to search for one lost sheep. These shepherds would have invested their whole livelihood into their flock. They would not jeopardize their investment on a fool's errand, chasing one sheep. Forget the one; it's an acceptable loss.

The Father's perspective is fundamentally different.

Let us take a moment to reflect on who the older brother was in the parable and who these older brothers are in our parishes. Start by considering where the older brother had come from when he asked the servant what was happening. He came from the fields. He was working.

We discover that the older brother is dutiful. He never left home; he followed all the rules. In fact, he is so upset at the father's response to the prodigal son that he tells his father that he himself worked like a slave. Clearly he is hardworking, dedicated, and faithful. These are all wonderful things.

Yet if we look beneath the words of the older brother, we see what is going on in his heart. Underneath his dutiful obedience lie bitterness, anger, and resentment. That is why the older brother goes into a rage when he finds out that the father has killed the fatted calf and is throwing a party in honor of his brother. He worked hard for the father, but he never felt he received anything in return. This is not the mindset of a son but the mindset of a servant or slave. That is the core problem with the older brother: he does not know who he is!

Thus when the father pleads with the older brother, he is trying to restore his son's identity in a way that is different from how he handled the prodigal son but based on the same principles. Both the prodigal and the older son suffer from identity issues. They are acting and living in a manner that is inconsistent with who they are.

The father used robes and rings, the symbols of family, to let the prodigal know who he was and to restore him. As he pleads with the older brother, he tries to confirm his identity as well: "You're my son. Everything I have is yours. What do you mean, I never gave you gold, or killed the fatted calf for you and your friends? It's your gold and your calf. It all belongs to you. Don't you understand? You are not a slave! You are my son!"

We hear this message throughout the Scriptures, especially in Paul's Letter to the Romans: "You did not receive a spirit of slavery to fall back in fear, but you received a spirit of adoption, through which we cry, 'Abba, Father!'" (8:15). St. Paul also speaks of being freed from the slavery of sin, and this imagery resonated with people in the ancient world. During that time, you either owned a slave or were a slave yourself. Also, your fortunes could change. If, for example, you did not pay your debt, you could be sold into slavery.

This was the economy of Paul's day. Yet he spent a great deal of time letting the world know that it had been bought and paid for. Jesus paid our debt, not with something perishable, like silver or gold, but with his own body and blood. He did not stop there, however. Jesus did not just set us free, but he adopted us into a family. Not just any family, but the family of the King.

It gets better. We have been adopted, and the King has promised us that we will receive an inheritance. For this we do not need to wait, for he has made a down payment on this inheritance by sending us his Holy Spirit, so that we can know that we are truly sons and daughters, not slaves.

Yet in the Church today, there are perhaps many slaves: dutiful believers who have met every obligation placed upon them by the Church. Perhaps they have never disobeyed a single commandment. They "work in the fields" out of duty, not understanding their identity. And so they become frustrated and angry when we start celebrating the return of prodigals.

These believers fail to realize that they are sons and daughters not because of their good behavior or correct belief but because of the scandalous nature of God's mercy and grace. That mercy and grace is brazenly laid before them in the celebration of the unworthy prodigals who come back to us.

I confess that I sympathize with their frustration. After all, God's mercy is not fair. It does not make sense from a human perspective. However, this is the mind and heart of God. If our Church is to be renewed at every level, mercy must be infused throughout all our systems and structures.

The Church cannot simply dismiss the outrage and agony of our older brothers. We need to have compassion for them, as the father of the prodigal son had compassion on the older brother. We need to plead with them to join the party, to recognize and celebrate the miracle of the return of those who were lost and have been found.

He Insists on the Party

While it is true that the father has a heart for the older brother, the party must go on. Here is the point: the father does not back down from this key value. The fatted calf is killed, and the household is going to party.

The great drama of this parable stems from the fact that we do not know how it ends. We do not know if the older brother joins the party or storms off in a rage.

A year ago, I spoke to a group about this parable, and I made this specific point. At a break, a man came up to me and said, "Fr. James, I beg to differ with you, because we do know how the story ends."

I asked him to tell me, and he replied, "The older brother kills the father."

Now, that may seem like a shocking and unrealistic turn of the narrative, and yet the scribes and the Pharisees killed Jesus. From an earthly perspective, the religious leaders of Jesus' day played an active role in the death of Jesus because he was hanging out with tax collectors and sinners instead of confirming and affirming the religiously faithful.

Within every religious structure lies the possibility of self-righteousness, especially for those who feel they must make themselves acceptable before God will bestow his love. Add in the belief that we become acceptable to God through hard work, performance, and obedience, and you have the ingredients for our current situation: we literally believe that we make ourselves righteous.

A Church that misunderstands grace becomes a self-righteous Church. It does not make room for the broken, the lost, and the less than perfect, and it is intolerant of those who do.

In order to become a Church that is motivated by and reflects the Father's heart as revealed in the parable of the prodigal son, we must allow our hearts of stone to be transformed into hearts of flesh (see Ezekiel 36:26). Only the Holy Spirit can bring about this change as he brings us into the embrace of the Father. If we are to be a Church that reflects the compassion of the Father, we need to be a Church made up of people who have encountered the merciful heart of the Father.

A Prodigal Comes Home

I want to conclude with a story of a young woman at Saint Benedict Parish. Three years ago, this woman went through a difficult time in her life. She had gone through a marriage breakup and found herself, as a single mother, suffering from postpartum depression. She had also sustained a brain injury in an accident.

This woman had been raised in the Church but had walked away from it when she was a teenager. One day she walked past Saint Benedict, and she decided the following weekend to come to Mass.

Over a year ago, I was at a gathering of parish leaders when one of our staff members read a letter that he had received from her. I would like to share a bit of Jen's story with you. She started off:

> I am probably the most under qualified person there is to write anything about God. I don't know a whole lot about religion, so to speak. I don't know many Bible verses by heart. I don't know the details of Catholicism. I don't even know how to say the Rosary, but I'm eager to learn. That being said, these are the things I do know, as sure as I am breathing: I know that the power of God is amazing. I know that I am not in control of my life. I know that God is always with me. I know that God uses people in beautiful ways, and I know that God isn't trying to punish me. I know that God loves me—although that was a tough one to accept.

This letter was filled with hard-won wisdom, of which this was just a part. She continued to describe her life's journey to that point:

> One Sunday morning, when my daughter was just about a year old, I found myself at Saint Benedict Parish. Those months were such a blur that

91

I don't even know how that happened. I was well enough to function, but nowhere near out of the darkness. I remember walking through the doors and being so scared. I was desperate. That was my last hope, and I was terrified, because I knew that if this last-ditch effort to give God a chance and give my life a chance failed, I didn't know if I would bounce back.

I don't know how many months I attended Mass in the foyer. My daughter was barely one, and I thought, what if she makes too much noise? What if these people realize I'm a complete mess? Or that I'm a single mother? What if they're unkind? I couldn't take the chance, so I didn't go any further, but I stood in the foyer and hung on every word that was spoken. I cried every time the band would sing about God's love or brokenness. I desperately wanted to believe in God's love, but I didn't think it was for me.

I remember Fr. James and Fr. Simon speaking about God's love with such conviction, but I was convinced they were talking about someone else. I wasn't worthy. I was ashamed. God couldn't love me.

Eventually I built up enough courage to go inside, not ready to take the plunge yet and actually sit. We hung around the back of the church. I wanted so badly to be a part of whatever this was. I remember thinking, is this for real? These people are so nice. Where is the hidden camera; what's the catch?

There are people like Jen all over our communities: people who are desperate, who feel lost. They may not be able to use those words, they might not be able to put their finger on what they are experiencing, but they are lost.

Sadly, many people see our parishes as the last place they would want to go. They believe they would not be welcomed. They see our parishes as places where they would experience condemnation and judgment, not as places where they could encounter the compassion of God the Father. I find this truly tragic.

Jen went on to describe how she eventually sat in the pew and experienced welcome during her time visiting our parish. In her time with us, she heard me (and other parishioners) speak over and over again about Alpha. She decided to attend and had a profound, life-changing encounter with Jesus and experience of God's love.

Today Jen is very active in our parish. She often comes to weekday Mass. She leads a ministry to reach mothers in the community and is the emcee at our Alpha right now. She is impacting many people around her. Some of the mothers from her group who were not churchgoers took Alpha. One came into the Church at the Easter Vigil last year and another is serving on the Alpha team this year.

Jen's is one of many incredible stories that I could share with you. I believe hers is a story that can help us imagine what kind of Church we can be, what kind of fruit we can bear as parishes and dioceses when we more fully reflect the Father's heart.

PART 2

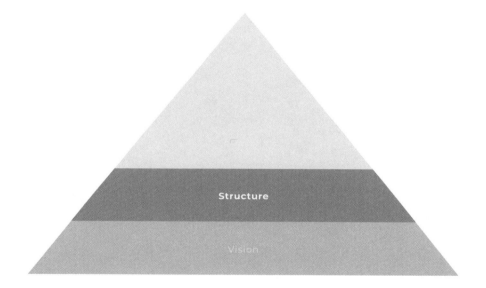

Structure

Vision

STRUCTURE

CHAPTER 6

Our New Reality

We have spent a great deal of time laying out the importance of a theologically grounded vision and the necessity of gathering our communities around a life-giving, outward-focused picture of the future. Forming and communicating a vision takes time, and with the pressing concerns facing our parishes and dioceses, leaders may resist investing that time; they just want to get going, even if they have not yet established a clear direction. However, it does not matter how fast we move if we have no destination in mind!

Yet as essential as vision is to renewal and renovation, it is but the beginning. We need a framework that can support that vision, a way of deploying the various levels and organizational structures of the Church that focuses our efforts. This is not about adding layers of work to this process of renewal but about laying a foundation that can sustain growth and transformation that will nurture fruit that lasts. To do that, we must turn our attention in this section of the book to our structure and models.

Asking the Fundamental Questions

I have heard it said that all organizations and systems are perfectly designed to get the results they are presently getting.[32]23 If this is true, then we must ask ourselves the following question: "Are we happy with the results we are presently getting?"

If the answer is yes, then we do not have to change a thing. If we keep doing what we are doing, we are going to keep getting what we are getting. If, however, the answer is no, then we have to address our structures and systems, which are rooted in our history.

We have already noted that the modern era has witnessed the most profound and accelerated social change in human history. For the Church, this change has been dramatic. We are now firmly at the end of Christendom—a time in Western history when popular culture and faith were aligned. This period extended from about the late fourth century up until roughly fifty years ago.

We can no longer presume many things that we could presume while living in a context that was at least culturally Christian. Yet many of the basic models of how we do Church—our policies, procedures, and structures (including, literally, our buildings)—are built upon presumptions that no longer reflect reality. Our parishes and dioceses are designed to reach a world that no longer exists. And we wonder why we are not bearing fruit.

Rather than get defensive, circle the wagons, and bemoan our new reality, today's cultural context gives us an opportunity to embrace mission with a new vitality. We are in a new apostolic age, an era where missionary territory is not in some far distant land but outside our doors. In fact, missionary engagement might also be required *within* the walls of our buildings, as we cannot assume that people in the pews have a living, intentional relationship with Jesus Christ or that they think with the mind of Christ.

Not only our structures but also many of our principles, pastoral modalities, and methodologies are based on reaching a nonexistent world. That is why we began this book by asking whether we are more attached to our model or to our mission. The question of structure aligns with the question of model. Any organization more attached to its model than to its mission will soon die.

Consider the iPhone. We have all heard of built-in obsolescence, a technology-related reality that affects most of us. App developers constantly push to increase the capacity of their programs, putting more strain on the operating system (OS) of a device. The more advanced the software, the more you have to upgrade the OS to keep pace with the increased capacity of the applications. If you keep upgrading the OS, sooner or later problems with the hardware occur. Either the OS makes your current hardware sluggish and unresponsive, or the device will no longer be compatible with the latest OS, which means you cannot use the latest apps.

In many ways, that is where we are today as a Church. We do not simply need updated versions of our "apps" (our programs, methodologies, and strategies); we need entirely new apps to engage this very new world. Our current operating system (namely, our parish and diocesan cultures) cannot run these apps, so we will need to change our OS. To do this, however, we will need new hardware, and this hardware is our structure.

The hard truth is that mission should drive structure. Therefore we need to ask the following question without flinching: Does our current structure serve the mission, or is it holding us back?

Often we do not have to think too long to answer this question. Most parishes and dioceses choose structure over mission 90 percent of the time. In fact, if you look closely, you might assume that the end game in many dioceses is to keep the structure at all costs. Time and time again, we sacrifice mission efficiency and effectiveness to keep the structure going. In fact, we sacrifice health, personnel, fruitfulness— pretty much everything at the altar of the status quo. When structure hampers our ability to live out mission and we do nothing to change the structure, we do not bear fruit.

Perhaps looking at this through the lens of warfare will make the point clearer. (Obviously, I'm not advocating war, but parish and diocesan renewal is often a bit of a battlefield experience.)

Think about an army about to be overrun by the enemy's forces. Typically, in a situation like that, an army will order a strategic withdrawal and concentrate its forces in a more defensible position. If it tried to defend everything and maintain its current position, that army would be obliterated.

Likewise, if an army retreated but chose an indefensible position, it would be overrun. You cannot simply retreat from one losing position to another losing position. If you do, you keep losing!

In terms of the Church, if our current structures are inadequate for our mission, are we willing to be intentional about creating new structures? In other words, are we willing to take a hard look at our resources and our current reality? Are we willing to make difficult decisions, perhaps withdraw from where we are and find a defensive line we can actually hold?

Remember, however, that Jesus gave us instructions to "go!" The purpose of a tactical withdrawal is not to "hold the line" forever; our goal is not to take on a perpetual state of defensiveness. The goal of a strategic withdrawal is to regroup and then move on the offensive.

Strategic withdrawals are sometimes necessary. Often in the Church, we are not willing to do what needs to be done to hold the line or go on the offensive because of the pushback, anger, and negativity that come from our people. Our unwillingness to deal with these realities holds our future health and fruitfulness hostage.

In the early years of the American Civil War, the Confederate States won the majority of victories, even though they had fewer soldiers, poorer equipment, and less training. They had no business winning anything. The leadership of the Union army, however, was incredibly cautious. Historians believe that Union forces could have won the war in the first year. The cost in human life would have been devastating: forty thousand to fifty thousand soldiers. The Union general William Tecumseh Sherman wrote that the cost of a prolonged war would be horrific. He was mocked and accused of being insane for taking that stand.

Union leaders tried to play it safe, not willing to commit their resources and pay the price of victory, and so the war ground on and ultimately racked up more than 620,000 military deaths.[33] There is a lesson here. Union leaders were too cautious; they were afraid to do what needed to be done.

I am not advocating chewing through your people, treating them like cannon fodder, and sacrificing them for the greater good. Yet we must come to terms with the larger principle that when leaders are afraid to do what needs to be done, our parishes and dioceses end up paying a price. We need leaders with courage and pastoral fortitude: men and women, rooted in a relationship with Jesus Christ, who have the determination to create a vision and the courage to follow through with *decisions that support that vision.*

Not by Our Power

The beautiful thing about parish and diocesan renovation is that we are not in this alone. God does not expect us to bring about Church renewal through human inventiveness and willpower alone. This work of transformation is ultimately a work of the Holy Spirit. We must cooperate with that divine power, bring our human wills into alignment, and give the Holy Spirit space to work. We must ask ourselves, are we are willing to give the Holy Spirit permission to act in us and through us?

Our answer to that question has repercussions. Jesus says that pruning will be inevitable. "He takes away every branch in me that does not bear fruit, and every one that does he prunes so that it bears more fruit" (John 15:2). The fruitless branches will be cut away, collected, and burned. If the structure is bearing no fruit and is dragging us down, then it is like a branch that needs to be cut off and thrown in the fire. I think this is part of what we see God doing in the Church today, and he is asking us to cooperate with him in the process.

Even parishes that are somewhat healthy and bearing fruit cannot escape the knife. Pruning is not a punishment; it is a process that enables plants to absorb nutrients and deepen their vitality. If we do not prune, the result is a weak and mediocre plant. As we prune, however, we must be careful about what we cut away.

Models of Restructuring

Our ministry has given us the opportunity to see both Catholic and non-Catholic communities struggling with the issue of restructuring. Let us take a look at three different models of diocesan restructuring that I have seen in various places throughout the world:

Clustering

Clustering can mean different things in different places. I use the word to indicate the bringing together of multiple parishes under a single pastor. Each parish remains a separate entity with, for example, its own finance and pastoral councils, but one priest is the pastor of all the parishes in the cluster. I have met priests who are responsible for two, three, five, and even seven parishes.

When parishes cluster like this, the weight of a dysfunctional system is simply multiplied and placed on the pastor. A millstone is placed around the neck of the priest, and often millstones continue to be added even when it is obvious that the priest is not doing well with that weight. This model of restructuring is the worst of the restructuring scenarios and takes a terrible toll on priests and their communities.

Regions

Many Catholics are familiar with this model, because many dioceses are divided into particular regions called deaneries. The purpose of a deanery is to increase communication and collaboration on particular initiatives. Usually there is a nominal coordinator for the region, often called a dean or a vicar, who has at least some leadership authority.

In my nearly twenty- five years of priesthood, the last five or so working with many priests on renewal, I have seen that this structure is generally not helpful. It is based on the presumption that geography is the primary thing that parishes have in common, that being physically near each other fosters a common experience with common needs. That assumption breaks down today, as people are much more mobile than in previous times. In a consumer-minded culture, individuals "parish shop." They often end up attending the parish that "fits them" rather than the one in whose geographical boundaries they live.

There are two other elements that impact this reality. One is the "distance" between where parishes are on the continuum of maintenance and mission. In other words, one parish community will have much more in common with another parish that is at, or near, where they are in this journey toward mission—regardless of where they are geographically in the diocese. If you are a parish heading out on mission, and you are surrounded by parishes that are mired in maintenance, your regional structure is going to be a millstone; it is going to be painful.

The other element that influences the regional structure is size culture. The experiences and elements of a parish are rooted in how large or small the parish is. These experiences shape expectations about how leaders exercise their authority, the structures of leadership, and the processes of ministry.

For instance, in a small parish, ministry is often undertaken by relatively few people, and decision-making stays close to the community. Usually there is fairly direct access to leadership.

You can feel the difference in a larger parish. Ministry is done by more people. There may be regulating bodies that support ministries, volunteers, and even staff, while major decisions are made by relatively few people.

We can be somewhat oblivious to size culture, trying to make the same leadership structure work in parishes regardless of their size. When a parish looks at the size-based elements of their culture, however, they will see that they have much more in common with a similar-sized and structured parish than with others that are simply in their geographical region.

When these regional structures were first formed, there were no issues—mostly because there was no urgency or need to be on mission within a parish's own area. Missionary work took place in far-off lands. Parishes maintained the flock, and that was sufficient. Most parishes had a similar structure, with a pastor, an associate pastor, and maybe a housekeeper.

We have largely inherited our current regional superstructures from a bygone era. Lately, however, some dioceses have restructured using a version of the regional approach. The diocese asks a group of independent parishes near each other to work together, share resources, and maybe even share staff.

This may sound like a solid move to consolidate, but it ends up having all the issues of regional structuring—with a new wrinkle in the mix. These grouped parishes do not have a single leader. Independent pastors (and their respective staffs) must work together without any structural incentive to work together or any clear lines of decision-making, authority, or accountability. It is leadership by committee, and guess what happens?

Nothing. Time and resources are wasted, and people become frustrated and discouraged.

Amalgamation

This third and final model of restructuring seems to be the one model of renewal that can work. Amalgamation can mean many things, but I define it as one canonical and legal parish with one pastor, finance council, parish council, and so forth. Several parishes, for example, could amalgamate into one parish, with perhaps multiple locations, church buildings, or campuses. It would be a sort of regional parish, and it could contain multiple associate pastors who work with the pastor.

The configuration will likely differ depending on whether it is in an urban or a rural area. No matter the form, its critical component is the presence of an acknowledged leader and a structure deliberately created to serve the Church's mission. I think that this is the path we need to follow.

As we can see in all our discussions about structure, we are not yet speaking about what to do with buildings or about redrawing parish boundaries.

Structure also deals with expectations of leadership: how a priest leads his team and supports key people. It should also challenge diocesan leadership to look at how their structures support leaders at all levels. It is not enough to ask parishes to restructure and change if those at the diocesan and regional levels do not take this same journey. If we want parish renewal, we must also work toward chancery renewal.

Every organization is perfectly suited to get the results it is presently getting. Is it not time for new results?

CHAPTER 7

Our Journey

Now that we have laid the foundation to talk about structure, let us look at what restructuring for mission can look like in practice. To do that, I want to discuss what we have been doing in my own diocese, the Archdiocese of Halifax-Yarmouth. First, however, we need to address a fundamental issue.

The decline of our parishes is part of a bigger story, as we have seen: the decline of Christendom. Remember earlier when we explored the Berkana Two Loop theory? The Two Loop theory posits that as a dominant system declines, innovators appear who begin to see a new way of doing things. If those innovators can connect and form networks, there is a greater chance that this new system can begin to take root. The dominant system that we have inherited from the era of Christendom continues to decline, but as it does, the Lord is connecting people and networking people, allowing something new to emerge.

In order for us to live in this new system, though, we have to travel through what the Two Loop theory calls a transition point, where we let go of not just the old ways of doing things but the old ways of seeing things and the old ideas associated with them. In other words, we cannot just renew our physical structures and processes; we must renew how we live within them. As the British economist John Maynard Keynes once said, "The difficulty lies, not in the new ideas, but in escaping from the old ones."[34]

My very first weekend at Saint Benedict Parish, I asked the people, "What will stop the decline that necessitated the closure and amalgamation of our three buildings from continuing to happen in our midst?" even as we were celebrating Mass in our new building. I told the parishioners that if we simply did what we have always done, then there would be nothing that would stop our continued decline.

It is not enough to change your address or your furniture. As critical as the creation of new structures is, we must change how we live within those new structures, or we will simply become more efficient versions of parishes that are not bearing fruit. Decline will continue, and we will find ourselves having to retrench, retreat, and cut away again in another decade.

We have talked about amalgamation of parishes as the model for experiencing renewal. However, amalgamation alone is not a magic bullet. The journey toward renewal is fraught with difficulty.

A number of years ago, the Boston Consulting Group studied secular businesses with regard to what happens when organizations go through what they called "transformation programs."[35] What they discovered is more than a little disconcerting: 75 percent of business turnarounds done through restructuring ultimately fail. Just think about that for a second: a 75 percent failure rate!

Remember, when a diocese or an individual parish experiences decline, that decline has momentum. When you are in decline, even if you had the ability to flip a switch and immediately do everything you need to do perfectly, you are still going to move in the direction of decline. Hopefully that decline will slow down, and eventually the parish or diocese will begin to move in the direction of health, but something particular needs to happen first.

We see this in both the business world and in the Church. A downturn leads to an operational turnaround designed to arrest the decline and begin a new period of growth. This often happens in a process of amalgamation and restructuring. Operational efficiencies appear. Instead of three administrative assistants, you now have one. Instead of three offices or church buildings, you now only need one. You now have multiple pastoral staff members who can focus their efforts on a single community. Due to this, there is an initial boost of life, a sense of newness and possibility, as three communities, for example, come together as one. All of a sudden, Sunday Masses, instead of being only a fifth full, are now half full. There is a "buzz," an excitement that sets in.

Over time, however, this excitement dies down. Dreams of future possibilities get lost in mundane reality. During this period, we see that the operational moves that brought you to your current state have less and less effect. Things begin to level out.

This is a critical moment. Once an organization completes its restructuring and its administrative changes, and the sense of newness wears off, that organization stands at a crossroads: it can choose to employ a new vision, model, or strategy; or it can continue to do what it has always done.

Now ideally, an organization creates a new vision and restructures based upon that vision, but if they have not done that—if they began with administrative moves—they can still choose to live differently within that new structure and reach an inflection point. If they can do that, there is a real chance of new life and sustained fruit.

However, failure to innovate over the long term leads to a possibly accelerated decline, and it is here that we see the 75 percent highlighted by the Boston Consulting Group at work. Even though this failure rate comes from an analysis of secular businesses, I believe the same principles hold true for Church amalgamations attempted without a reorientation of vision, culture, and strategy—as seen by the results of actual dioceses who have tried to foster renewal.

Reality Check

About two years ago, the Archdiocese of Pittsburgh began a reorganization in order to focus on mission and evangelization. It was a strategic withdrawal, with the hope that they could stop losing parishioners and start living out their mission. It is important to note that this was not the first time Pittsburgh had restructured. In the period between 1992 and 1994, the archdiocese moved from 332 parishes down to 218.[36] Looking at that move now, they did not experience a turning point in vision and strategy. With the new restructuring operation, the diocese hopes to move from the current 188 parishes to a total of 48 parishes by 2022.

Just look at the trend over the past 36 years—from 332 to 218 parishes, and now from 218 parishes to 48. Correspondingly, as with other dioceses, Mass attendance has dropped precipitously over the last 16 years—from 246,000 in the year 2000 to 138,000 in 2016. That is a 44 percent decrease. Looking more closely, we see that 50 percent of their parishes are operating in the red; and over the next 8 years, they will experience a 50 percent drop in the number of active priests.

Clearly they are bleeding. Here is the critical question: What if they do not get this restructuring right? What if they fail to live out of a new vision and new model, and they keep doing what they have been doing? In another ten to fifteen years, do they retrench to fifteen parishes, or five? How many Catholics will still be attending Mass by the year 2040?

As you may know, it is not just Pittsburgh; this narrative is being played out in dioceses all over North America and Europe. In 1970 the Archdiocese of Chicago had 462 parishes, and by the end of the 1990s, they retrenched to about 348 parishes. In 1995 they had a Sunday Mass attendance of 554,000, which decreased by 27 percent by 2016, for a total Sunday Mass attendance of 401,000. They are also looking at a 35 percent drop in active priests over the next ten years.

The Archdiocese of Chicago is certainly not the worst-case scenario, but it is important to note that they have tried to manage their decline many times in the past, focusing mostly on structure and not the deeper reality. Again, what happens if they miss the mark this time? This haunting question has led their leadership to embrace a more courageous and thorough transformation that moves beyond the question of structure.

Many dioceses elsewhere—in Canada, the United States, and Europe—face this same issue. Recently, at a Divine Renovation Conference in Germany, I spoke with a priest from Austria who told me that his diocese was downsizing from five hundred to forty parishes. Another priest from Germany reported that his diocese planned to move from seven hundred parishes to thirty-two.

We cannot totally predict these things, but the trend is maddening— not simply for Pittsburgh and Chicago but for the Church all over the world. In spite of the data in front of us, which points to the critical importance of new vision, models, and strategies, we have mostly failed to deal with the realities beyond our structure.

Now we at Divine Renovation have the great blessing to work alongside archdioceses like Chicago and other dioceses globally, and we are beginning to see some fruit. The struggle, however, is intense—and for all of us it begins at home.

The Archdiocese of Halifax-Yarmouth

The statistics for the Archdiocese of Halifax-Yarmouth, where I serve, are similar to the ones that we have already discussed. As previously mentioned, between 2001 and 2016, my archdiocese experienced a decline in church attendance perhaps as high as 50 percent. In 2004, the Archdiocese of Halifax began an amalgamation process that sought to move from seventy-five parishes and missions to twenty-four parishes.

That attempt to restructure was not fully realized, and after being amalgamated with the neighboring diocese of Yarmouth, we ended up with ninety parishes and missions that were functioning as forty-three parishes or cluster parishes. After all this effort, we are experiencing a continued decline. We are blessed to have an archbishop who is committed to renewal, and through his leadership, we are making difficult decisions and cutting away what needs to go in order to arrive at a healthy place, a position from which we hope to expand via missionary activity. Therefore our goal in the past year was to move to a total of twenty parishes through amalgamation.

Examining what went wrong sixteen years ago in our original amalgamation may shed some light on what dioceses should and should not do in the journey toward renewal. The first thing we should realize is that, even though we are a universal organization spanning the globe, we are just not that organized. When people tell me that they are not fond of organized religion, I often quip, "Well, then you should become Catholic." Sure, we are hierarchical, and there are lots of levels of authority and reporting, but when it comes to actually doing something, we are like a lumbering ox.

Many people outside the Church think that if a bishop or the pope says, "Jump," Catholics ask, "How high?" In reality it does not work that way. My own archbishop likes to say that he wishes he had a fraction of the authority people think he has.

At every level, however, the Church is an organization with voluntary membership. When it comes to the bishop promoting an event, wanting his priests to show up for something, laying out a direction, or encouraging parish-based initiatives, about one-third of the priests or parishes do it, one-third will try to do it but will eventually stop doing it, and one-third will not even try to do it. That is generally how it works, and it is generally how it played out in my archdiocese.

So fourteen years ago, our diocese produced a report called "Forward in Faith." It was an attempt to place the infrastructure of the archdiocese at the service of the mission. In that sense, it was a phenomenal plan. The leadership examined every single region in our archdiocese and made recommendations to amalgamate parishes. Then they said to parish leadership: "Now you figure it out. You decide what you're going to do. Are you going to keep all your buildings open, or are you going to close one? Are you going to have different uses for the same building? Are you going to move into one?"

Some of you might recognize this story, because it really is the origin of Saint Benedict Parish, which came into being after three existing parishes amalgamated into one. Under the leadership of the pastor at that time, the parish decided to sell their three buildings and build a new facility, which would enable the new parish to live out its life in a tangible way. It was a bold and prophetic move, but once the parish moved under one roof, it still needed a new set of values, a new model for being Church.

Looking back on the original amalgamation plan from the archdiocese, you can probably tell what did not happen. The archdiocese made these key decisions but left it up to parish leadership to make it happen. Diocesan leaders did little to help parishes or hold them accountable. A third of the parishes made an attempt and were, to some degree, successful with their amalgamation plans.

One-third tried to do it, met with very loud and obstinate resistance, and eventually gave up. Even when there was a desire to fight through the resistance, the weight of maintenance bore down on leaders. Leadership, staff, and volunteers were exhausted from dealing with regular Sunday liturgies, funerals, religious education, and the various needs that aging buildings and populations present.

On the other hand, one-third of parishes and leaders did nothing. They did not even try seriously to amalgamate.

What were the results overall? Parishes that did not try, as well as parishes that started but never finished—they all, obviously, failed to amalgamate. Some of these parishes made it as far as a cluster, and many others just remained separate parishes. However, even the one-third that pushed forward did not bear much fruit. Remember the

75 percent failure rate noted by the Boston Consulting Group study? That is exactly what happened.

Other parishes in our diocese who sold their buildings, as Saint Benedict did, and built new ones continued to suffer decline several years later. They may have successfully changed their structure, but they did not change how they did things. They were under the illusion that changing their structure and moving into a new building would solve their problems. Such choices can get you to the starting line, but by themselves they do not guarantee victory.

With almost all our parishes continuing to decline, and with a growing number of priests leaving active ministry because of age or illness, the strain on the system grew. This led our current archdiocesan leadership to look again at restructuring in conjunction with a new pastoral plan. The previous pastoral plan, "Forward in Faith," had its positive points, but it failed to lay out a strong vision or strategy for interior transformation.

Our current pastoral plan is called "Equip the Saints," named for St. Paul's discussion in his Letter to the Ephesians about the various offices or charisms in the Church that equip the saints for her building up (see Ephesians 4). "Equip the Saints" is a plan for total renewal, including focus on mission and investment in leadership support. In order to get to the starting line of that renewal, however, we had to do some restructuring.

During the time that this new pastoral plan was conceived, I was not yet serving as episcopal vicar for leadership support and parish renewal. I was still the pastor of Saint Benedict Parish and had just become the chair of our council for priests. Even then, I had a sense from my brother priests that all the sacrifices we had made through-out the years in order to maintain our structures came at a great cost. Priestly morale was exceptionally low; the priests were discouraged because they were working extremely hard yet not seeing much fruit from their ministry.

So much seemd to be dying—not just parishioners. The priests gave their life to this, only to see it fading. One young priest said to me, "James, I feel like I've married a dying woman. That is not why I became a priest. And the tragedy is, I don't believe that my wife needs to be dying. It's just that we're not willing to do what needs to be done to save her."

Looking at the dip in morale and the low degree of trust that existed within the archdiocese, I remember thinking we should slow down the implementation of the strategic plan. How could we possibly roll out this plan if the leaders at the local level felt disengaged and discouraged? I thought it was going to be a train wreck.

So, with input from the council of priests, the diocesan leadership decided to slow things down and invest in building up trust levels, engaging our priests, and supporting them. We decided to use the Q12 Employee Engagement Survey from Gallup, an organization primarily devoted to optimizing organizational health and employee engagement. (If you are familiar with *Divine Renovation*, you will know that within Saint Benedict Parish we also used Gallup's ME[25] Survey).

The word engagement has various meanings, depending on the context. People might speak of "engagement," for example, as something like involvement or busyness. Gallup understands engagement, however, as psychological buy-in, and they classify people as belonging to one of three camps relative to engagement:

- Engaged members of an organization are highly passionate about the organization, and they are enthusiastic and excited about what they are doing as part of that organization. Engaged members align themselves with the vision of the organization and will make sacrifices so that vision can be achieved.

- Unengaged persons, on the other hand, are basically neutral. They are not enthusiastic, nor are they overly upset by the direction an organization might take.

- Actively disengaged persons, even though they may be involved, oppose the vision of an organization and work directly against it. These members express anger, bitterness, and resentment, and they try to tear down what is being built. Essentially they are destructive.

Since Gallup works with so many organizations globally, they have the responses of forty million people in their database.[37] These have helped Gallup learn about the importance of engagement and its overall impact on the effectiveness of organizations.

Gallup leadership told us that we were the first diocese in the world to use the Q12 Survey to measure priestly engagement, and so they were especially interested in working with us. They helped us with two items in particular. First, they helped us customize the language of the Q12, which was business focused. We knew that some of our priests would be sensitive to that corporate feel, considering that kind of terminology to be in opposition to the spiritual life.

Second, Gallup helped us customize the structure of the survey by differentiating among the various categories of priests. For example, we could look at the data from priests in active ministry compared to retired priests. We differentiated priests who were leading a parish from priests in some other role, such as associate pastors or chaplains. Other distinctions we used were rural or urban, French- or English-speaking, "international" priest or "non-international." We also had categories for years of ordination (0 to 5 years, 5 to 10, 10 to 20, 20 to 40, and 40-plus). When we received the results, therefore, we could dig into an enormous amount of detail.

The Q12 Survey Question Breakdown

As the Q12 questions are so critical to an organization's health, it is worth exploring each of them briefly in the context of priestly ministry and parish life.

Do I Know What Is Expected of Me at Work?

This is a big issue for priests today. The tremendous changes in contemporary society have led to even greater expectations for the Church and the role of the priest. There are expectations from those who grew up in the 1940s and 1950s, a generation who often still want their priests to be Bing Crosby. Expectations also come from the bishop, from leaders in the chancery, from our priestly formation in the seminary, and from our brother priests.

In addition, we experience expectations from our own hearts, as we try to discern the type of priest God is calling us to be. Finally, we have expectations set on us when we recognize that the world is changing, and we have to lead differently.

If we do not do a good job managing expectations, they will crush us. Many dioceses have not clarified these expectations—especially those related to living with a new reality. Therefore priests live their ministry trying to guess at how they should minister rather than moving forward in a clear direction. This takes a great toll on many priests.

Do I Have the Materials and Equipment I Need to Do My Work Right?

What happens if you are asked to do something, but no one gives you the tools and the equipment to do it? What happens when you are then held accountable for doing that job and doing it well? What does that do to your heart or your sense of enthusiasm?

In many ways, this is how the archdiocese handled the first attempt at restructuring, back in 2004. They wanted several parishes to become one parish, for example, but left those parishes to figure it out on their own.

This approach leads to disengagement. On the other hand, if we ask people what they need and surround them with support, giving them the tools they require, engagement increases.

Do I Have the Opportunity to Do What I Do Best Every Day?

Every person has gifts and talents that allow them to excel in particular areas. Aligning people's strengths with areas of ministry and service allows them to concentrate on doing what they do best. Not only does this strength-based approach to ministry produce positive fruit, but it also provides a life-giving experience for people.

Of course, everyone has to do things outside their areas of strength at some point in life. However, if most of your job, ministry, or volunteer service requires you to do things that you are not good at and do not enjoy, it is going to suck the life out of you.

Often in ministry, we do not spend enough time discerning people's strengths and roles. I think many of our current issues related to the health of our parishes and dioceses come from the fact that we have placed priests in positions of leadership or in roles for which they do not have the gifts. We need to get better at discerning strengths.

In the Last Seven Days, Have I Received Recognition or Praise for Doing Good Work?

We all have a need to be recognized. For most of us, this need for recognition is not the driving force behind our vocational choice, and we will not fall apart if no one tells us we are doing a good job. However, most of us want to have an impact, to make a difference—and receiving recognition is one way that we evaluate whether our actions matter to others. When we are recognized in appropriate and meaningful ways, it makes a difference.

Likewise, when we toil and sacrifice, giving of ourselves, without any recognition, we can start to wonder if our labor is worth it. This leads to discouragement and disengagement. Many priests and pastoral leaders assume that because this is ministry, there is no need for recognition. This attitude, however, leads to disconnection, staff turmoil, and burnout.

Does My Supervisor or Someone at Work Seem to Care about Me as a Person?

When we customized the Q12, we encouraged the priests to think of their supervisor simply as "the leadership of the diocese." We left it relatively vague, though of course it includes the person of the bishop and what we affectionately call "downtown"—the chancery office, the staff of the bishop, and the leadership structures of the diocese.

The fact is that sometimes a priest can feel like an anonymous cog in a giant ministry machine. We might hear from downtown only when they launch a new policy or receive a letter of complaint about us. It seems that the mistakes we make are amplified, and all the good work we have done goes unrecognized. Helping our people understand that we genuinely care about them is a critical component of fostering engagement.

Is There Someone at Work Who Encourages My Development?

Great leaders build up their team members, helping them grow professionally, psychologically, and spiritually. They also encourage healthy boundaries, foster a balanced life in those they lead, and support activities that promote physical health as well. Well-grounded leaders understand that with the authority of leadership comes the responsibility to nurture and care for their employees, volunteers, and team members.

Unfortunately, many parish priests, leaders, and staff struggle to maintain health in these areas. Often our parishes and dioceses are tangles of toxic relationships and unhealthy coping mechanisms. The way we manage decline makes this worse, as we sacrifice the health of our people in hopes of maintaining our structures at all costs. If we want to change this dynamic, we must commit ourselves to the development and well-being of our people.

At Work, Do My Opinions Seem to Count?

When people buy into an organization and its mission, they usually experience a sense of ownership about that organization. Often that sense of ownership stems from the fact that their opinions count. The more people feel as if their opinions do not count, the more likely they are to be unengaged or actively disengaged.

I use the word "feel" here intentionally. We like to think of ourselves as rational creatures, but in truth, our attitudes and our engagement in everything that we do are more rooted in our feelings than our thoughts. Allowing our people to express their opinions and taking them seriously can help build a foundation of engagement.

Does the Mission or Purpose of My Organization Make Me Feel My Job Is Important?

I think that this is a question on which, universally, a diocese will achieve a high score despite how much it may be struggling. This is because we are about the mission of Jesus Christ and his kingdom. Our archdiocese was no exception.

Are My Colleagues Committed to Doing Quality Work?

A lack of accountability within our parish and diocesan staff and teams results in a culture of mediocrity. When we are immersed in a culture of mediocrity—when we are not evaluated, coached, held accountable, rewarded, and challenged to grow—we become disengaged. We become more engaged, on the other hand, when we work in a culture of high-performing people who are held accountable and are committed to producing high-quality work that bears fruit.

Do I Have a Best Friend at Work?

We encouraged the priests to think about this relative to other priests. The ME[25] Survey poses a similar question: Do I have a best friend in my parish?

People asked, "Why does it say, 'best friend'? Why couldn't it just say 'friend'?" Gallup responded by noting that basic friendship does not seem to impact engagement. Having a deep friendship, however, corresponds with organizational health.

A priest once said to me, in regard to church work, that we're not here to be friends, but secular studies show that forming deep friendships at work fosters a healthier and more efficient organization. Jesus himself thought friendship was essential. "I no longer call you slaves," he said to his disciples, "because a slave does not know what his master is doing. I have called you friends" (John 15:15).

In the Last Six Months, Has Someone at Work Talked to Me about My Progress?

Once again, this is about accountability and growth. Tragically, in many of our dioceses, no one talks to priests about their progress. No one sits down and asks them about their goals, their vision, the ways they have grown, or how diocesan leadership can help them. This is really basic coaching.

The lack of support for priests is appalling—especially at such a crucial time in the Church's life, when so much is being asked of priests and other leaders. If we want to bear fruit, we must pay attention to this critical question.

In the Last Year, Have I Had Opportunities to Learn and Grow?

Some dioceses more than others provide these kinds of opportunities for their priests and pastoral leaders. If people get the sense that we are simply trying to squeeze as much work out of them as we can, with little regard for their passions and desire to improve, this leads to a growing disengagement. However, if people understand that we care for them, that we are willing to invest in them and nurture their future growth, it changes how they see their work, the parish, the diocese, and ministry in general.

The Results

When we offered the Q12 Survey, 100 percent of priests in active ministry and the majority of retired priests participated. When we received the data back from Gallup, it not only confirmed our anecdotal evidence but offered us clear proof that we were in a more dire situation than we thought. The overall engagement level of our priests was not great; and as we analyzed the data based on particular roles, the alarm bells began to ring.

The segment of priests who had the lowest engagement scores possible (literally the bottom 1 percent of all the respondents in Gallup's global database) were homegrown priests from our diocese, ordained between zero and twenty years, who were leading a parish. That was a clear red alert! These guys were the future of our diocese.

On the other hand, retired priests who did not have a parish were the happiest priests. The priests who were active in ministry but were not leading a parish were really engaged as well. In addition, priests from other countries were actually quite engaged, and the priests who were still in active ministry for forty years or more were much more engaged. It was priests who were in the midst of leading parishes and who still had the rest of their lives as pastors ahead of them who were hanging on by their fingernails.

I have traveled to a great many dioceses all over the world, where I have had the privilege of speaking and ministering to priests. As alarming as our numbers sound, I believe that if these dioceses used a tool like the Q12 Survey, they would see strikingly similar results. We cannot confront a reality that we do not actually see clearly. That is why tools like the Q12 Survey are essential if we want to lead the change and transformation of our parishes and dioceses.

After we received our survey results, the bishop's leadership team and the archdiocesan council of priests spent time discussing next steps. Eventually we created a communication and feedback plan to inform priests of what we discovered. We also worked with a Gallup consultant to do an online seminar to explain the results.

In addition, we decided to hold an overnight gathering of priests facilitated by someone from outside the archdiocese. This gathering focused on four distinct questions. It not only gave diocesan leadership the experience of listening to the priests but also gave the priests the experience of being listened to by diocesan leadership.

In the Q12 Survey, respondents rate their reaction to each question with an answer from 1 (Strongly Disagree) to 5 (Strongly Agree). After gathering the priests together for a nice meal, prayer, and some fellowship, we broke up into different groups based on some of the categories of data used in the survey—priests of a certain age, those with rural parishes, and so forth. We then had each group go through four of the key Q12 Survey Questions and brainstorm about what needed to happen in order for them to answer the questions with a 5, thereby keeping discussions positively focused.

Each group reported their feedback for each of the four key questions to the larger group. We collated that feedback into different categories, eliminating any redundancies, and captured it all on paper. Finally we looked at the action points under each category. In the end, we discerned four basic categories for action. I would like to share these with you.

- The bishop: 14 percent of the feedback from the priests pertained to the leadership of the bishop himself. It took great courage for the bishop to listen with an open heart and mind to this feedback.

- Downtown: 22 percent of the feedback related to the bishop's staff and the structures of the chancery offices.

- Priests: 19 percent of the feedback had to do with the priests themselves. We needed to own some critical changes—especially in terms of how we related to each other and supported each other.

- The system: 45 percent of the feedback revolved around changes to the structures and processes of the diocese.

If you include "downtown" as part of the larger diocesan structure, then 67 percent (more than two-thirds) of the changes we believed should happen in order to move us to a place of health related to our structure.

So where are now?

This feedback from our priests gave us a more-than-compelling reason to continue to develop and execute a bold and exciting strategic plan. This plan has not been without its difficulties. Our people, like most folks, have struggled with change; they fear loss, and the process of change is difficult. Our plan focuses on future growth through mission, but it requires that we embrace the paschal mystery, that we live out the experience of dying before we can reach the resurrection.

I have already mentioned that we have moved from ninety parishes and missions to twenty parishes. These ninety existed on paper, but we had actually been functioning as forty-three parishes or pastoral groupings, or clusters. These clusters did not form intentionally. When we opted for an amalgamation model sixteen years ago, these parishes defaulted to clusters because their leaders experienced resistance and pushback. They opted to stop the process and ended up with a cluster.

As I write this, in February of 2020, the archdiocese is only a few months into the consolidation of these forty-three parishes into twenty. This may sound like a radical move, but remember, our goal is to retreat to a defensive line that we can hold, so that we can eventually become healthy and move forward on mission. Most of these parishes now consist of multiple sites, basically one parish operating in different vicinities and out of different buildings.

In the non-Catholic world, multisite communities often arise out of a cycle of health. These Christians expand to different sites as they evangelize, make disciples, and grow. Our current approach in the archdiocese aims to manage decline with an eye toward future growth. We are making a good attempt to cut deep enough. Therefore we have looked at the entire diocese and broken its territory up between these twenty new parishes. Many of the forty-three previous parishes have combined with others to become one, and from this process, we now have a total of twenty canonical parishes, most with new names.

Under this structure, for example, you might have a newly formed parish—let us call it St. Thomas—made up of five previously existing parishes. St. Thomas parish might have church buildings spread across a region, with a number of other different buildings. However, these buildings would all belong to one parish. St. Thomas would have one pastoral council, one finance council (with one bank account), and one pastor.

The archdiocese is also providing clear guidelines around structure, in that no more than 30 percent of the ordinary income of the parish is to be spent on buildings, so that the majority can be invested in mission. Parish leadership will have to make decisions accordingly.

Our goal is to staff each of these new parishes with at least two priests who will work collaboratively, with one of them being the pastor and therefore in the leadership role. This recognizes that there is a uniqueness to the task of leadership: something will be asked of the person in the leadership role that is different from what is asked of the other priests.

Too often in the Church, we view the role of the priest as generic. A priest is a priest is a priest—and we give very little attention to the particular weight of responsibility and requirements that come with leading. Our hope is to have two priests in every single parish and to structure the parishes so that they have the critical resources to support a staff. Right now, many of our parishes do not have any staff, but moving forward, every parish will have a deacon, perhaps, and lay staff working as a team. No pastor will be forced to go it alone.

In addition, every parish is expected to have a "senior" or "parish" leadership team. We will cover this in more detail later in this book, but in essence, this kind of team consists of three or four people who come around the pastor to help make tactical decisions and to share responsibility and leadership. This is not leadership by committee; the pastor is still the leader. However, as we often say in Divine Renovation ministry, there is no such thing as a well-rounded leader, but there can be well-rounded teams. No one has all the gifts. We need to break from the lone ranger, benign dictator model of priestly leadership.

Each parish will also have a mission-oriented pastoral council and finance committee.

Most exciting of all, our diocesan center can now offer these twenty new parishes a greater degree of support than we could our ninety different parishes or missions. We will assign diocesan staff directly to the parishes, and their jobs will include supporting, assisting, and facilitating the life of each of these parishes. I will also be out in the field, supporting pastors and pastoral leadership.

Finally, our vision is that once a month the priests will gather together with the bishop for a day of prayer and formation, including frank discussions about successes, failures, best practices, open questions, and so on. We want to hold these monthly formation meetings because we are entering uncharted territory, a place for which we have no map. We are going to try new things, and we are going to fail. We will encounter new problems and new realities, to which we will need to prayerfully respond. We will explore details of these gatherings later in the book.

As I write this, I recall a brutal scene in the movie *Saving Private Ryan*, when the soldiers are disembarking from their landing craft onto the beach at Normandy. There is bloody carnage everywhere, and at one point the soldiers are pinned down by enemy fire. Shaking with fear and unable to move forward, one of the soldiers says to another, "We've got to get off the beach. We're getting murdered out here!"

As a Church, we have got to get off the metaphorical beach. If we stand still, we are going to die. We might get wounded or even killed as we move off the beach, but remaining where we are is a death sentence.

No plan or strategy will be perfect. We cannot wait for that perfect plan to show up. What we have done in the past, the ways that we have supported each other—all that must change. We have to move—and we have to do it together.

Structuring our dioceses so that leaders and their collaborators gather together regularly increases our chances of moving forward fruitfully. We will not figure it all out at once, so let us move forward together, united with Jesus in the power of his Holy Spirit.

CHAPTER 8

Breaking Through

Whatever structural approach we take to diocesan and parish renewal, the bottom line is that it should foster and reinforce authentic leadership (which we will cover in depth in the next section of this book). In other words, the models, processes, and organizational architecture we use must, in themselves, remove obstacles to the function of leadership: decision making, communication of vision, accountability, growing leaders from the next generation, to name a few, so that the Church may be able to fulfill her calling. Pope Francis called us to take up the task of submitting our structure to mission in *Evangelii Gaudium*:

> There are ecclesial structures which can hamper efforts at evangelization, yet even good structures are only helpful when there is a life constantly driving, sustaining and assessing them. Without new life and an authentic evangelical spirit, without the Church's "fidelity to her own calling," any new structure will soon prove ineffective. (2613)

We have explored ways that diocesan leaders can approach the structural reorganization of parishes so that these renewed parishes can, in turn, have a missionary impact on the diocese. In many ways, this is what Divine Renovation ministry focuses on: the "making new again," or renovation, of parish life, so that these enlivened parishes breathe new life into surrounding neighborhoods, parishes, and the world. Parish transformation is perhaps the primary way through which dioceses will experience renewal, because transformed people transform parishes, and transformed parishes transform the dioceses of which they are an integral part. There are, however, other innovative initiatives that can and are being undertaken by diocesan leaders to bring missionary renewal at a diocesan level.

Any path to renewal includes facing some challenges that the Church has never had to face before. The apostolic age in which we now live includes universal literacy, high-speed communication, and the pervasive effect of social media on popular culture. Cynicism, skepticism, and a massive disconnect from personal modes of relationship color Western society today. The world has gone "virtual," and the Church needs a compelling response.

Four Responses to Uncertain Times

Whenever God's people have faced massive cultural and societal change, we have reacted in one of four ways: with agnosticism, cynicism, a turning to the past, or breakthrough. We see these same responses occurring in the wisdom literature of the Old Testament, and it might be useful to explore these roots as we try to rise to today's challenges. This wisdom literature includes the Book of Job, the Psalms, Proverbs, and the Book of Ecclesiastes. Catholics and Orthodox, who use the Greek canon of Scripture, also include Sirach and the Book of Wisdom. These books represent a five-hundred-year dialogue of Jewish theology and spirituality with what some call theodicy, and what most experience as the fundamental mystery of human suffering: why do bad things happen to good people?

The Torah—the first five books of the Old Testament—and early Jewish theology offered no clear teaching about life after death. For most Jews, there was no sense of an afterlife or eternal judgment as we think of those today. It follows then that in the Book of Deuteronomy, we find a simplistic viewpoint regarding worldly consequences in relation to the moral life. Namely, if you respected God's commandments, good things would happen to you; you would be blessed with a life free from suffering. If, however, you disrespected God's commandments, you would experience punishment. Those who suffer or experience illness in their life must have displeased God.

Yet the author of Psalm 73 sees something quite different. "I was envious of the arrogant," he writes, "when I saw the prosperity of the wicked" (Psalm 73:3). Though there is a belief that the wicked are punished in this world, the psalmist's experience tells him otherwise. There are many not-nice people who are healthy and wealthy, and there are many innocent and just people who are suffering. The only way to square this circle is to believe that the wicked will pay for their transgressions before they die.

This belief persisted even up to the time of Jesus. We see it reflected in the Gospel of John, when Jesus heals the man born blind. "His disciples asked him, 'Rabbi, who sinned, this man or his parents, that he was born blind?'" (John 9:2).

Human experience seems to come up against what was revealed to the Jewish people. We see that tension expressed in the Book of Job, which is an extended parable of a just man who loses everything and suffers greatly. In the course of this book, the author puts Job on trial and ultimately the Lord on trial for allowing the righteous to suffer.

Job is truly a just man, so the author rejects the belief that only the wicked suffer. The book's conclusion, however, takes the *agnostic* approach. Job repents of questioning God and puts on sackcloth and ashes as a sign that God is beyond him. Human moral reasoning cannot come close to God's knowledge or experience, and we simply cannot presume to know the mind and heart of God. In other words, the mystery of suffering is beyond us, because God's reasons are beyond us.

The next wisdom book that takes up this question of suffering is the Book of Ecclesiastes. This book represents what I call the *cynical* response. The famous saying "To everything, there is a season" comes from this book. In other words, suffering is simply a part of life. We just have to accept it.

"Vanity of vanities," the author of Ecclesiastes writes. "All things are vanity!" (Ecclesiastes 1:2). Life is full of hardship; trying to resist that reality is simply a waste of time. You live, and then you die, and some undeserving slob gets all your stuff. From the perspective of this book, life is seemingly pointless and patently unfair. Trying to glean any kind of meaning out of suffering is a waste of time.

Historically speaking, the next wisdom book to raise the question about human suffering is the Book of Sirach, which dates to between the years 200 and 175 B.C. Its author returns to the more simplistic view presented in Deuteronomy and the other books of the Torah, that suffering is the result of sinful behavior; it is a punishment levied against the wicked. In many ways, Sirach's approach is a reaction against the approach in Job and *a return to the past* for easier and simpler answers to the question of suffering. This approach reduces uncertainty, eliminates mystery, and doubles down on the beliefs of the past.

The final voice comes from the Book of Wisdom, which is the last book of the Old Testament before the birth of Jesus. This book appeared so close in time to the incarnation that the Gospels refer to the Book of Wisdom several times. Within the pages of the Book of Wisdom, we witness several theological breakthroughs.

For example, Wisdom makes it clear that death is not a part of God's original plan for humanity but came about as a result of our rebellion. This book also clearly notes that God created the universe out of nothing. Most importantly, Wisdom makes clear reference to an afterlife that will either be reward or punishment, as opposed to everyone dwelling in the pit of Sheol (see Isaiah 38:10-20).

Under the inspiration of the Holy Spirit, the Book of Wisdom presents a new synthesis of previous revelation, informed by human experience. In other words, even though from a worldly perspective it may seem that suffering just people are being punished, ultimately justice will be served in the next life.

Why are we spending so much time talking about the problem of evil within the Wisdom books of the Old Testament? To highlight the reality that the four responses that we see from God's people in times of uncertainty—agnosticism, cynicism, a return to the past, and breakthrough—are the same ones that we wrestle with in our current situation. Knowing this allows us to resist the temptation to respond in ways that are not helpful.

In the face of contemporary culture and the uncertainty of our present moment, for example, there are Church leaders who become paralyzed by trying to find a way forward. There is no clear path, and they feel as if they will never have clarity. Parish renewal is beyond them, and they proclaim their agnosticism: that there is simply no way to know what may or may not work.

We need to resist this agnostic response. We might not know everything we need to know in order to chart a clear way forward, but we do know that there are actions we can take that make a difference, approaches that will allow our parishes to move closer to a place of health. We might struggle with implementation of these things or with the development of a strategy, but we can communicate what actions, activities, and approaches have an impact on parish culture and the lives of other people.

The temptation to cynicism is quite real. I explored this in depth in the last section of the book. Some leaders have well-thought-out reasons why certain approaches will not work, reasons often rooted in experience and a kind of hopeless fatalism. This is why grounding ourselves in prayer and in our relationship with Jesus is so crucial. In the midst of our negativity, loss, and trial, we can keep our eyes on the Lord and maintain real hope. Remember the Berkana Two Loop theory: even in the midst of the dying process, something new can emerge.

We also need to resist the temptation to pin all our hopes on returning to the past: when Christendom held sway, when people respected the Church, and when we had clear and easy answers to the problems we faced. This temptation seems to be a strong one. Many of our leaders (and our people) believe that if we can reproduce the Catholic culture of the 40s and 50s, with all the trappings, everything will be fine.

I believe that if we can successfully resist falling into these temptations and live out God's will for us, we can experience breakthrough and find a new synthesis. We can take the richness of our Tradition and apply it to contemporary realities in new ways. As we cooperate with God's grace, we can bring to birth a new, mission-focused communion of churches.

What might this look like?

I have already laid out our plan for the Archdiocese of Halifax-Yarmouth. As we move from ninety-three parishes and missions to twenty, we believe that if we can help just 30 percent of those new parishes begin to evangelize and bear fruit, transform their cultures and move to a place of health in the next ten years, then our efforts will have been successful. What happens to the other 70 percent?

In truth, we will likely end up managing the decline of the majority of our parishes that may never become healthy; we will become effective and efficient at gracefully dying. I do not write this to be provocative or scandalous. I mention this reality because authentic leadership is one of the keys that will move a parish managing decline towards becoming a healthy and growing parish.

Within this realm of leadership, three things will be necessary for parishes who want to grow rather than manage decline:

1. For leaders—priests, laypeople, and deacons—to grow in self-awareness.

2. Learning to lead out of a team, an approach we will explore in the leadership section of this book.

3. Some form of ongoing accompaniment.

The presence of these three things will be essential to navigating this new territory. The question remains, however: what does a diocese do with the parishes that simply continue to decline over the next five or ten years?

One of the biggest problems for our Church today is that, although we are experiencing decline in a slow process of dying, we are not yet dead enough. We comfort ourselves in thinking that, compared to the Church in other regions or countries, we are not doing so badly. As we have said, however, if you do not alter your trajectory, it does not matter how far along you are in the process of decline. It all ends the same way. All you need is time.

In many places throughout the world, the Church lacks a sense of urgency, often because leaders there have yet to acknowledge the problem. If our downward spiral were to become more obvious, it would be difficult for Church leaders to maintain a spirit of denial. The desperation phase of the dying process can be filled with grace, however, because we might finally be willing to do whatever we have to do in order to see new life.

Seeds of Renewal

Imagine a diocese that, years from now, has a group of parishes bearing fruit in terms of making, forming, and missioning disciples. These healthy parishes could now begin to bless those parishes in decline by sending lay leaders to them as missionaries, after a fashion. These missionaries would apply the principles of renewal that they learned at their parish to the parishes in decline.

These healthy parishes would also start producing vocations—including vocations to the priesthood—at a higher rate. Thus, in many ways, the small number of healthy parishes in a diocese can seed the health and growth of parishes that are in decline.

For this to happen in the most fruitful way, diocesan leaders must be intentional about this process. Here are four possible models for how dioceses could help their healthy parishes bring life to dying parishes, once these declining communities recognize that they need assistance.

Growing the Church

When non-Catholic communities grow, they manage this growth in one of three ways. Some just keep adding members and become megachurches, eventually moving to bigger and bigger buildings. Others choose to open multiple sites around the city or geographical area they are in, while remaining one single church (multisite). Still others identify and equip leaders in order to send them out to start new and completely separate communities (church planting).

In *Divine Renovation*, I shared what has been happening in parts of the Anglican Church in England through Holy Trinity Brompton, the Anglican Church that started Alpha. HTB (Holy Trinity Brompton) began to church plant. They would identify maybe twenty to thirty people and an ordained leader and send them into a church that was essentially dead. They would provide some financial and prayer support as those "missionaries" worked to bring new life to the church. Now that they have been at this for several years, many of the churches that they renewed are planting other churches. This is a healthy life cycle.

About six years ago, some of our parish staff and I were part of a cohort with the Parish Catalyst organization. During the two years we were involved with this cohort, we received tremendous blessings through their guidance and ministry. During one of our sessions, a non-Catholic church leader gave a talk on church planting.

This may be an unfamiliar term to many Catholics. The easiest way to understand the concept is to look at gardening. When you have a healthy plant and want to start another plant, you take a cutting from the healthy plant and place it in a new pot. If this cutting is placed firmly in good soil, it will begin to grow.

During the presentation on church planting, the facilitator asked us what this might look like in a Catholic context. Thinking about it,

I knew we would have some challenges implementing this, because our understanding of church was so different from that of the speaker.

For example, in the Catholic Church, most parishes exist in a particular territory; in one sense, every inch of the globe falls within some parish's boundaries. Therefore you could not just plant a new parish anywhere, because you would be doing it in another parish's backyard, so to speak. In addition, the foundation of parish life revolves around the celebration of the Eucharist, and you need a priest for that.

Transplanting

Our parish team knew these restrictions, so instead of "planting" a new parish, we began to explore what "transplanting" might look like. Think of a kidney transplant. What does someone need for that transplant to be successful?

First, an available and healthy kidney donor. In other words, we need to have something to give. In a healthy, evangelizing parish that has created a culture and systems to make, form, and equip disciples for mission, we have something to give: passionate disciples who are willing to surrender their preferences for the sake of the mission.

The second thing we need for a successful transplant is a willing recipient. If I walked up to a healthy person and asked them if they wanted my kidney, chances are they would say, "No thanks." However, if I approached someone who was diagnosed with kidney failure, he would most likely take me up on my offer.

Unfortunately, there are many places that are still in denial and not willing to change anything. Until a community faces the issues before them and truly believes the prognosis, they will not be motivated to do what it takes to reverse course.

The third thing you must do for a successful transplant is actually make the switch, integrating the new kidney into the body in place of the dysfunctional one. We talked about that at Saint Benedict quite a bit. We hoped to apprentice an associate pastor for a year or two, immersing him in our evangelization and leadership cultures and letting him learn our systems. Then, after this apprenticeship, that priest would be missioned to become pastor of a different parish. We would send this priest—with the archbishop's permission, of course—and a group of parishioners who discerned their call to participation, to bring life to a parish.

This would be a true sacrificial offering for the life of this other parish. We would not send just anyone with the priest. Rather we would invite our best givers and most active families to pray about embracing this mission. Then we would send them with a big check.

At HTB, they send their outgoing missionaries with a check for fifty thousand pounds. That is a lot of money. Remember, however, that as parishes evangelize and make disciples, giving goes up, which allows them to share that abundance with other struggling communities.

Let us return to the image of a transplant. Once the operation is complete, the biggest danger to the recipient is organ rejection. In terms of the parish transplant, the declining parish leadership may welcome the influx of missionaries, but when they arrive, many parishioners may feel they are being invaded by aliens. If leadership does not navigate this reality well, this could lead to division and, ultimately, rejection.

The missionaries themselves must be very self-aware. They will need to arrive at their new parish with humble, servant hearts. They must honor the history and accomplishments of this community, while seeing themselves, ultimately, as serving the people. They must be there to pour themselves out for the parish, not to take over.

We never had the chance to do this at Saint Benedict. I started to work half-time with the archbishop, serving the other parishes in my archdiocese, and half-time with Divine Renovation ministry. Our apprenticing associate pastor, Fr. Simon Lobo, CC, became the pastor of Saint Benedict. We still believe, however, that such a transplanting model would be possible within a diocese.

The challenge will be finding willing recipients. By the time some of the churches were willing to work with Holy Trinity Brompton, for example, these communities were down to something like twenty people, with the average age of their youth group being seventy-five! I hope we will not have parishes wait that long to receive a transplant.

Transfusion
This is a similar model to that of transplanting. We deliberately mentor an associate pastor in a healthy parish and send him out to a struggling community. Rather than sending that priest with a contingent of parish missionaries all at once, we gradually transfuse that parish. Perhaps we send one or two families during the first month,

and then throughout the year, we continue to send missionaries at a controlled pace.

This process would not have to be officially announced. It is perfectly normal in Catholic parish life to have families and individuals follow popular priests to their new assignment. Generally that happens without much discernment. In the transfusion model, we would be intentional about it. Those considering leaving the healthy parish would pray about it first; they would deliberately answer a call to mission and not just follow their preferences.

Adoption

This is another way in which a healthy parish can make a gift of itself to a struggling parish, and it may be less challenging for a declining parish to accept this kind of approach. In this model, a struggling parish recognizes that it is declining and may not have the resources needed to move toward health. So they ask to be adopted into the family of a healthy parish. They retain their identity but have access to the other parish's resources.

This is a real partnership. The healthy parish recognizes that they must give of their human and financial resources to help the adopted parish become healthy. The struggling parish maintains its identity, but its leadership has to be open to being mentored and attending formation sessions: like staff meetings, leadership summits, and Alpha training, for example. The adopted parish would need to reform its leadership structure in many ways as well.

We have experienced something like adoption in Divine Renovation ministry, though we are an entirely separate organization from Saint Benedict Parish. The work we do with our networked parishes, and those in leadership coaching, is a form of adoption. However, even before we formed DR as a ministry, other parishes in our diocese and elsewhere approached Saint Benedict Parish and asked for help. They did not want to simply copy us, but they did want a mentoring affiliation that would allow them to receive the kind of leadership formation we were putting into place

Signs of New Life

These four models—three of which could work within Catholic ecclesiology—may sound theoretical, but some amazing things are beginning to happen right now in these areas. These new initiatives are only going to grow in the future.

We see this in the Berkana Two Loop model. There is a moment in the process when the dominant system continues to decline, but something new starts to grow. When these two moments coexist, something called the composting effect can happen. We still have resources that might be legacies from a time when the dominant system thrived, and we can use these resources to support the new initiatives. New initiatives have developed within lay movements for several decades, and one of the fundamental beliefs in the Divine Renovation approach is that what has been happening in the movements can happen within the parish and within the diocese.

Here is one of those new initiatives. I met a priest named George in London, England, in 2019. He is originally from Vancouver, British Columbia, but has served in the Archdiocese of Vienna in Austria for the last fifteen years. He shared with me that only 3 to 5 percent of people in his area go to church, with only 8 percent of Catholics attending Mass. He estimated that there are only about two thousand people under the age of thirty-five who are active in the Church across the whole diocese.

Furthermore, most of the active young people belong to lay movements. The vitality and energy present in these movements is not present in diocesan or parochial structures. For example, one priest of the diocese had created a First Communion process that had over three hundred families participating. Most people thought he was successful, but unfortunately, after First Communion, only five of those families remained. This was typical, according to Fr. George. In his diocese, they sacramentalized but rarely evangelized.

These realities kept Fr. George up at night. About six years ago, he began to read some books on leadership, most from a non-Catholic perspective. He began to be exposed to different ways of thinking—including some ideas about church planting. Then, around five years ago, he read *Rebuilt* by Fr. Mike White and Tom Corcoran; this moved his imagination.

In August 2015, Fr. George started what was effectively a "church plant," with the permission of his bishop: a Sunday evening Mass specifically for students. Not to be discouraging, but only two students turned up! After an extended period of time, the Mass experienced fivefold growth: ten to fifteen students regularly attended, along with four or five families.

Around that time, Fr. George pitched a vision for a mission-focused parish to that small group of people. He posed the question: what would it look like to be a parish for people who do not go to church regularly?

Now, this small community, being a kind of church plant, was already somewhat missionary. To live out Fr. George's vision would not require moving a parish from pure maintenance to mission. The community took up the vision and began to live it out. They had three pillars: Eucharistic Adoration all day, every day; a focus on the weekend experience; and eventually, after reading *Divine Renovation*, Alpha as a tool for evangelization.

Five years later, the community has experienced incredible growth. They have about two hundred people, mostly young, attending Mass regularly; they have reached the capacity of their current building. About 50 percent of parishioners now attend small groups regularly, and eighty members are active in ministry. They even started an initiative in 2015 called *Shut Up, It's Christmas*, which focuses on reaching out to other people and bringing them in. By 2018 they had nine hundred people, most of whom did not attend church, show up for a Christmas-themed evangelistic event.

On one hand, these numbers may seem small, but I think they tell an important story. Remember, Fr. George started with two people! They had a clear identity as being missionary, focusing on mission rather than maintenance. They implemented changes around their weekend experience and focused on leadership. Finally, they started using a proven tool for evangelization. All these things helped them experience growth and engagement far beyond what other parishes in their diocese knew.

Trying to transform a maintenance parish into a missionary one is exceptionally difficult. Yes, it is what we focus on in Divine Renovation ministry. We recognize that not every parish will be able to make the transition, but Fr. George's experience demonstrates that it is possible to create a missionary-focused parish from scratch. The beautiful thing is that the Lord is not finished with them; this story is far from complete. The Archdiocese of Vienna is perhaps at a place of desperation as they continue to experience decline, and they are open to new initiatives.

Another initiative taking place in that diocese comes from a priest named Fr. Bernard, who spent a year in London, England, on an internship at one of the Anglican church plants from HTB. He celebrated Mass on Sundays at the local Catholic parish (which was in our Divine Renovation Leadership Coaching network), but he was apprenticed with this other community.

Fr. Bernard is a member of a new religious community called the Loreto Community. The Archdiocese of Vienna is partnering with him; it recently sent him and thirty or forty other Loreto Community members into a dying parish in the inner city of Vienna. This parish, known as the Schubert Kirche, has a seventeenth-century church building that is famous because the composer Franz Schubert played there. This is a very traditionally built church, but the parish only had about eighteen regular members. Fr. Bernard and his group of on-fire young disciples will be transplanted into this parish and attempt a kind of HTB renewal.

Another initiative that seems very encouraging comes from Sheffield, England. Several years ago, the archdiocese there proposed buying a plot of land and renewing the building that sat on that land. That seems fairly unremarkable, except that this plot of land is right in the center of the student residence area for the local university. As the archdiocese renovates the building, they plan on creating what they call a "mission hub." The design of the building has been completed, and they have identified a priest chaplain, who will help lead this missionary community.

The entrance level of the building will be a coffee shop, while a chapel for Eucharistic adoration will be located upstairs. This future community plans on using Alpha as their core evangelization tool. The beautiful thing is that men and women from around the country have discerned a call to be a part of this initiative. This is a work in progress, something new for the archdiocese. They are intentionally creating a community with missionary DNA right from the start.

Please pray for all these initiatives, and allow them to plant the seeds of hope in your heart. We do not have to be trapped in cynicism or agnosticism; we do not have to settle for the belief that we cannot escape our decline or that renewal is a mysterious process that we can never understand. Nor do we have to pin all our hopes on a return to the past, a past that may no longer have much relevance in our contemporary situation. Rather we can push forward and embrace new models, breaking through to become missionary parishes, missionary dioceses, and a missionary Church.

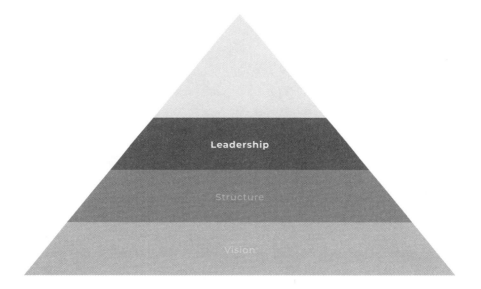

PART 3

LEADERSHIP

CHAPTER 9

Leadership Essentials

You may remember the movie *Castaway*, which featured Tom Hanks as a FedEx employee marooned on a desert island. During the Super Bowl in 2003, FedEx presented a TV ad based on the movie; I often show the video of this commercial to parish leaders during a talk. The video opens with a Tom Hanks–like figure—complete with wild hair, scraggly beard, and a disheveled FedEx uniform—holding a rather battered FedEx box as he stands in front of a house. He looks around, as if searching for something, while background music swells. He catches sight of the house address, matches it to the package, and rings the doorbell. When the owner opens the door, he explains to her that he was marooned on a desert island for five years with only this piece of mail but that, as a FedEx employee, he wanted to make sure he delivered it.

The woman, for her part, is astonished and thanks the man for his dedication. The FedEx employee begins to turn away but then asks the woman what was in the box. She opens it and says, "Nothing really. Just a satellite phone, GPS locator, fishing rod, water purifier, and some seeds. Silly stuff!"

Then the commercial ends.

That FedEx employee had everything he needed to thrive on the island. He had all the essentials for building a new life right at his fingertips, but he never knew it because he never bothered to open the box.

I like to show this video to parish leaders, because I believe that every parish already has everything it needs to experience renewal:

all of the gifts and talents needed to become healthy and grow. The question is: will we open the box?

About seven years ago, in New Zealand, I visited Te Puke (with apologies to my Kiwi friends, pronounced "T-pooky"), a town that claims to be the kiwi capital of the world. It was the beginning of harvest season. I discovered pretty quickly that there is such a thing as a male kiwi tree and a female kiwi tree, and it was easy to tell them apart. The female trees were absolutely loaded with fruit. In many cases, they were bent over from the weight of the fruit, which practically begged to be picked. The male trees, on the other hand, were standing tall and straight, carrying no fruit whatsoever. Driving by the fruit-laden kiwi trees, it was as if I heard the Lord speaking to me: "James, these trees resemble most parishes, laden with fruit that no one ever picks."

I think that most parishes harvest only about 5 percent of their fruit. I mean the gifts given to the baptized that are never recognized, affirmed, nurtured, and called out for use in manifesting God's kingdom in the world.

This is largely the result of living with a clerical model of ministry for many years: the notion that fulfilling the mission of the Church is primarily the role of priests, religious men and women, and deacons. We have not considered this the work of the baptized layperson.

In the clerical model, the primary role of laypeople is to pray, pay, and obey. Parish renewal, however, requires that we embrace the apostolic identity of the *entire* people of God, helping laypeople encounter the love of the Father in Jesus Christ, experience the power of the Holy Spirit, discern their gifts, and receive the formation they need to live a mission- and holiness-focused lifestyle.

To move in this direction requires authentic leadership.

Leadership is the gift and discipline that, if done well, unleashes all the other gifts; it allows us to harvest the fruit from our trees, to mobilize parishioners for mission. When Jesus said, "The harvest is abundant but the laborers are few; so ask the master of the harvest to send out laborers for his harvest" (Matthew 9:37-38), he was talking about the harvest to be reaped not in the Church but in the world. The laborers are to be sent out, but we only have a few, because we have never mobilized them. If you practice authentic leadership, however, you will mobilize the men and women in your parish to become effective missionaries who transform individuals and cultures *out in the world* through the power of the gospel.

Within the Church, leadership can function as either a bottleneck or a bottle opener. Sometimes our parishes work from a command-and-control model, led by people who centralize everything around themselves, micromanage others, and control information flow and decision-making. They create a bottleneck, which slows transformation and renewal. Bottleneck leaders fill their daily schedules with the details of controlling a complex organization; in the process, they frustrate others, burn themselves out, and blunt the impact of their community on the world around them.

Bottle-opening leaders, in contrast, raise up other leaders, affirm their gifts, and invest in others by giving of their time, experience, and support. The goal is that others might bear even more fruit. In my experience, bottle openers are rare creatures within Church structures. The habits of a clerically centered leadership often repeat themselves, even in the work of the laymen and laywomen hired by the pastor to serve on staff.

Equipping *All* the Holy Ones

Paul writes in Ephesians:

> He gave some as apostles, others as prophets, others as evangelists, others as pastors and teachers, to equip the holy ones for the work of ministry, for building up the body of Christ, until we all attain to the unity of faith and knowledge of the Son of God, to mature manhood, to the extent of the full stature of Christ. (4:11-13)

St. Paul is talking here about some core gifts or charisms—gifts for apostolic work, prophetic gifts, gifts for evangelization, gifts for shepherding or pastoring others, and gifts for teaching. Certainly in the Catholic Church, we recognize that these gifts have been associated with particular ecclesial offices, like those of deacon, priest, and bishop. I would never deny that. Equating these charisms with the offices in an exclusive way, however, places those gifts in the hands of a select few—the professional ministerial caste—and directs that their use be primarily for work on behalf of the baptized.

There is a substantial difference, though, between having the "office" of an aspect of ministry, or the responsibility for it, and having a particular charism for that ministry. Every ordained person has the office of preaching or teaching, for example, but not every ordained person has the gift for this.

Paul's letter is not addressed only to the leaders in the church at Ephesus. Rather he is writing to the whole community, including mothers, fathers, children, free people, and slaves. These gifts, therefore, are present within the whole community—among all the baptized—so that all can be channels of God's love and mercy to the world.

When parish leaders take seriously the charisms of all the baptized, when they help the people of God discover, discern, nurture, and use those gifts, the Church will grow to maturity in Jesus. This is about becoming bottle openers, who will "uncork" the grace that God has poured out on every baptized person, not only for their salvation but also for the salvation of the world.

Look closely at the Ephesians text. The charisms, offices, and roles St. Paul talks about are given to equip the "holy ones," the baptized, for their essential part in the mission of the Church in the world. Some translations of Ephesians 4:12 would seem to infer that this passage speaks about the body of Christ being built up when holy ones receive ministry from a select few, rather than being equipped for the purpose of ministry.[38] All lay men and women have a missionary call on their lives by virtue of their baptism; God has gifted them to bear fruit as they live out that call. The idea that the work of mission belongs only to the ordained, religious, or particular holy men and women creates a passive laity who see themselves as religious consumers.

Passive parishioners—prominent in many parishes today—fail to understand that they are called to take their place in the Church's mission and serve the world in the name of Christ. Many work from a transactional understanding: "I come to the parish to receive ministry. That's the job of priests and parish staff. I put money in the collection basket so that you can do ministry to me. Don't disappoint me. Give me what I want, when I want it, and I will keep my end of the bargain and drop a few bucks into the collection."

If we attempt to mobilize our people into mission, these religious consumers perceive it as a break in the agreement. They push back—or start looking for another parish that will honor the bargain.

This is the challenge we currently face as leaders, but we can address it and equip our people to move joyfully into mission. The pastoral plan that we are currently living in the Archdiocese of Halifax-Yarmouth seeks to do just that. As I mentioned in chapter seven, the bishop chose to ground the plan in the principles found in Ephesians 4. He understands that leadership in the Church is not simply about feeding the sheep who show up but about equipping them to do the work of ministry and mission proper to the baptized. This is a different paradigm from a clerical model; it is one we must embrace if we, as the people of God, are to reach "the full stature of Christ" (Ephesians 4:13).

Two Leadership Approaches

Many of us, when we hear the word "leader," immediately think of those who occupy *positions* of leadership. Yet the reality of leadership is far richer.

There is a big difference between *positional* leadership and *character*—or what I call "authentic"—leadership. In other words, you might function as a leader in an organization or a group by virtue of the position that you hold, but you might not actually exercise authentic leadership: few may actually be following you. Positional leadership relies on power to get things done, while authentic leadership relies on influence to accomplish things.

Positional leadership and the mechanisms of power can get you only so far. They can perhaps remove some obstacles, but they do little to move hearts. Someone once said, "If you have to constantly remind people that you're the leader, then maybe you're not." Authentic leadership forges relationships, fosters loyalty, and inspires people to action.

Positional leadership relies fundamentally on institutional authority. It uses policies and procedures as external stimuli to compel adherence. I have heard of workplaces where the managers spy on staff; the underlying office dynamic is distrust. Managers believe they must monitor employees and compel their behavior externally, or the employees will rip them off by not doing a full day's work, stealing supplies, and so on. Positional leadership therefore tries to control behavior through reward and punishment—which ultimately grounds this type of leadership in fear. If you do well in your job, you will be rewarded. If the person in a position of authority believes you are not doing a good job, you will be punished. Naturally, employees tend to be a little afraid of that type of authority figure.

When we experience fear, cortisol floods our system and evokes a fight-or-flight response. The hormone sends out signals that prompt the body to move blood away from the rational centers of our brain and into our fists or our feet. We are either going to run away or become aggressive in order to protect ourselves—depending on the situation and our general personality.

This is why we often say things that are not helpful when we are upset, afraid, or angry. Once we are past that particularly fearful situation and look back, we may wonder why we said something dumb or failed to think of the perfect response. The reason? Our brain had prioritized fight or flight, shutting down cognitive function and leading us to rely more on instinct.

We see this reality lived out and reinforced in the Church. When a priest gets a call from the bishop saying, "Could you come and see me?" the priest's first thought is often "I'm in trouble."

I saw that fear play out a number of years ago, in one of the parishes where I served before Saint Benedict. We hired a new office manager who had completed a course on administration at a community college but had never worked in this area before. She was a wonderful, gifted person, and she was shocked when we offered her the job. She did not realize how good she was.

About three weeks into her role, I asked her to come to my office. I wanted to tell her what an amazing job she was doing and how delighted we were to have her on our team. I wanted to affirm her, but I did not realize the impact of calling a new employee to my office. The woman was trembling when she arrived. She thought I was going to fire her!

I have never forgotten that. Our experience of those in authority is often colored by our history of working within a culture that largely lives out of positional leadership. This woman's past experiences with positionally focused leaders led her to assume something awful was about to happen.

That culture, however, is radically changing. The positional leadership approach worked more effectively in the past because thirty or forty years ago, there was much more respect for institutions and institutional leaders. Things began to shift in the 1960s, 70s, and 80s, and they have continued to shift today. This is evident in an increasing cynicism and suspicion of politics, institutions, and people in power. Even Church leadership positions do not hold the same respect that they once did.

A young father in my last parish said to me, as the clergy sex-abuse scandal unfolded again in the news, "Fr. James, when you leave, I won't simply not trust the new guy. I will actively distrust him until he earns the right for me to simply not trust him."

When it comes to authority and leadership in the Church, we are starting in a deficit position. We have to win the right to be not trusted as opposed to actively distrusted! Positional leadership never wins trust. That is the role of character—authentic—leadership.

Character leadership is ultimately about relational authority. I do not have authority over you because of my position. I have authority because I am in relationship with you.

Think of the authority that your grandmother had over you. Was she your boss? No. She had a certain authority because you knew she loved and cared about you. We will listen to that kind of authority because it is not based on reward or punishment; it is based on love and respect. Within the framework of relational authority, we understand that we are not just nameless cogs in a giant wheel or objects to be used. We are cherished and respected.

Character leadership is trust based rather than fear based. When people experience love and respect, it creates trust—and trust goes both ways. The person in leadership trusts the employees or other staff members, and the team members trust the person in leadership. Rather than releasing cortisol into our bodies, as the fear-based positional leadership approach does, character leadership evokes the release of oxytocin and dopamine, the bonding and pleasure hormones in our bodies. We sometimes describe the experience of these hormones as "the warm fuzzies"!

Some of you might be saying, "Wait a minute, Fr. James! What about the importance of having a vision, aligning with that vision, and holding people accountable? Have you gone soft on us?"

I have not gone soft. Creating a vision, fostering alignment around that vision, and holding people accountable are all critical if we want to experience renewal in our parishes and dioceses, but those things must happen in the context of character leadership. When team members understand that they are loved and respected, they do not do things because they *have to*; they do things because they *get to*. They have a growing desire to move in the right direction. When you exercise this authentic leadership, you will often get the very best from people; they will go the extra mile time and time again.

Unfortunately, some leaders believe that investing in relationships and building trust is a waste of time. We need to ask ourselves, how effective and efficient are our large staff turnovers, which often stem from the reality that people do not like working for parishes and dioceses in which they are being controlled by fear? How much work are we losing to dysfunction and to obstacles created by a primarily positional approach to leadership?

At heart, positional leadership changes behavior, but character leadership changes people. I am not saying there is no place for actual positions of leadership. There will always be a need for those, as well as policies, procedures, and structures of authority that help us remain true to the Church's discipline and teaching, as well as her mission. I am not arguing for doing away with any of those things. But people in positions of leadership will only be effective if they live out their authority in the form of character leadership. Such respectful leadership will help us navigate the great external cultural shifts we see around us and foster the kinds of internal cultural shifts we need in order to bear the fruit of holiness and mission.

Character Leadership as Servant Leadership

After I wrote *Divine Renovation*, one reader commented that she was a bit disappointed that I did not speak about servant leadership. I think she made a fair point, but in that moment, I remember thinking that in a Christian context, the only form of legitimate leadership *is* servant leadership. This is Jesus' model. The fact that we have to specifically name servant leadership in the context of the Church is a sign of our failure to live out authentic leadership.

Jesus communicated about leadership in his words and certainly in his actions. I want to look at two places in the Gospels where he spoke explicitly about leadership.

The first occurs in the story of the washing of the feet in the Gospel of John, chapter thirteen. We read this story every Holy Thursday. The night before Jesus dies on the cross, he takes on the role of a slave and kneels down to wash the feet of the apostles. Peter is offended by Jesus' actions, declaring that the Lord will never wash his feet. When Jesus finishes, he turns to his disciples and says:

146

You call me "teacher" and "master," and rightly so, for indeed I am. If I, therefore, the master and teacher, have washed your feet, you ought to wash one another's feet. I have given you a model to follow, so that as I have done for you, you should also do. (John 13:13-15)

Although John's Gospel does not speak to us about the institution of the Eucharist at the Last Supper, we know from the synoptic gospels—Matthew, Mark, and Luke—that the institution of the Eucharist did occur at the Last Supper. Looking at this through the lens of John's Gospel, we see that Jesus institutes the Eucharist and then shows us what the Eucharist looks like when it is lived out. Jesus does not deny the titles of teacher and master. These are, in a sense, symbols of positional leadership. Through his actions, however, he demonstrates that living authentically as Christians means being a servant and caring for others. Jesus shows us that character (or servant) leadership is the basis for how we live out positions of leadership.

The second time Jesus explicitly talks about leadership occurs in the Gospel of Matthew, chapter twenty. A similar story occurs in the Gospel of Mark, chapter ten. In the story, James and John ask Jesus to place them at his right and left when he comes into his kingdom. Their conception of Jesus' kingdom was an earthly one. In secular kingdoms, sitting at the right and left hands of the king meant you were the king's second and third in command.

Jesus tells James and John that they do not know what they are asking. In order for them to ascend to those positions, they would have to suffer what Jesus will suffer. The two respond that they can do that. Jesus tells them that they will suffer, but they will not be at his left and right.

The other ten apostles hear this exchange and grow angry with the two brothers. Jesus calls them together and says,

You know that the rulers of the Gentiles lord it over them, and the great ones make their authority over them felt. But it shall not be so among you. Rather, whoever wishes to be great among you shall be your servant; whoever wishes to be first among you shall be your slave. Just so, the Son of Man did not come to be served but to serve and to give his life as a ransom for many. (Matthew 20:25-28)

Here we have Jesus' most explicit teaching on leadership. We are not to lord our authority over others: "it shall not be so among you." In his Gospel, Mark uses the present tense *"it is not* so among you" (10:43, NRSV). The disposition of Christian leadership in the Church, and by Christians in the world, must be servant leadership.

In spite of Jesus' clear teaching, the Church has gotten this wrong throughout history. In the Middle Ages, for example, Church leaders started to take on the titles reserved for the nobility. This is when we started calling bishops "Your Excellency"; cardinals "Your Eminence"; and others "Your Grace" and "My Lord." This is what the secular world called their civic leaders at the time.

We have these titles to this day. Even the honorific title of monsignor is simply the French construction for "my lord." In the twentieth century, it was still fashionable to call cardinals "princes of the Church," and bishops lived in "palaces." In the twenty-first century, we still have a cultural tendency in the Church to treat cardinals, bishops, and priests with exaggerated deference.

Over a year ago I spent an evening with a cardinal who is one of the humblest servant leaders I have ever met. It was rather odd to hear some people calling him "Eminence." I could see him almost wincing.

The Middle Ages also saw bishops and Church leaders beginning to live as noble lords at the papal "court" and even within dioceses. They owned land; enjoyed the prerogatives of earthly power; adopted a personal coat of arms, which they used on the banners and shields of their household guards; and often lived in actual palaces. They imitated the trappings of earthly power. Does this sound like Jesus' instructions on leadership?

If we want that kind of culture to change, then we have to change our language. We already have that language in our tradition—a beautiful, simple word for the ordained: father.

Another way in which we can fall prey to the temptation to imitate worldly leaders is by embracing a kind of CEO model of leadership. I am aware that many CEOs live out this role as authentic leaders, but with all due respect, the position is often perceived as being at the top, removed and disconnected from the company minions.

In many organizations, it is common to have an org chart in order to track the network of accountability and authority that flows through an organization. I believe organizational charts are good things to have: they foster clarity in decision-making and organizational "architecture." Many org charts position the boss at the top, with every other person placed in descending order, in relation to the top dog. Again, these are useful, but I believe that we Christians should flip our org charts like this:

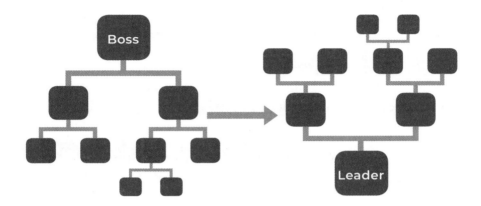

Part of changing our language means changing the symbols we use to talk about leadership—and an org chart is a symbol. The leader, therefore, should occupy the bottom position of an organization. In this servant model, leaders do not have direct *reports* but direct *supports!* How successful you grow within such an organization is not based on how many people report to you but rather on how many individuals and teams you serve and support.

For example, you might have five people supported by you, and you would offer support in the context of character leadership. You can still talk about goals, performance, and accountability. You will still have to make decisions and still have critical (and sometimes) difficult conversations with those you support in an effort to help them grow. All those things, however, emerge from a different starting point: you are not the boss but the servant leader.

This is Jesus' model.

Ten Signs You Are the "Boss" and Not the Leader

Tony Morgan, a consultant and church health strategist, has written an article that can help bishops, priests, lay staff members, parish ministry leaders, and others in Church leadership examine their approach to ministry. The article is titled "10 Signs That You're 'the Boss' . . . But Not the Leader."[39] I have added some commentary to help explore his ten points.

1. You have to make every decision.

Bosses often feel they have to micromanage and second-guess the decisions of those who work for them. They may rationalize that, because of their experience, they are most qualified to make all the decisions. This behavior often stems from a lack of trust in team members or from a need to control.

If you find that this statement is true of your leadership style, then you are not empowering others to make decisions in their sphere. Chances are, you are a bottleneck—and you may not even know it.

2. You know people fear you, and you are okay with that.

When I started at Saint Benedict Parish, an older priest took me aside and said, "James, just remember: when working with your staff, you've got to make sure that they're afraid of you." I respected that priest, but his was the boss model. "Do what I want, or I'm going to punish you."

If you agree with this second statement from Tony Morgan, it is a red flag that you are functioning as a boss and not a leader.

3. You have an agenda for today but lack vision for the future.

This is one of the main differences between a boss and a leader. A vision for the future drives leaders. Today's issues must be addressed, and activities done, but everything that we do must be in service to our future state. Bosses work from to-do lists: they will accomplish this year's goals, but what those goals have to do with a future destination is hazy at best.

4. You "lead" a team, but your life is isolated from other people.

In other words, you have a team in name only. A group of people gathered around a table for a particular purpose does not necessarily make a team. We are going to examine the dynamics of a team later, but if you are in charge of a group yet lead from an ivory tower, divorced from the messiness of team dynamics or the lives of your team members, you are living firmly in boss land.

5. You think that once you get the title, you will have influence.

I see this a great deal: leaders who believe they will be able to move people once the promotion is official, the business cards are printed, and their name is on the office door. People are not going to give a fig about your title if you do not demonstrate that you want to invest in them, treat them with love and respect, communicate a dynamic vision, serve them humbly, and empower them to make decisions.

6. You believe the volume of your words is louder than the impact of your behavior.

Our words often communicate one thing, and our actions another. Our actions, of course, will have far more impact than our words, which is why, as authentic leaders, we should want others to hold us accountable when we get this wrong, and we will most likely get it wrong sometimes. That is the nature of sin and our wounded human nature. Leaders try to create integrity between their words and actions, and they cultivate relationships with others who will hold them accountable when there is a disconnect.

7. You blame others for mistakes and take credit for the wins.

We see this in every organization: bosses who seek to shift the blame to other teams, people, or cultural forces rather than own it themselves. Authentic leaders understand that they are ultimately responsible for missed goals, mistakes, and poor team performance.

On the flip side, when there is success, it comes from the team's performance, facilitated by the leader. The leader did not accomplish those wins; the team did. It seems unfair to be responsible for the losses and yet not be able to claim the wins. Perhaps it is unfair, but that is simply the cost of leadership. Those who live out of a servant's heart embrace that reality. Bosses, especially insecure ones, take the praise and deflect the blame.

8. You do not ask your subordinates or peers for input or advice.

Bosses—whether they be laypeople, priests, or bishops—tend to think that they have a direct connection with God or that they alone are the oracle of wisdom for an organization. True leaders surround themselves with people who are smarter, more experienced, and more talented than they are. Recruiting, nurturing, and helping these high performers reach an even greater level of performance or growth is a hallmark of a great leader.

9. You are focused solely on the mission and not the people who are on the mission with you.

I have had to learn this lesson over the years—sometimes in rather painful ways—as I have been very mission focused and blind to the unintentional ways in which I have hurt people. Bosses, whether intentionally or unintentionally, often treat team members as objects to be used or resources to expend in pursuit of a goal. Leaders hold the success of the mission and the good of their team members in balance.

10. You are the boss, but no one is following you.

An old adage goes something like this: If you think you are a leader, but no one is following you, you are simply going for a walk. The greater truth is that leadership is not just about having people follow you. The true measure of leadership is whether you have other leaders following you: people who have, in turn, people following them.

Leadership vs. a Clerical Model of Ministry

When I first came to Saint Benedict Parish as pastor, I told the staff that we could no longer be doers of ministry: we had to become leaders of ministry—and leaders who do not simply lead other doers but who also lead other leaders of ministry. When you can make that shift, leadership starts functioning as a bottle opener by raising up other leaders.

Often these leaders will not be front and center when things are happening. Sometimes, the best leaders in parish life operate in the background. They are not generals; they are sergeants and corporals, quietly organizing, training, and forming others. You might wonder what some of your best leaders even do on a day-to-day basis; they always seem to have other people doing their work for them. The truth is that they are busy raising up, equipping, and giving others real authority at different levels of ministry.

This is Jesus' model: How can I serve you? How can I equip you? How can I support you? How can I help you grow in your leadership capabilities?

The clerical model of ministry functions quite the opposite way, as we have seen. This model is really all about the person at the center saying, "Watch me. Cheer for me." People will respond to this unspoken invitation and tell you how wonderful you are, because they are not being challenged to do anything but remain passive recipients of your ministry. It can become very easy for a priest, deacon, or even a lay leader to get caught up in this, because it is very affirming. In many parishes, there are plenty of laity who are quite happy with this kind of arrangement. There can be a symbiotic or codependent relationship between parishioners and their leaders in this regard.

Not long ago, I filled in at a parish on a weekend when there had been an ordination in our diocese. One of the prayers of the faithful was for the newly ordained priest, "that he may meet the needs of his parishioners, and that his parishioners may affirm him." That is a classic example of the codependency that lurks behind the clerical model of ministry. We boil down the job of the priest to "meeting the needs of parishioners."

That is the very definition of maintenance. A maintenance-focused priest meets the needs of parishioners, and in return his parishioners affirm him, telling him how wonderful he is. This simply does not reflect a mission-focused mindset.

If we want to move into mission fruitfully, we must meet the challenge by shifting away from a clerical model of ministry. Character leadership—authentic leadership—can help us do this. Leaders come in many forms; they are not limited to those who hold a particular office in the Church. As we will see in the next chapter, an exploration of leadership as influence may help us make this transition.

CHAPTER 10

Leadership as Influence

In the twenty-first century, technology has expanded the possibilities for exercising leadership. Consider, for example, the video-hosting website YouTube. Any individual with a camera and access to the Internet can create and upload content on any topic imaginable—and there are billions of people waiting to consume that content. In 2018, the top ten YouTubers collectively grossed 180.5 million dollars in revenue from their YouTube channels. Beyond their revenue, each of these YouTubers has amassed tens of millions of followers, who listen to their advice and recommendations. Marketers from major companies have taken notice, and now they actively partner with these YouTubers—even going so far as to shape product development strategies based on their input.

None of these YouTube stars are CEOs, titans of industry, investors, bankers, or politicians. They do not hold positions of authority in large companies. In fact, most of them started at home using a simple camera. In 2019 the highest-grossing YouTuber, for example, was Ryan, an eight-year-old boy who reviews toys. All of these individuals wield influence. So much so that marketing experts refer to them as Influencers—and influence is the currency of authentic leadership.

The word *influence* comes from the Latin word *influere*, which means "to flow into." Even if we do not hold a position of authority, we all have influence that allows us to guide or sway decisions in some areas of our life—among family and friends; in organizations, clubs, and associations; or at work. Likewise, if we are not conscious of the reality of influence, or if we operate primarily out of a positional approach to leadership, we can be in a position of authority and yet wield little to no influence.

Again, it is not that positional leadership is unimportant; but the only way we can exercise positional leadership in a fruitful way is by understanding that the heart of leadership is influence. Kenneth Blanchard, a world-renowned leadership consultant and author, acknowledges this: "The key to successful leadership today is influence not authority."[40]

Influencers do not lord their positions over others in order to force them to do what they wish. As Christian speaker, pastor, and writer John Maxwell said: "To be an influencer, you have to love people before you can try to lead them."[41] This is the reality of servant leadership, an approach that will allow you to be a bottle opener in your parish or diocese.

Seven Influence Traits

I wrestled for many years with this concept of influence, wondering what it looked like under the hood. Then I came across the work of Dr. Karen Keller, a clinical psychologist who has studied influence for many years. I have since come to know Karen. She is a committed Catholic and a woman of deep faith.

In her book *Influence: What's the Missing Piece?* Dr. Keller identifies seven traits that make up the reality we call influence. She also created a research-based tool called the KII (Keller Influence Indicator) to measure the degree to which an individual possesses the seven traits. Dr. Keller believes that individuals can grow in their degree of influence by actively and intentionally concentrating on these seven traits. (This approach is similar to how we understand growth in human virtues—by working at them.)

Within the parameters laid out by Dr. Keller, I would like to provide my own reflections on these traits as they relate to the Church's life and mission.

1. Confidence
To have confidence is to believe that God has really called you to an area of service—whether you are in religious life, ordained, or lay.

This mental attitude is also about having faith in your identity as a child of God sent on mission by the Father. A priest mentor of mine once said, "James, when times get tough—and they will—you've got to be convinced that you're called to this role as much as the apostle Peter or the apostle Paul."

We have to be rooted in our calling to ministry and even more rooted in our identity in Jesus Christ. Before we minister in a particular role, first and foremost we are children of God. We are loved and redeemed. Our confidence is in who we are, not in what we do or how well we do it.

If we do not have this kind of confidence, we can easily grow insecure, and insecurity creates a minefield in terms of working with others—particularly the types of talented people we should bring alongside ourselves. Insecurity breeds false competition and the desire to limit the work and influence of others so that we do not look bad. The more confident we are, the freer we will be to raise up and rely on gifted people. This in turn will increase our influence.

2. Commitment

This trait is a kind of "stick-to-it-iveness" or perseverance in the face of adversity. Often it is the result of having a clear sense of purpose, related to confidence in our vocation. We each have a general vocation (to married life, single life, religious life, ordained life), and this provides a general sense of purpose. Within that general vocation is our specific call or specific purpose.

For example, though there are many couples fruitfully living their vocation to marriage, no two couples live that vocation identically. It is essential that we understand our personal sense of purpose—our call within our vocation—whether it be in family life, ministry to the people of God, or something else. The more clearly we understand this sense of purpose, the deeper our commitment in the face of adversity, opposition, and stress—and, in the long term, the greater our influence.

3. Empowerment

This is about equipping the saints to do the work of ministry, a trait we have explored previously. When you empower others, you do not simply delegate tasks; you delegate responsibility and give others the authority to make decisions—even decisions that you may not like.

While there is certainly a time for leaders to step in and correct the decisions of team members, leaders who empower others recognize that simply because somebody approaches a problem or strategic goal differently than you, it does not mean their approach is wrong. It is a lot like being a parent: you form your children the best you can and gradually empower them to make decisions for themselves.

Sometimes in parish and diocesan life, this idea of empowering the laity comes across as a threat to the leadership of the priest. This will generally occur if that priest lacks confidence or operates out of a largely positional, controlling approach to leadership. The irony is that the more you release your authority and empower others, the more your influence grows. Conversely, the more you hold on to your authority, the smaller your influence becomes, until eventually you end up as a leader with a title and no followers.

4. Courage

This is the discipline of pressing on and doing what needs to be done in the face of difficult circumstances. Courage is not the absence of fear. We will experience fear on this journey of parish and diocesan renovation, because we are stepping into new territory as we move from maintenance to mission. Fear of failure, of being misjudged, of being criticized—these are all real reasons for fear. This fear can lead to habits of avoidance, preventing those in authority from having difficult conversations or confronting important issues head on. Not only does this lead to dysfunction, but it also limits influence, because people will not follow leaders who do not demonstrate courage.

Authentic courage means pressing forward in the face of fear. To do this, we need the presence and gifts of the Holy Spirit. In his exhortation to his disciples, Jesus said: "I will not leave you orphans" (John 14:18). Jesus' promise of his Holy Spirit in Scripture is a promise to us as well. We have not been orphaned. God does not call us into mission, into leadership in his name, and then abandon us.

We have received the promised outpouring of his Spirit at our baptism. We must lean into that Spirit, take heart, and press forward. When we do that, our influence grows, as does our capacity for courage.

5. Passion

According to Dr. Keller, this trait is the expression of eagerness and enthusiasm that flows from our human spirit. This is a natural kind of passion, and it is good and holy because it comes to us from the Lord. The Holy Spirit, however, gives us supernatural passion, and this is the passion that drives our Christian life and ministry.

Remember that grace, according to St. Thomas Aquinas, builds on nature. The natural passion that we may have to help others, serve the Church, or change the world is perfected and amplified by the supernatural passion imbued in us by the Holy Spirit. I have experienced this countless times in my life—especially in times of great trouble. When I call on the Holy Spirit, he renews my passion.

In the secular world, we will often describe someone who is passionate as being "on fire." As contagious as this natural fire can be, it is only a shadow of the supernatural fire of the Holy Spirit. Jesus said, "I have come to set the earth on fire, and how I wish it were already blazing!" (Luke 12:49).

The fire of faith, healing, wholeness—the fire of the kingdom of God—fell upon the earth at Pentecost, when the Holy Spirit came as tongues of fire to the Church. St. Catherine of Siena said, "Be who God meant you to be, and you will set the world on fire." If we want to grow in our influence as leaders, we need to ask the Lord to stir up our passion and help us guard against the things that can destroy it.

Without passion there can be no vision. We will lose sight of where we want to go or end up with a vision that is purely human, a vision that could be accomplished apart from God. The vision God has for us and our communities is much greater than anything we could come up with out of our human imagination.

6. Trustworthiness

The core of trustworthiness is authenticity and vulnerability. When we become vulnerable to others, acknowledging our weaknesses and discussing our failures, we become easier to relate to, more accessible on a human level. People open their hearts and minds to us.

Trustworthiness is also about integrity, about doing the things we say we will do, about being on time and following through. Within that framework, we all get a few passes. If someone fails to live up to what they promised to do, we may let it slide. Perhaps it has been a tough week. Then it happens a second time. Well, we might be a little annoyed, but again, we give them a pass. Then it happens a third time, and we start to wonder if that person will ever follow through.

Similarly, we need to hold ourselves accountable and value accountability to such an extent that we ask others to hold us accountable. Becoming open to being held accountable and acknowledging to others when we have failed to follow through will deepen our level of trustworthiness. Failing to follow through means that we must go to those we have let down and ask their forgiveness. It also means allowing others to help us move from a place of overpromising and under-delivering to a place where we honestly assess our capacity, so that we take on the work that we are able to accomplish.

7. Likability

This trait is more than being friendly, outgoing, or the life of the party. Likeability is the ability to elicit positive attitudes in those around us. People may not remember what we said or the specifics around what we did, but they do remember how we made them feel.

When we enter a room, what is our impact? Do I bring hope? Do I bring doubt and fear? Do I raise others up or bring them down? Am I a problem bringer or a problem solver? Do I add to the stress levels of those around me, or do I lessen them?

Dr. Keller says that the brain is hardwired to remember these things. It generates feelings that make us like or dislike, based on how the other impacts us. The more we grow in this area, the greater our influence.

Influence vs. Manipulation

Leadership is fundamentally a part of our baptismal call. The ordained are configured in a particular way to preach the Word of God, to celebrate the sacraments, and to lead as they occupy particular offices and roles within the Church. The baptized also share in the priestly, prophetic, and royal dimensions of the life and ministry of Jesus, although in a different way.

Every baptized Christian is called and empowered to live prophetically, telling forth the heart and mind of God for the sake of the world. We are all called to live as priests, offering ourselves—our material goods, time, experience, talents, and gifts—as living sacrifices to the Lord for the sake of his mission. We are also called to live out the royal dimensions of the life we share in Christ, ordering society and culture in light of kingdom principles such as justice, peace, and integrity.

We all share a degree of influence, whether or not we occupy an official or recognized leadership role. Christ has placed us where we are so that we might be salt, leaven, and light, exercising our God-appointed influence to *flow into* the lives of individuals and society. If we embrace the reality of our leadership consciously, we can grow in our ability to influence. We can do this in a spirit of integrity rather than manipulation if we deliberately cultivate the seven traits—becoming more confident, committed, empowering, courageous, passionate, trustworthy, and likeable.

As a leader, I initially wrestled with finding the difference between influencing people and manipulating them. We never want to manipulate, but we live in a fallen world where it is always possible to succumb to temptation because of our brokenness. The difference between influencing and manipulating, however, is not that difficult to determine.

Influencing people within the kingdom of God happens within the context of service. We want to influence people because we want what is good for them. That is the essence of love, according to Aquinas in his famous *Summa Theologica*: "to will the good of another." Authentic leadership involves acts of love that nurture and serve others, promoting their well-being.

When we manipulate people, on the other hand, they become objects from which we extract what we want, with little thought for their good. We want to believe we would never manipulate anyone, that we are so spiritually and psychologically mature that this is not an issue for us. The truth is that we are all imperfect; we struggle with sin and make decisions that benefit us primarily rather than others. At the heart of sin is rebellion against God, and when we commit sin involving another person, we compound that rebellion through our willingness to use other people. People become a means to an end. Ultimately this approach is a rejection of love.

In order to exercise authentic leadership—this is true especially for those of us in official positions of authority—we have to regularly ask ourselves, "What's in it for me?" This side of the grave, there will not be a time when our motives are 100 percent selfless; there is usually going to be something in it for us. Generally I consider a day a success if I can finish it at somewhere around 51 percent pure motivation. I have made peace with that.

When we ask, "What's in it for me?" we must answer not only to ourselves but also to God and to other people. Accountability in our relationships will help us see whether we are moving into manipulation as opposed to influence. A spiritual director, a confessor, and especially the team members we work with most closely can all help keep us accountable.

What's in It for Me?

Let us dig a little deeper into the "What's in it for me?" question. Despite our best efforts, and even with the assistance of God's grace, we will be tempted. We might fail to choose love. I would like to explore a few of the more common pitfalls in this regard.

These are pitfalls not because they are wrong in and of themselves. Rather, they can slowly gain the upper hand in our lives and motives. I offer a brief reflection on the following areas to help you determine if you are on the right side of the "What's in it for me?" line.

Ego

Anyone who dreams big and believes that God wants to use them to do great things probably has a larger-than-average ego. We all have an ego: we want to be recognized for the work that we do, for our experience and accomplishments. Problems begin when our ego becomes the primary source of our motivation.

One of my good friends and colleague, Ron Huntley, often tells me not to believe my fans. Having friends who speak the truth plainly like this, in the midst of excessive praise and success, will help us keep our egos in check. We should surround ourselves with such friends. They are invaluable.

Power

As the old saying goes: "Power corrupts, and absolute power corrupts absolutely." Power can lead us to manipulate others as we pursue selfish ambition. Ambition itself is not bad, but selfish ambition can destroy us and those in our power.

J. R. R. Tolkien's *The Lord of the Rings* illustrates the dark side of power and ambition. The trilogy tells the tale of the one ring forged by Sauron and giving him the ability to gain control of the world—the elves, men, hobbits, dwarves, and others. Sauron lost the ring in battle, and those who found and wore it discovered that it took control of them, drawing them into darkness. Some of them wanted to use the ring to wield power benevolently, but the lure of unrestrained power proved too much for them. They found it nearly impossible to refuse the temptations offered by absolute power.

We need to remain vigilant, alert to any possibility that we are following a path to power in pursuit of our own selfish ambition.

Control

This pitfall is a close cousin to power. Those with an excessive need to be in control will be unable to grow as leaders beyond a certain point. They will be burned out by their inability to delegate and to release decision-making power to others, and they will drive everyone on their team crazy in the process.

Control can be a healthy thing, personally and organizationally—until it is not. An inordinate desire for control can stem from such things as negative experiences or deep trauma. These can cause an excessive fear of vulnerability and a felt need for protection. The result is a control freak who seems happiest when completely dominating a situation. Control is ultimately elusive, however. The controlling approach never works out positively in the long run.

Praise

Deep within the human heart lies a desire for affirmation. We want to know that our actions have had a positive impact on a person, situation, or issue.

A healthy relationship with praise can lead us into a virtuous cycle, whereby we set out to do good, receive positive affirmation, and become even more committed to doing good. A healthy relationship with praise, however, can turn into a darker kind of dependence, which prompts us to change our decisions or avoid hard ones so that we continue to receive praise. Praise then becomes the major motivation behind our actions.

A dependence on praise is somewhat pathetic. To be honest though, when I give a talk, part of me is looking forward to the praise I hope to receive afterward. It is kind of embarrassing that, after all my years of traveling and speaking, I am still this oriented toward praise.

I recognize, however, that this is who I am, and I work hard at growing detached from feedback. To counter the longing for praise, it helps if I stay grounded in the reality that only one person can satisfy the desires of my heart—and that is the Lord.

Prestige

This is closely connected to praise, but prestige is primarily about the affirmation we receive based on the position that we hold. This is an especially strong pitfall for clergy and those in full-time ministry, because people often confuse the fact that we do holy things with personal holiness.

This has been an issue in my ministry. Since I travel so much with Divine Renovation ministry and talk about the fruit that we have seen, people sometimes put me on a pedestal. When people come up to me with that look that signals they will treat me as if I am a particularly holy person, I want to shout, "You don't know me. You have an idealized image of me, but you don't know the real me. In fact, if you did know the real me, you'd probably run away from me!"

I may do holy things, but sometimes I do not act holy. I am just another broken sinner trying to do the best I can through the grace of God. We must all guard against the desire to be recognized and treated in a special way just because we hold a particular job, office, or role within the Church or any organization.

Money

Scripture says that "the love of money is the root of all evils" (1 Timothy 6:10). All of us struggle in some way to put money to its proper use and remain detached from it. Jesus spoke about our relationship with money more than he spoke about any other issue, and he summed up his concerns this way: "For where your treasure is, there also will your heart be" (Matthew 6:21).

This can be an issue even for those of us in the priesthood, who have forsaken "everything" to follow the Lord and to serve his kingdom. Traditionally priests were not paid a salary; instead they survived on the tithes of their people and any income derived from the parish. This often led to an unhealthy connection between the pastor and the collection, which had the potential to deform pastoral practice. Think about it: if the priest said things that pleased his people, they might give more than they would if he spoke hard truths.

In my present ministry, I chose to receive the same salary as that of a parish priest, the expense shared between my diocese and Divine Renovation ministry. No matter how often I speak at events, I make the same amount of money as I did when I was a pastor. Therefore, I generally do not deal with finances. When organizations, dioceses, or parishes pay Divine Renovation ministry, they work directly with our office, not me.

Several years ago, I was in another country giving a series of talks. After the final night of the conference, one of the priests from the sponsoring community dropped me off at the hotel and handed me a thick envelope with my name on it. I asked him what it was, and he said it was for me, and I should take it up to my room. Imagine my surprise when I opened the envelope and found a large stack of $100 bills. I threw the envelope down in shock. As I thought it over, I concluded that this was a portion of my speaking fee and had been given to me by mistake instead of being sent to our office. I thought that I would hand it in to the office when I returned home.

As I stared at the envelope though, another conclusion took root. Perhaps this was a personal gift from the conference organizers; after all, the envelope had *my* name on it. I wrestled with that temptation for a bit. In the end, I put the money back in the envelope, sealed it, and returned it to the priest the next day as he drove me to the airport. I told him I would rather have him send this to the office directly.

I share this story with you because none of us are immune to this kind of temptation. This is especially true for those in ministerial leadership positions, where there are few other perks associated with the job.

Pleasure

Taken as a whole, there is nothing wrong with pleasure—in fact, the Lord created it, so it must be good. We were not made for a life of misery but for a life of joy. All of creation is a gift to us, and the Lord gave us our bodies and minds so that we might enjoy beauty and take pleasure in the gift of created reality. The psalms and many other books in the Bible celebrate these created things, and Jesus himself came as one eating and drinking, demonstrating the goodness of created life.

We must be measured in our enjoyment of creation, however, and detached from the experience of pleasure rather than bound up in it. This is true for priests as well. Even though we have obviously given up certain pleasures, we can overcompensate for that sacrifice by indulging too much in other ones—like eating and drinking. We have to take a measured approach.

Sexuality

Our sexuality is a beautiful gift from God that permeates our experience of life, regardless of whether we are single, married, or celibate. Our sexuality is much broader than genital activity. The truth is that, besides temptations against chastity (the right ordering of our sexuality), we can be tempted, even within chaste relationships, to be affirmed as a man or a woman, to feel that we are attractive in some ways. This is normal and can even be healthy, but we must be aware of it and make sure that we maintain a proper perspective and right order in regard to sexuality.

Gifts

Pastors often receive wonderful gifts from parishioners around holidays like Christmas and Easter. There is nothing wrong with this, but we must guard our hearts so that we do not grow too attached.

For a number of years, a parishioner would give me a nice bottle of single-malt whisky every Christmas. I happen to like single-malt whiskies. The first year I received this gift, I was very grateful. The second year, I was doubly grateful. The next Christmas, I wondered if I would receive my next bottle of whisky. I found this question interfering with how I related to the gift giver.

I was blown away by how easy it was for a gift to influence how I influence! We must be aware of this temptation lest we fall into a trap, manipulating the people we serve and tainting our influence.

Respect

Scripture tells us that we should live our lives in such a way that we are respected by people in the world. If we do not earn the respect of the people we serve, they are not going to want to follow us. It is actually quite simple, and it is a good thing. Yet we have to be on the right side of the line in terms of respect.

We do not want to be so attached to respect that we bend or deny the truth in order to receive respect from others. Jesus warned us against the danger of having others think too well of us: "Woe to you," he said, "when all speak well of you" (Luke 6:26). When everyone thinks well of you, you have probably become a people pleaser, speaking what people want to hear rather than what they need to hear. That is the sign of a false prophet.

When we are faithful to the Lord's will and to the message of truth, many people will not respect us. There will be opposition when we step out and lead change. People will gossip, say unfair and unkind things about us, and maybe even spread lies. If we are excessively concerned about receiving respect, this will drive us crazy. If we are overly concerned about what other people think of us, we will take criticism personally.

I once heard someone say, "If you let praise go to your head, you will allow criticism to go to your heart."

Fulfillment

This seems like the most benign of all the pitfalls, but beneath the surface of fulfillment is the same critical question: what's in it for me?

I had a conversation a few years ago with a rather wealthy person who had recently returned from several mission trips to Central America. As he was describing his experiences serving the poor, he kept referring to how good those trips made him feel about himself. I thought, "What if the poor whom you helped never thanked you? What if they were not grateful, or they didn't even know it was you who had helped them? Would you still have had such a positive experience?"

The rabbis used to say that the best kind of charity is when the giver does not know who received, and the receiver does not know who gave. This is echoed in the words of Jesus: "Do not let your left hand know what your right is doing" (Matthew 6:3). In other words, that is the purest kind of giving, because it empties the dynamic of the need to experience fulfillment.

There is nothing wrong with fulfillment in itself. In fact, when we live the vocation the Lord has for us, we will experience deep fulfillment. The danger arises when the need to feel fulfilled becomes the primary motivator. In the economy of God's kingdom, the one who seeks himself will lose himself, and the one who loses himself will gain fullness of life.

Knowing about these potential pitfalls will help us guard against manipulating others as we exercise our influence as leaders. We can use these points as a kind of examination of conscience, reflecting on them and bringing them to the Lord during our prayer time. Thus in all of these issues, we can be honest with ourselves and others about that challenging and provocative question: What's in it for me?

CHAPTER 11

Leadership as a Team Sport

The Church has a problem. Not in her theology or teaching but in the living out of her understanding of leadership.

We know that when it comes to the Church's mission to the world, all the baptized are called to lead. We are all baptized as priest, prophet, and king, because we receive these dimensions of Christ's life in that sacrament. The Church has a word for these three dimensions of priest, prophet, and king: *munera*. The word *munera* comes from the Roman Empire's system of government and means something like a task, delegated job, or office. In the Church's theology, however, these three *munera* are not simply tasks but rather make up the essential components of Christ's mission and, by extension, his Church's mission.

As Jesus is priest, prophet, and king, so are all those who bear his life. Priests, according to the Scriptures, offer sacrifice; Jesus asks all the baptized to follow his example and sacrifice themselves for the good of others and of the world. Prophets tell forth the heart and mind of God; all the baptized must live and speak prophetically, proclaiming the truth about justice, human dignity, and God's love for the world, particularly for the poor and vulnerable. Finally, Jesus is king; all the baptized, sharing in the royal dimensions of Christ's life, are called to use their influence to order the world according to the values of God's kingdom.

Leadership *within* the Church, as opposed to leadership in the context of mission *to* the world, functions in a more particular way. Bishops, priests, deacons, and those to whom they delegate authority exercise the triple *munera* in a particular way, as they have been uniquely configured to Christ to serve his people. Through ordination, their ministry is "ordered" to support the mission of the baptized in the world.

For example, priests exercise the priestly dimensions of Christ's life when we celebrate the sacraments, particularly the Eucharist. We exercise our prophetic office when we preach the Word of God and instruct the faithful. Finally, we exercise the royal dimension of Christ's life when we nurture, support, and call forth the gifts of the community and send the community out on mission.

That is why we say that the Church is hierarchical. The word "hierarchy" may conjure images of a complex, multi-layered bureaucracy with many levels of authority, each relating to another in a confusing network of relationships. That is not how the Church uses the word. If you think about hierarchy that way, the Catholic Church is actually one of the least hierarchical organizations out there.

If ordination is the requirement to exercise office, then there are only three levels to the Church's hierarchy—deacons, priests, and bishops. Deacons and priests are accountable to the bishop, and the only person the bishops are nominally accountable to is the pope, who is also a bishop. There are probably more hierarchical levels at your local bank or Walmart store.

Leadership and Management

The Church uses the word "hierarchy" because it comes from the Greek word *hierarchēs*, which in turn was constructed from the roots of two Greek words, *hier* (meaning "holy" or "priest") and *arch* (meaning "rule" or "lead"). In a strict sense, to say that the Church is hierarchical means that it is led by priests. Bishops possess the fullness of the priesthood of Christ, and priests possess a share of the bishop's ministry. Therefore, without the bishop's explicit permission, priests and deacons cannot fulfill their ministerial functions. That is why priests and deacons cannot simply move from one diocese to another under their own authority and exercise their *munera*. They need the permission of the bishops from both dioceses—the one they are leaving and the one they are joining—before they can minister according to their vocation and role.

I am laying this foundation because it is essential for us to recognize that we cannot bypass, in particular, the role of bishop or priest as leader. This reality constitutes a thoroughly Catholic understanding of Church. This is nonnegotiable. The fundamental question, however, is "How is this leadership exercised?" It is here that the Church has run into problems.

The royal dimension of Christ's life is often called "governance" in the Church's language. Unfortunately, governance within the Church has traditionally been reduced to oversight or management, at best. There is a huge difference between management and leadership, however. Authentic leadership mobilizes people, helping an organization grow and move from one reality to another. Management, on the other hand, concerns itself with the effective and efficient operation of an organization in its current form. You can have a very well-managed parish or diocese that is not going anywhere or is even suffering decline. You can have a well-managed parish or diocese that is very effective and efficient in doing things that no longer work.

There should be a healthy tension between management and leadership. Management needs leadership to provide vision and direction. Leadership needs management to accomplish things well.

If you had a bunch of people like me leading your parish, it would probably be over-led and under managed. You might have a phenomenal vision that set people's hearts on fire, but successful execution of the day-to-day and month-to-month tasks necessary to move in the direction of that vision might be lacking. I have learned over the years that I need to surround myself with strong managers. This is a difficult balance to achieve. If managers dominate an organization, movement will slow down and possibly halt under the weight of policies and procedures.

One of the ways we can help ensure this balance is to look at governance within the Church—by bishops and priests and their lay leaders—through the lens of leadership rather than administration. This is vital if we want to see transformation and renewal in the parish and beyond.

Culturally this will be a major challenge for us. If leadership is fundamentally about moving a community from one reality to another, then the history of Christendom works against us. With the exception of particular times and places, the Church—especially in the West— did not have to move in any particular direction. Our basic pastoral strategy for centuries has been to build a church, unlock the doors, post the Mass times, and then minister to the people who show up.

Outside of traditional mission territories, this was (and still is) our model: give pastoral care to the sheep who show up.

Help!

We currently live in a very different world. There is a kind of cultural tsunami headed our way; if we do not mobilize, if we do not move and prepare for it, introducing different models that support mission to the world, we risk being swept away. I believe that never in the Church's history, at least since the fourth century, has the need to recapture this call to authentic leadership been so urgent. That those of us holding positional leadership in the Church were never trained for this new reality is a pressing problem.

Remember, the essentials of priesthood are to preach the Word of God, celebrate the sacraments, and exercise leadership. Thinking back on my seminary formation, I can clearly see the gaps. I studied a great deal of biblical theology but only had one course on homiletics, or how to prepare and give a homily—and it was not even a good course. I spent a great deal of time studying sacramental theology and the philosophical principles that underpin this theology, but when it came to the nuts and bolts of how to celebrate all the sacraments in a valid and fruitful way, I took one course for a single semester. Finally, in terms of leadership, there was nothing. We had one class to prepare us for parish ministry. In that class, as I recall, we spent one two-hour session learning about parish administration (management).

To this day, most seminaries largely ignore the art and science of leadership in their formation approach. We see it time and again as we coach pastors in the Divine Renovation Network. Hardworking, passionate, talented priests tell us that they were not prepared for leadership. This reflects my experience when I was first assigned to a parish.

Honestly, my growth in leadership since ordination has been fueled by encounters with my incompetence. These encounters forced me to come face-to-face with my weaknesses and seek resources to become a better leader. Facing such weaknesses is essential for those who have not been formed to lead—especially the newly ordained, who get hit by this reality when they start their first assignments as pastors. They might be able to see when something is heading in the wrong direction, but they do not know how to fix it. Or their attempts to fix issues or grow their parish—in ways based on the training they received in seminary—have opposite effects.

I would like to share a story of what launching into ministry looked like for me as an underprepared young priest. Whether you are ordained as a priest and serving as pastor or you are in some other area of pastoral leadership, I hope this will speak to you.

When I was assigned to my first parish, I had three half-time staff members—a secretary, a janitor, and a pastoral assistant. I was kind of mystified as to what to do with them. I was essentially a loner and not much into collaboration. That situation changed when I came to my second parish. I had three full-time staff members to deal with, and the following year, my parish amalgamated with another parish, doubling my staff. I had six staff members and no idea what to do with them! I had never really led a team before, and I was clueless.

So I started to read leadership books. That is when I discovered the importance of vision and mobilizing a parish. As the team started to grow, I wanted to hire a full-time staff member who would oversee all aspects of administration: buildings, finances, policies, office management, and so on. My plan was to meet with this person once a week, and she would oversee all the commissions and committees, focusing on the managerial tasks. I was excited about this new position, because it was going to free me up so that I could focus on other areas.

We ended up hiring an incredibly intelligent, organized, articulate woman who had held this role at a church in western Canada. Not only did she have the skillset for the job, but she was also completely in sync with the vision. I was so excited! She started in her position on a Tuesday—Monday had been a holiday. I gave her the tour on Tuesday and introduced her to staff. I saw her on Wednesday, and then Thursday was my day off. I came in on Friday, looking forward to working with her—only to find her letter of resignation on my desk!

I could not believe it. I was absolutely stunned. I went to her office to speak with her about the letter and to express my confusion. "I don't understand," I told her.

She looked at me quite calmly and said, "I can't work for you."

"Why?" I asked. I thought I was a good priest and a pretty good boss, after all.

"I don't like the way you treat people," she replied. "I can't work for you." Then she reached into her desk and pulled out a brochure. "You need to take a leadership course."

I walked away incredulous. Obviously, I thought to myself, I hired the wrong person. I threw the leadership brochure in the garbage.

I had a choice right there: to ignore this woman's feedback and carry on as I had been doing or to take stock of my leadership style and make changes. Through God's grace, I chose the latter, and it became a turning point in my life. I recognized that I had a high turnover rate on staff. The truth is that I drive myself pretty hard, and I drive others that way too.

Even worse, I secretly possessed a pathetic kind of pride regarding how fast I went through staff. I thought, you see, that few people had the talent and passion to keep up with me. I had the ability to achieve a great many things as a leader, but often, when I turned around to celebrate, there would be bodies all over the ground.

Obviously I did not intend to hurt people as I exercised my leadership, but now I was coming face-to-face with the reality that I did—and regularly. I did not even know I was doing it! That might sound ridiculous, but it is true.

I realized that I needed people around me who could pump the brakes when my passion and drive were placing the completion of goals above the welfare of people. I needed people willing to call me out when my words or actions negatively impacted someone else: when I ostensibly gave someone authority to handle a situation, for example, and then cut their legs out from under them by micromanaging or overriding them. Perhaps I accomplished important things in my old style of leadership, but I probably was not building the kingdom of God. It was more like the kingdom of James.

This gets us back to the difference between influence and manipulation: leadership is about others; manipulation is about us. The more we grow in love, holiness, and wholeness, the more attentive we are to the nurturing and growth of the people on our team. This was a difficult and painful lesson, but it underscored for me what has become a Divine Renovation ministry principle: there is no such thing as a well-rounded person, but well-rounded teams can and do exist.

This assertion flies in the face of the prevailing educational philosophy, which has dominated Western culture in recent decades: you can do anything you want and be anyone you want if you try hard enough and have a positive attitude.

Frankly, common sense tells us that this is not true.

I would love to be as good at music as Mozart, but that is not going to happen. I could spend years practicing the piano for ten hours a day, and I might eventually become a mediocre piano player. I simply do not have the natural gift for music that Mozart had. He became a virtuoso at a young age because he had an innate gift that grew as he practiced.

When it comes to leadership, no one has all the gifts necessary to lead well. We all have strengths in some areas and weaknesses in other areas. This makes each of us unique. Sometimes people tell me that they want to have the same gifts that I have. I do have certain gifts, but you should see the gifts I am missing! Honestly, placed in a leadership role without anyone else around me, I'm a train wreck—and I have the stories to prove it.

The fact that I cannot do it all myself came as a real revelation for me. That fact might sound self-evident to most people, and you might ask, "Why did it take you so long to figure it out?" Culturally, the idealized goal of priestly formation is to shape the seminarian into the heroic leader who is well-rounded and able to handle the demands of priestly ministry, balance the parish budget, fix the boiler, and chant the Mass beautifully—kind of like a spiritual Lone Ranger. Our formation process focuses on helping us work on our weaknesses so that we can eventually overcome them enough to be well rounded. This approach to formation and education is deeply rooted in Western culture. There is another way.

Imagine that when you were a child, your parents recognized that you are gifted in math. You struggled with other areas of study, but you did your best, and your report cards reflected your one great strength as well as your weaknesses. What if your parents told you, "Don't worry so much about those other subjects. We can see that you love mathematics and have the skills and passion to become a great mathematician. Focus on the areas of your strengths and giftedness." That is a radically different way of thinking.

Leaning into your strengths, instead of primarily focusing on your weaknesses, can be life changing. Recognizing this was pivotal in regard to my understanding of leadership. Our natural strengths and gifts are ways that God has hardwired us, not only to experience his presence but also to serve the world.

If we want to lean into our strengths, however, we need to surround ourselves with people whose strengths compensate for our weaknesses.

Getting to a Well-Rounded Team

During my third year at Saint Benedict, things were beginning to shift in terms of culture, but I was still operating out of my old model of leadership. Sure, I had learned the importance of surrounding myself with people who would hold me accountable, but I was doing that in a haphazard way, without a lot of discipline. In many ways, I operated out of a Braveheart model of leadership: gather the troops, tell them where we are going, get them cheering, and then charge ahead! Every once in a while, I would turn around to make sure that people were still following me. That was my model of leadership, and it worked—at least for a while.

I came to Saint Benedict with ten years' experience trying to lead parishes from maintenance to mission. I had learned a lot along the way—mostly from my mistakes. I had also learned a lot about church renewal from both Catholic and non-Catholic sources. I had a proven track record for getting things moving, but I had never really succeeded in taking things to the next level. I was not naturally gifted in this regard, and I did not know how to get there. I constantly ran smack into a glass ceiling of sorts.

The same was true as I started at Saint Benedict. People were experiencing conversion through the Alpha process, lives were being transformed, people were stepping forward for ministry, prayer lives were deepening, the liturgy was coming to life, people were excited about the vision, and the parish was starting to mobilize. Things were changing. We knew, from using Gallup's ME25 tool, that upward of 85 percent of the parish was enthusiastic, or at least happy, with the direction in which we were headed. It was all going really well and moving in the right direction.

But then I ran out of strategy! I had implemented everything I knew based on my previous experience. I had no idea what to do next.

When you take a transatlantic journey on a ship, there is a certain moment when you lose sight of where you came from, and you cannot see the shores of your destination yet. Centuries ago, this part of a ship's journey was the most dangerous part, because it was where the most mutinies happened. I was far from shore, and I was terrified; I felt unsure and alone. I could not go backward, yet I did not know how to go forward.

The staff and I gathered for a retreat day, and I laid all my worries on the table. I admitted to them that I had no idea what I was doing anymore. That turned out to be a breakthrough. Allowing myself to become vulnerable with the men and women of my staff led me to discover a new way of leading.

One of our staff members, Tanya Rogerson, gave me a book by Patrick Lencioni, a world-renowned leadership consultant, faithful Catholic layman, and founder of Amazing Parish. I started reading more of his work, and his books blew me away.

We started to implement some of what we were discovering in Lencioni's work, and I made a total mess of it. The application and execution were truly bad. That did not stop us (and it should not stop you). Eventually we created a Senior Leadership Team, which has become the lynchpin of our approach at Divine Renovation ministry. In our work, presently with around sixty parishes in our leadership coaching network, we train pastors how to lead out of this kind of a team—and the results are transformative.

In the next chapter, I want to explore what a Senior Leadership Team does and how you can build a healthy, functioning, and effective one. Such a team will accelerate your parish's journey from maintenance to mission.

CHAPTER 12

Leading out of a Team

At its heart, the Senior Leadership Team (SLT) consists of a small group of people who gather around the pastor to help him make tactical decisions. In other words, the SLT helps the pastor lead.

The Senior Leadership Team model is more than a formal way for a pastor to consult with people, however. It represents the type of change the Church must make as it addresses the fact that we are living in a time of cultural upheaval. We cannot, as a Church, do things as we have always done them; the times require a radically different approach. Priests have not been formed for this; I was not formed for this in the seminary. We priests must gather people around us who can help us figure out what we should be doing.

Using a Senior Leadership Team requires the pastor to share his authority. The pastor must make the internal shift from talking about "I" to talking about "we."

Remember: vision is about where you are going; strategy is your plan to get there; and tactics are the decisions that you make as you execute the plan. Some tactical decisions can be made ahead of time, but unforeseen problems will arise, which will require you to make decisions that you might not be prepared to make. As Mike Tyson, the famous boxer, used to say, "Everyone's got a plan until they get punched in the mouth."

Trust me, as you begin to lead a parish or a diocese from maintenance to mission, you *will* get punched in the mouth, and you will grapple with issues you have never dealt with before. The Senior Leadership

Team members are there to help absorb these blows and help you wrestle with these problems.

When an SLT functions properly, the sense of isolation—of having the weight of everything resting solely on your shoulders as the heroic leader—disappears. In our coaching network, priests generally identify the Senior Leadership Team model as the single biggest game changer for them. Many of the pastors in our network report that this approach has transformed their priesthood. They no longer feel alone as leaders. There is no burden related to leadership that they cannot speak about with their teams, and they see greater fruitfulness in the growth and transformation of their parishes.

We need to be clear that with this model, the pastor (or bishop) does not abdicate leadership in favor of leading by committee. Neither is an SLT a kind of board of directors. The pastor is ultimately responsible for the decisions, but he shares his authority with a small group of people who help him make the kinds of decisions he previously would have had to make by himself. The goal of the team is not consensus but rather arriving at the best decisions. When you work toward consensus, you often end up "negotiating down" from the best decision, settling on a suboptimal approach in order to secure the support of the entire team.

Remember, the goal here is to make the *best* possible decisions. You are not going to make the right decision all the time. Rick Warren, the pastor of Saddleback Church and the author of *The Purpose Driven Life*, said that if you are going to lead, your options are to be a risk taker, a caretaker, or an undertaker.[42] The Church today requires leaders to be risk takers, to forge new paths and apply the richness of the Church's tradition in new ways in order to meet the demands of mission in the twenty-first century.

Leading as a risk taker means that sometimes you will get it wrong, but leading out of an SLT means that you have a greater knowledge and experience base from which to work. You gather the right people and hammer out the issues fully and forthrightly. It is no guarantee that you will always get it right, but it should lead to better decisions overall.

In order to foster better decision-making, Senior Leadership Teams need to meet every single week. Parishes sometimes form SLTs that initially meet only every other week, but as these parishes mobilize, the pace and depth of their discussions intensify. Within six months, they move to a weekly meeting of two to four hours.

Some of you might be freaking out at the thought of regular weekly meetings that last that long. After all, everyone knows that Church meetings are so boring that they might shorten our passage through purgatory. We have found that if you run these meetings the right way, however, they become the best two to four hours of your week.

The size of your SLT matters as well. Having too many members reduces the likelihood that you will have critical and honest conversations, and team members will have less time to bring their perspective to the group. Also, it is harder to develop and maintain deep trust among members of a larger group. A team that has too few members, on the other hand, risks becoming a kind of echo chamber, with little diversity in approaches, arguments, and points of view. Also, individuals can miss these team meetings because of illness, vacations, and life in general. When that happens on a very small team, the pastor and one other team member might be present for a meeting, and two does not make a team.

In our experience at Divine Renovation ministry, we believe these teams should have a minimum of four people and a maximum of six. We have witnessed team dynamics beginning to break down once you have more than six people in the group. Therefore we recommend having no more than the priest and five other team members on the SLT. The sweet spot is probably five in total, which allows you to preserve team dynamics and minimize problems because of illness- or vacation-related absences.

If you are in a big parish with lots of staff, the ideal is that your Senior Leadership Team members be staff members—because they are the ones closest to the action. It is as simple as that. We do have network parishes that use a mixture of staff and committed, nonpaid lay leaders. Multiple configurations can work, provided that the dynamics of your SLT meetings are on point.

What do I mean?

In some of his work, Patrick Lencioni talks about a "good" meeting consisting of one-third advocacy and two-thirds inquiry. Advocacy is about advancing your ideas and arguing for them in discussion with other team members. Team members should be passionate about their ideas and points of view, and they should feel comfortable speaking up and advocating for them—especially in front of the pastor, who may disagree. That is advocacy!

Inquiry, on the other hand, is about shutting up and listening. For example, if you are in a meeting and another team member says something you disagree with, inquiry demands that you refrain from jumping down her throat with your objections or rehearsing your rebuttal while she is talking—in other words, closing your mind and failing to wrestle with what she is actually saying. Using inquiry, we ask questions of the person, to clarify her position, rather than attack her argument.

God gave us two ears and one mouth. So two-thirds inquiry and one-third advocacy. This is the dynamic that makes the SLT work.

In fact, Patrick Lencioni often points out that a key role of a leader is not only to provide space for disagreement but also to mine for conflict, to bring out hidden or suppressed areas of disagreement so that team members can engage in inquiry and explicitly tackle the issue together. Here is where the size of your SLT really matters. The more people you have on your team, the less time individuals have to contribute and interact. So if you are at a meeting, and you know you will only have one chance to speak, are you going to spend it inquiring about another person's point of view or advocating your own point? The vast majority of people will make their own point—which breaks down the healthy dynamic of the team. Therefore you want to keep the Senior Leadership Team from becoming too big.

The Four Nonnegotiables of a Senior Leadership Team

In our experience, healthy, fruitful Senior Leadership Teams share the following characteristics: *Unanimity of Vision*, *Balance of Strengths*, *Vulnerability-Based Trust*, and *Healthy Conflict*. These characteristics define an SLT. It can be challenging to foster these elements within the Senior Leadership Team, but they are so important that, without all four of these characteristics, you do not have a real SLT; you simply have a working group that meets regularly. This will become clearer as we explore each of these in depth.

Unanimity of Vision

Remember that vision is a view of the future that produces passion. As a leader, how do you picture the future for your parish or diocese? What vision for your community makes you so excited you cannot sleep at night?

It is critical to unearth the dream that God has placed in your heart. If you do not, how will others be able to embrace the vision? Sometimes, in the midst of *doing* the things of ministry, it can become difficult to discover (or rediscover) that passion-producing vision. If you find it challenging to develop your vision, I suggest that you reflect on what drives you nuts in relation to your ministry, parish, or diocese. The things that elicit a negative response from you are the opposite of what is going to make you excited.

Once you have discovered that vision, begin to articulate it. Spend time in prayer, perhaps before the Blessed Sacrament. Ask the Lord to reveal more of the vision to you, and then start writing it down. This is not a vision statement. Vision rallies and inspires people. A vision statement clarifies; it comes later.

Try to avoid turning your vision into a strategy. Do not talk about how you will accomplish this vision; just describe the vision itself.

I once spoke in a diocese led by a wonderful bishop. At the end of our sessions, he stood up and said he wanted to share his vision for the diocese with the priests. He went on to describe a four-point strategy, not a passion-producing vision. Do not confuse the two.

It is not that plans are unimportant. In fact, plans are necessary. Without a plan, you cannot execute, and as Thomas Edison once said, without execution, vision is simply hallucination. Now is not the time to plan; it is the time to create and articulate vision.

When inviting people onto your Senior Leadership Team, remember to gather those people who share the passion that you have regarding this picture of the future. You cannot fake passion—at least, not in the long run. The hearts of your SLT members must burn with the same fire that you have in regard to the future. This shared passion will help see you through the undoubtedly difficult moments in the transformation process for your diocese or parish.

In order for your team members to share your passion, however, you must present it to them in an engaging way. Your passion for this picture of the future must shine through and be contagious when you talk, write, and communicate about it. You cannot point people to a book and say, "Read this, and two weeks from now, I want you to be passionate about it." This is not an intellectual exercise.

Each of us is uniquely created by God; we have been hardwired differently from one another. Different aspects of the vision, and the ways it can be lived out, will touch different people more than other aspects. Nevertheless, a healthy Senior Leadership Team shares a core passion for the overall vision of a mission-focused Church that evangelizes and disciples people and experiences deep community, where members commit their gifts for the mission and come together for dynamic, life-giving liturgies.

It may be difficult to find those people in your parish or diocese. If this is the case, resist the temptation to place someone on the SLT simply because they hold a position of leadership in your parish or diocese. Folks who do not share the passion can often give only intellectual assent; their hearts remain unmoved. Sooner or later, the things that they are passionate about will surface, and you may find yourself frequently disagreeing about tactics and strategy. The problem is that you will not really be disagreeing about tactics and strategy; that is just a symptom of the larger disconnect. The true issue is a disagreement of vision.

Think of a canoe holding several people headed to the north shore of a lake. The only way this canoe will arrive at its destination is if every person commits to that direction. If half the team paddles for the north shore, and the other half for the east shore, what will happen? The canoe will go in circles or possibly even capsize.

Similarly, unanimity of vision is essential for a Senior Leadership Team. Intellectual assent is not enough. A dispassionate neutrality is not enough (and it is exceedingly rare). If the leaders who make up an SLT do not agree to and share passion about the vision, sooner or later the result will be sabotage—whether intentional or unintentional.

We have seen this happen with associate pastors in particular. Team members and parishioners share a vision, and the pastor brings his newly appointed associate into the SLT simply because he is the new associate pastor. If that associate holds a different vision for the parish, the results are disastrous. Believe me, we have coached many parishes through this.

This same dynamic can happen at the diocesan level. You might have a bishop who is passionate about his vision, but his right-hand person, the vicar general, does not share that passion. The bishop might be able to bring him in intellectually, but the lack of passion becomes a problem in the long term.

When the associate in the parish or the vicar general in the diocese is not passionate about the vision, it is best to put him on a different team, not the SLT. Things often work better for everyone when he serves in a different area, where his gifts can shine.

The question is, how do you find the men and women who can become passionate about your vision? This takes time. First, pray. Pray for the grace to recognize those whom the Lord is preparing for your team. Then you have to invest in people. You have to be willing to articulate your vision and help people see it. You have to plant seeds and then water and nurture them.

You will eventually find the people in whom this vision takes root and starts producing passion. You should focus your discernment on those people.

If you want to explore unanimity of vision further, I encourage you to check out *Divine Renovation Guidebook: A Step-by-Step Manual for Transforming Your Parish* (Twenty-Third Publications, 2016).

Balance of Strengths

Finding team members who will bring a balance of strengths to your SLT will not happen at random. You need to be careful and deliberate as you build your team. Most people tend to associate with those who are like-minded—who believe the same things they do and who act in ways that are similar to their own. If you choose people for your team who think as you do and are hardwired as you are, you will end up with a team that is collectively blind. Leading out of a team compensates for your blind spots—that is the point of this structure. Healthy SLTs tend to have a 360-degree view of things.

In my experience working with parishes, many teams skip this essential characteristic of an SLT. They presume that because they agree on vision and perhaps even like each other, they must already have a balance of strengths. Most often they do not.

So how can we ensure that our leadership teams have a balance of strengths? You might already be familiar with many of the tools that can help you with this.

Myers-Briggs Test. One of the most popular tools is the MBTI Personality Assessment Instrument (commonly called the Myers-Briggs test). Other well-known tools include the Birkman Method Assessment and the DISC Personality Test. In general, all of these create a profile of an individual based on four major types. Some of the tools are more complex than others, some offer more detail, and they all use slightly different language, but as a whole, they agree that in terms of leadership profiles, four types predominate.

The *executing* type gets things done and drives plans to completion; the *relational* type tends to maintain harmony; the *influencing* type mobilizes others; and the *strategizing* type has a penchant for big-picture thinking and planning. While you cannot reduce the mystery of a person to a simple profile, understanding how you and other team members are wired strengthens teamwork and communication, and it allows the team to place its strengths at each other's disposal.

CliftonStrengths Assessment. The tool that has had the greatest impact on the work of Divine Renovation ministry and the parishes we coach is the CliftonStrengths Assessment (formerly called the Clifton StrengthsFinder). Don Clifton, the behavioral psychologist who created this tool and a faith-filled Christian, identified over three hundred talents: things that we do well and ways of approaching problems and situations that come naturally to us. When we "lean" on the talents we have received and hone them, we generally achieve a predictive level of success.

Clifton then grouped these talents into thirty-four themes and organized these thirty-four themes into four domains—executing, influencing, relational, and strategic. Mapping each team member's top themes of talent across these domains is a great help to building a balanced team.

A diagram might make things clearer. I used this in the *Divine Renovation Guidebook*, and I present it in many of my talks and workshops.

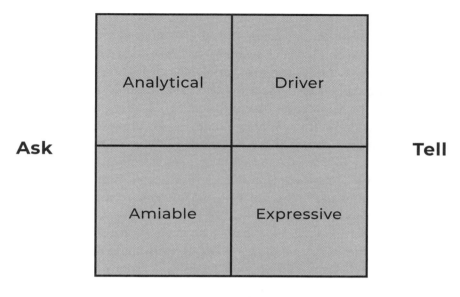

Task

Ask

Analytical

Driver

Amiable

Expressive

Tell

People

This diagram is known as the Tracom Social Style Model, and it is useful for underscoring the importance of team balance. When I use this at a workshop, I ask participants whether they are a task person or a people person. Most people hate having to choose between these two things, so I make sure that they decide quickly. Then I pose the following: when you work with others, do you *ask* them nicely to do things or *tell* them nicely to do things? Once someone answers these questions, they can easily place themselves on one of the four quadrants of the Social Style Model.

After people have answered this question and identified a quadrant, I ask them to immediately turn and get in groups of four without any discussion. Once these groups are formed, group members share where they are among these four quadrants. Whenever I have done this, no matter the workshop size, 95 percent of the groups discover that they are imbalanced.

Now, this is a simplistic and somewhat crude way of trying to drive home the point, but the reality is that if we do not deliberately create a good balance on our teams, we have a high chance of doing it wrong.

The CliftonStrengths Assessment is a simple way to start. We recommend having the pastor take the assessment and plot out the five top themes that appear in his profile. It is rare for an individual to have top themes that appear in all the CliftonStrengths' quadrants. Chances are, he will have a predominance in at least one of the four quadrants. Once the pastor has a clear idea of his strengths, he can invite other members onto the team who have different strengths. This is an enormous help in attaining balance.

In the Church, we frequently find that staff and key volunteers have strengths predominately in the relational and executing quadrants. Our parishes are often filled with nice people who are busy doing stuff. These very busy people, however, may not be mobilizing others for mission, and they may not be working toward a clear goal or following a developed plan.

On the other hand, you can gather people together in the Church (whether at the parish or diocesan level) with the express purpose of creating a plan and end up with a preponderance of people with strategic strengths. When that happens, the group consists largely of idea people, who may not be good at executing or following up. They may also not be good relationally, making plans but alienating and frustrating the rest of the parish or diocese in the process. Another scenario may be that they do not have influencing strengths. They have a great plan, but no one wants to follow it.

Lots of pitfalls become apparent if we do not take care to create balanced teams.

APEST. Another useful assessment tool that we have used when working with parish teams is known as APEST (apostle, prophet, evangelist, shepherd, teacher). It is the work of Alan Hirsch, an evangelical Protestant theologian and missiologist (someone who studies mission in the church).

Before we turn to APEST, let's look again at the passage from St. Paul's Letter to the Ephesians that we discussed in an chapter 9:

> And he gave some as apostles, others as prophets, others as evangelists, others as pastors and teachers, to equip the holy ones for the work of ministry, for building up the body of Christ, until we all attain to the unity of faith and knowledge of the Son of God, to mature manhood, to the extent of the full stature of Christ. (Ephesians 4:11-13)

As we consider how Alan Hirsch breaks open this passage, we must keep in mind our Catholic understanding of what St. Paul presents here. First, St. Paul was not trying to create a systematic ecclesiological structure. Therefore we must be careful to not read too much into it. What is clear from Paul's writing, however, is that when the Church authentically exercises all of the charisms or functions about which he writes (apostles, prophets, evangelists, pastors, and teachers), she experiences unity and grows into maturity, into the "full stature of Christ." In other words, the Church is living as the Church was created to live, from the local level to the universal level.

Second, in Catholic Tradition, the *office* of apostle, prophet, evangelist, shepherd (pastor), and teacher properly belongs to the ordained. However, when we speak about the function or charisms of apostleship, prophecy, evangelism, pastoring, and teaching (particularly, but not exclusively, in regard to the action of the Church in the world), we are speaking about what is proper to the baptized. To hold the office of teacher, pastor, evangelist, and so forth is, at the least, to bear the responsibility for ensuring that these functions are being carried out. Bishops, priests, and deacons might not do all the teaching in a parish or diocese, for example, but they make sure that it is happening by partnering with laymen and women.

These are important distinctions for us as Catholics. When we look at Alan Hirsch's breakdown of these five-fold functions, keep in mind that we are not examining them through the lens of ecclesiological structure. Rather we are considering them in the context of balancing strengths. It is a way of looking at the gifts, interests, and passions of our team members.

1. Apostle: As previously mentioned, the apostle is literally a "sent one" or missionary. In Hirsch's framework, an apostle is a person who is passionate about the mission. Often an apostle will push against the status quo, against any tendency to be self-referential or inward-focused as a parish or diocese. Apostles create new initiatives and drive toward innovation.

   We see this dimension at work even in secular organizations. When an organization's growth levels off, the apostle goes into new territory and pushes the boundaries. That is the apostle.

This apostolic initiative is seen throughout the history of the Church, even beyond the initial Apostolic Age. Many of the great saints and heroes of our tradition, the great founders of religious orders and movements, had an apostolic charism.

2. Prophet: A prophet is one who communicates the heart and mind of God to the people. Prophets call God's people to listen to the Lord and follow his will. If an apostle is one who pushes against the status quo, a prophet is a person who reminds us of truths that we would rather not deal with.

Often prophets annoy others, because their actions and words tend to prick consciences. We might treat prophets the same way we treat mosquitoes—as pests. Most of the prophets in the Scriptures were persecuted, thrown in prison, or put to death. They were inconvenient, calling God's people to remember inconvenient truths. In the Church today, the prophetic role involves speaking uncomfortable truths, reminding the Church of her missionary identity, calling people to be rooted in prayer, particularly intercessory prayer; to be mindful of the poor; and to engage with issues of social justice.

3. Evangelist: An evangelist is a proclaimer of the gospel message. The Greek word *euangelion*, from which we derive the word "evangelist," literally means "good messenger": *eu* (good) and *angelos* (messenger). Evangelists carry the message of Jesus Christ and his life like a burning flame in their hearts, a flame that must be shared so that the new life of God's kingdom will "set the earth on fire" (Luke 12:49). An evangelist wants to share the gospel message with others, both within and outside the Church. They are natural recruiters, and they will often do whatever is necessary to communicate the love of the Father in Jesus Christ to others.

4. Shepherd: A shepherd is one who cares for the people of God. We are much more familiar and comfortable with this function than with any of the others, because the Latin word for "shepherd" is *pastor*. Remember, though, we are not using this framework to focus on ecclesiological structure. Someone who exhibits

care and concern for others, particularly the spiritual growth of individuals as they relate to others in a group, often has a gift of pastoring. Shepherds value inclusion and are the arms of the parish, gathering people in. On a one-to-one or even a small-group level, the canonical pastor of a parish cannot be in a deep relationship with every member of the parish. Therefore a healthy parish will have a number of people with pastoral gifts. They directly care for God's people in a way that supports the ministry of the pastor.

5. Teacher: A teacher is concerned not only with the truth of God but also with the passing on of that truth. Like shepherding, Catholics are comfortable with this function because we value teaching—especially as it relates to catechesis.

Why is it important to spend time exploring these various functions and charisms? Because the Church needs all the charisms for the sake of her mission, and when they are not balanced—when some are underdeveloped while others are overdeveloped—the body cannot grow to the full stature of Christ. Furthermore, without this balance, the Church cannot experience the unity of Christ, according to St. Paul.

Culturally within our Church, we have an overdevelopment of the function of shepherd and teacher—especially among ordained leadership and even among traditional lay leadership. I once led a session with almost four hundred laypeople, and after giving a brief description of these five charisms, I invited them to identify what they thought was their primary charism. I was not too surprised when the vast majority of people felt they had shepherding and teaching charisms.

That same dynamic exists among the ordained. I think this is why so many ordained priests struggle with the idea of leaving the ninety-nine to go in search of the one. It goes against our instinct as shepherds. Even being the leader of a missionary parish—one that leaves the ninety-nine—can be a difficult experience. If you are a bishop or pastor whose primary charism is shepherding, moving the parish or diocese from maintenance to mission will be exceptionally challenging. It means that you need to be more concerned about the sheep you do not yet have than you are about the ones you do.

So too if your primary charism is teacher. Many pastors today and many people in Church ministry identify primarily with this charism; I think that is why they are much more comfortable with catechesis than they are with evangelization. In fact, I read recently about a bishop who said that, in order to carry out the new evangelization, we need a new catechesis. I wanted to smack my head in frustration. They are two different moments on the journey toward life in Christ.

If teaching is one of your primary charisms, however, it will be difficult for you to move beyond the importance of catechesis. That is how you are hardwired; it is what God has placed on your heart. We hear over and over again from our leaders, ordained and lay, that we need to communicate the truth. I certainly agree. However, someone with the charism of teaching sees this as the primary and burning need for the Church today.

If we want to live more fully in unity and maturity, we must recognize that, in the Christendom model of Church, we have placed a disproportionate emphasis on the function of shepherd and teacher. We have made them the most important functions. So much so that our diocesan seminaries have basically formed diocesan priests to be shepherds and teachers and have also tended to discern priestly vocations almost exclusively among those who have shepherding and teaching charisms. In fact, it is quite possible that men with more apostolic, prophetic, and evangelistic gifts who find their way into the seminary system may end up feeling as if they do not belong there.

Historically it seems that men with an apostolic gift who were called to the priesthood often joined religious orders that were more apostolic or started their own missionary orders. Likewise, men and women with prophetic or evangelistic gifts would join religious orders that allowed the exercise of that ministry.

In the past, it might be true that all we needed were shepherd-teachers. During the time of Christendom, we did not need to lead. In this post-Christendom age, however, we urgently need apostolic, prophetic, and evangelistic leaders. When we find balance in this, it will foster health in our parishes and in our dioceses, because we will come to the unity of faith noted by St. Paul.

Further, understanding these five functions will help us address the terrible disunity in the Church today. In many ways, we are our own worst enemy, breaking into tribes and taking potshots at any Catholic or other Christian not in our tribe. When we understand these five characteristics and how they work in the lives of our fellow Christians, we can be less judgmental toward priests and laypeople as they exercise their charisms in the Church.

We are all uniquely gifted, and we see the world through the lens of our gifts. Therefore we presume that the way we see the world and the Church is the way everyone should see the world and the Church. If others do not act accordingly, we conclude there must be something wrong with their character or possibly that they have an agenda that we must oppose at all costs. They become the enemy.

Take, for example, someone with the charism of teaching. God has placed on her heart a burning desire for others to know the truth of God. She values clarity and the need to transmit truth to others. If she meets someone who does not share those priorities, who does not seem to be concerned about the truth in the same way, she can easily conclude that the person must not care about the truth.

Similarly, if I possess the charism of evangelism, I experience a deep desire to communicate the message of the gospel. I want to tell everyone about Jesus, and I see that as the most important and critical thing that I and, by extension, the Church can do. We can get to catechesis later; right now we must proclaim the gospel. If I meet someone operating with different gifts, who does not seem to share my priorities, it is easy to conclude that they do not love Jesus as much as I do.

Looking at our teams through these five functions is similar to examining our strengths. We must make sure that our teams consist of people with charisms that balance one another. Alan Hirsch has a wonderful website called 5qcentral.com, which provides a number of assessments, including his APEST assessment, to help individuals discover where they have been gifted. Using this tool can help a team achieve a balance of strengths and gifts, which in turn will help them function in a healthy and fruitful way.

Vulnerability-Based Trust

Healthy teams need trust in order to enter into fruitful conflict. Patrick Lencioni often points out, "Conflict without trust is just politics."[43] Sound familiar? When we do not trust each other, we cannot create a safe space for disagreement—and people will not enter conflict if they do not feel safe.

This kind of trust emerges out of vulnerability, being authentic with one another, being real. I am not saying that the Senior Leadership

Team becomes your therapy group, but authentic vulnerability might mean admitting that you are wrestling with an issue and you do not know what to do, or that you are scared. It might mean saying, "I hear where you're coming from, but that strategy terrifies me. I am finding that really difficult to deal with."

Sometimes trust means apologizing for not meeting commitments; it means being willing to submit to accountability. This kind of vulnerability is important for every member of the team—including priests and bishops.

We have found that vulnerability-based trust often leads to authentic friendship, and this friendship is important. At Saint Benedict, the Senior Leadership Team members became good friends. Members knew that they were cherished, respected, and loved. For some people, those words might seem like platitudes. It was that experience of friendship, however, that allowed us to really challenge one another, to passionately disagree, and to come up with the best solutions and decisions. On those occasions when members may have messed up or betrayed the trust of another member, our vulnerability-based relationships allowed us to ask forgiveness and reconcile with one another.

If you have even one person on your team not willing to open up and become vulnerable, it can be disastrous. The person may agree with your vision and balance the strength of other team members, but if he holds back or puts on a mask, it kills the dynamic of the team. If you let this go on for too long—if you are unable to challenge that team member and help him move forward—the team bogs down.

I know this from experience. That is why I always ask parishes starting out on this journey to call their SLT an *interim* Senior Leadership Team. The individual team members are learning how to be vulnerable with one another, and it is quite possible that the team does not yet have all the right members.

Vulnerability-based trust leads to our final nonnegotiable characteristic.

Healthy Conflict
Earlier we talked about the two basic responses to conflict: fight and flight. I am not sure what your response is, but I have to tell you that I love a good fight. Maybe it is my Scottish heritage—you know, that *Braveheart* thing. I find conflict quite energizing.

Other people prefer flight. When you are in a closed room, though, it is really hard to flee. So what happens? People clam up.

What fight and flight share is that both responses make us stupid. We move into a more instinctual place. Blood moves from our brain to our extremities so that we can either run away or start fighting, and our capacity for reasoned discourse vanishes.

Why do we want healthy conflict? The answer, again, is that we want to make the best decisions. Remember, the first nonnegotiable characteristic of a functioning leadership team is unanimity of vision. In an SLT that is healthy, we are not in conflict about where we are going; we are not in disagreement about our destination, about what kind of parish or diocese we want to become. Disagreements are about strategy and tactics—how we can arrive at our destination.

These kinds of conflict are critical. They force proponents of a particular path to consider all the angles, to defend their position, and to modify the plan based on the truth behind opposing arguments. When it comes to tactics, if you are not in conflict, you have a serious problem. Perhaps the team has succumbed to groupthink, or people are not authentically sharing their points of view.

Every team must grow in its ability to achieve healthy conflict. The American psychological researcher Bruce Tuckman, in his study of group dynamics, talked about forming, storming, norming, and then performing. You have to bring your team together (forming), then you have to develop your capacity for conflict (storming). During the storming process, team members have to figure one another out.

It is like learning to spar in boxing. You have to learn how hard you can hit someone to maximize the fruit of training without seriously hurting the other person. This is particular to each team—and you will make mistakes. That is why trust is so important!

Once the storming process is over, the team's unanimity of vision, its balance of strengths, the depth of its trust among members, as well as its capacity for conflict become standard operating procedure (norming). After that, teams start to bear a lot of fruit (performing).

The pastor has a critical role in facilitating this. A healthy, functioning Senior Leadership Team requires the pastor to not only tolerate conflict but also unearth it. If everyone seems to agree, someone should play devil's advocate and start arguing against the prevailing thought of the group.

This is often where SLTs break down. People rarely want to argue against their pastor—especially if he is a bishop. We are culturally conditioned as Catholics to respect that office. So we generally do not say anything in disagreement, and we do not challenge the thought and perspective of the ordained.

I saw a video some years ago that was produced by a diocese and presented its bishop and his content in a rather unflattering manner. I thought, on viewing it, that his chancery staff responsible for the video did not embrace healthy conflict. Perhaps they did not know how to disagree with the bishop, and so they failed to address the problems with the presentation. The large audience I was watching the video with burst into laughter at a particularly awkward moment.

Sometimes, in the name of respect for a position, we do not respect the position enough. Remaining silent when feedback would improve a situation demonstrates a lack of care and respect. In contrast, speaking truth to power—disagreeing with a leader to his or her face and engaging in debate—can be a profound act of respect and love.

This unfortunate dynamic is also apparent in secular business. When the boss presents an absolutely stupid idea, very few employees stand up and call it as it is. Either no one gives much input, or people nod their heads and agree with the idea—despite the fact that it might be a dumb one. Why? Because they know they are not in a safe space. They do not feel free or empowered enough to directly disagree with the boss.

We are unlikely to disagree with someone if we know they will become angry or curl up in a fetal position and weep—particularly if that person has positional authority over us. Nor do we want to disagree with leaders who will stare us down and give us the silent treatment for the next week.

So what happens after a meeting in which team members are unable to engage in healthy conflict? They call, text, or meet up with people they do trust in order to share what they really think. This happens so often in the Church that the result is a splintering. We end up with hidden factions that never address the fundamental issues. These factions gather in diocesan and parish meetings, nod their heads in agreement with each other during the meeting, and then hustle back to their respective corners to start quietly opposing each other.

What happens, however, when a team can create a safe place for disagreement? We begin to disagree—often passionately! We have heated, intense, critical conversations. Since everyone on the team loves and respects the other team members, passion can be directed at ideas, strategy, and tactics. Such dynamics are actually quite fun when you get used to them. What is more, they lead to the sharpest and best decisions.

The presence or lack of appropriate conflict in an SLT is one of the easiest ways to identify if the team is healthy or not. I will often ask the priests we coach if they experience conflict in their Senior Leadership Teams. Sometimes they say, "No. We have great meetings that run smoothly, and we work on issues with no drama." I think to myself, "Wrong answer!" Either team members are not engaging in a healthy way; there is a fundamental disagreement about vision or a major imbalance of strengths; or everyone is on drugs.

So let us review.

1. Disagreement Regarding Vision. There are times when disagreements about vision do not manifest as direct opposition. Usually this happens when there is no actual buy-in of the vision, simply intellectual assent. Intellectual agreement lacks passion, and dispassionate people will not openly disagree. It is not worth it. The Greek translation of "dispassionate" is *apathos*, which is, literally, "apathy." You will never experience healthy conflict among apathetic people. They do not have the energy or willpower for it.

   By the way, when I use the words "disagreement" and "healthy conflict," I am not necessarily talking about polite and genteel discourse. At Saint Benedict, for example, there were times when I thought Ron Huntley and I were going to throw punches at each other. Our conflicts were passionate, energetic, and intense. Often we raised our voices, and sometimes we had to apologize to each other after the meeting. All of this, however, took place in the context of love and friendship. Seriously.

2. Imbalance of Strengths. When you have a balanced team, other team members will drive you crazy. For example, I am a very driven personality. I become impatient when things seem to take too long. I would rather jump into action than wait for the creation of a detailed plan. People on the Saint Benedict team were exactly the opposite, and they drove me nuts.

Often the impulse to plan and the impulse to jump in and do something clash in a team setting. I understand now, however, that I benefit when people call me to greater organization and planning, and they benefit from my sense of urgency. Together our strengths help ensure that we make the best decisions possible. Yet these strengths exist in a kind of tension, which must be sought and honored. That is healthy conflict. If you are not experiencing this tension, your team is probably not balanced.

3. Lack of Trust. If your team members are not yet in a safe place, it may be because of another team member, but often it is because of the leader—the priest or the bishop. A leader might say he is open to being challenged, but as soon as someone disagrees with him, he gets defensive, raises his voice, gives the challenger the "stink eye," or becomes sulky.

4. Remember the "two-thirds, one-third" rule—two-thirds listening, one-third advocacy. If someone disagrees with the leader, and that leader starts arguing without taking the time to listen, that sends the signal to other team members that the meeting is not a safe place. Once that happens, healthy conflict disappears.

Leading as the Leader

As the responsibility for fostering healthy conflict falls to the leader, a priest or bishop who wants to lead out of this model must do everything he can to facilitate disagreement and invite people to challenge his ideas. Remember, though, the SLT is not leadership by committee. On the other hand, I cannot tell you the number of times I went into one of these meetings convinced that I had the right perspective on a particular topic because, after all, I *am* a priest—only to leave the meeting convinced otherwise.

During those meetings, I had to fight the temptation to bang my fist on the table and say, "Look, I'm the priest, and I am making this call." Good leaders do not do that. If you surround yourself with talented people who share your vision and have a balance of strengths, and then you sweep away their concerns and ignore their arguments, do you think they will stick around for the long haul? If you keep acting in a unilateral way, eventually they will leave and go somewhere else.

There were times, as I embraced healthy conflict, that I had to deal with personal challenges to my leadership style. These were the one-out-of-ten times in which the process of healthy conflict did not yield a clear solution to the problem under discussion. In those cases, the final decision rested with me, as the pastor. In the absence of agreement, the leader must make the call. I have found in these situations that strong bonds of trust among team members allow people to rally around the decision of the leader. In addition, when people feel they have been listened to, they are more inclined to follow the leader's decision—even when it goes against what they would have chosen.

This is where inquiry is such a powerful tool. When a leader who encounters strong opposition takes the time to understand the perspectives of the other SLT members, the team can more readily own the final decision. This also minimizes the chance that people will leave a meeting and work on undermining a decision, or say, "I told you so," if the decision does not turn out well.

There have also been times when everyone on the leadership team disagreed with my idea. I had a choice to make: either ignore what they had to say and press forward, or listen to their ideas and change my own. In some of those cases, I was tempted to ignore my fellow team members. The reality, however, is that a leader who rejects the unanimous opinion of his entire team is generally acting like an idiot. If a leader did that, even on a semi-regular basis, they would have a Senior Leadership Team in name only

In the end, every leader gets the team he or she deserves. If in spite of what you say, your actions communicate that you want a bunch of "yes" people around you, then that is exactly what you are going to get. If you want people around you who are going to be better at things than you are, who are going to balance you out as a leader, who will help you maximize the chance that you make the best decisions possible to lead your parish or diocese forward, who are going to hold you accountable and love you enough to not let bad decisions or unhelpful behavior go unopposed, then you will end up with team members who can help lead the movement from maintenance to mission.

And that is one of the greatest gifts of all.

CHAPTER 13

Incarnating Leadership

Leadership theory is good.

Applying that theory to real life and seeing positive effects in terms of cultural transformation, fruitfulness in mission, and changed lives is even better. Some people, however, resist the application of solid leadership principles within the Church because those principles might come from the business world or other secular sources, and they do not seem very "spiritual." Perhaps this stems from our current imbalanced focus on holiness at the expense of mission. This imbalance manifests as a belief that holiness alone is sufficient and that a more deliberate approach to mission is somehow anti-spiritual. Grace, however, perfects human nature but does not replace it.

Effective leadership principles help a community: they remove obstacles that prevent community members from receiving and growing in the grace of God. In other words, good leadership helps dispose a community to the movement of God's loving action.

Think about it on a human level. If your organization is in chaos, praying more will certainly help, but it is not going to solve the problem. We need to pray, of course—*and* deal with the human stuff. We live this out in other areas of our life as Catholics.

For example, we believe that we can learn a great deal from psychology and sociology. Indeed, both disciplines have informed pastoral ministry within the Church to great effect. This does not mean that we disconnect from the sources of grace and spirituality within our

Tradition; rather we use the principles found in other areas that are in harmony with the Church's approach.

We do not want to copy the business world wholesale, but we can learn from the many examples of healthy leadership and organizations in the secular world. In fact, we have to become humble enough to see that we can learn from almost anyone—if we are willing.

Flipping the Org Chart

Applying these leadership principles in the diocese and parish is not rocket science, but we must live them too, and that is the challenge. Living them means embracing the leadership model of Jesus: we exist to serve others. Embracing a model of servant leadership means we serve each other by being vulnerable and committing to difficult conversations and accountability for the sake of the team as a whole—and each person in it. This will foster the growth and function of a healthy team, whether at the parish or diocesan level. In fact, if we want to inspire our parishes to embrace this kind of leadership model, we *must* live it out at the diocesan level first.

Nowhere is this approach better represented visually than by the "upside down" organizational chart, such as we spoke about in chapter nine. Priests and bishops who bear canonical responsibility make the final call in a situation, of course, but this flipped organizational chart demonstrates the basic structure of servant leadership. By the time I stepped down as pastor at Saint Benedict, for example, 1,400 people attended weekend Mass, and we had 865 parishioners serving in some form of ministry. Here is the point: I only directly supported four of them.

That was not my experience in earlier years. At that time, the parish had just started mobilizing and our liturgies and ministries were coming to life and bearing fruit. The problem was that I had twelve people "reporting" to me, and everything seemed to be a hair's breadth away from disaster. Honestly, it was unsustainable.

The servant leadership model we moved to is much healthier. I became much healthier, and the model was sustainable. It allowed Saint Benedict to mobilize as never before.

The Senior Leadership Team (SLT) model sits at the heart of this servant leadership approach. Whether you try to live this out at the parish or diocesan level, the essential elements remain the same. We found that it works best when the SLT members function as leaders of other teams within the parish or diocese.

The figure[44] below illustrates how we did this at one point at Saint Benedict. Although the exact shape may not be transferable to most parishes, the underlying principles are.

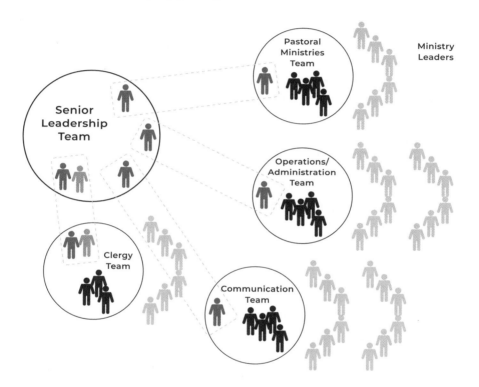

By the time I stepped down as pastor, we had five members of the Senior Leadership Team: myself; Fr. Simon Lobo, the parochial vicar; Ron Huntley, head of the pastoral ministries team; Rob McDowell, head of the operations team, and Kate Robinson, head of the communications team. Ron supported the staff who engaged in pastoral ministries, such as the directors of children's ministry, youth ministry, catechesis, evangelization, and engagement. Rob supported the office manager, the finance manager, the building manager, and some leaders of ministries associated with operations. Kate supported staff and parishioners who dealt with marketing, website, communications, and publishing.

Each staff member supported volunteer ministry leaders, who coordinated the roughly seventy different ministries we had at the parish. These ministry leaders supported a team of people for their particular ministry, which, depending on the size of the ministry, could be further divided into teams. We had a linked structure of leadership that supported the 865 people serving in ministry—all the way down to me with my team of four.

We did not arrive at this structure overnight. It took us several years to put it in place. Ultimately this approach changed my experience of leadership and expanded my sense of what is possible if we mobilize our dioceses and parishes.

You will have to wrestle with what works best in your situation, though if you have a big enough staff, you should be able to make something like the above work. When you have identified key leaders and made them part of the Senior Leadership Team, you must meet with them regularly, one-on-one. Supporting these key people means investing your time and energy in them.

That can be a challenge for those of us who have a hands-off approach to leadership. In the early years of my time at Saint Benedict, Ron Huntley asked me repeatedly who my key leaders were. This confused me; I could not understand what he was asking. One day I finally said, "You are, Ron."

His reply stunned me. He said, "Well, if I am, then we're in trouble, because I'm not feeling that at all." He was right.

In those days, I spent little time with my key people. My idea of leadership was to let people know where we were going, ask them if there were any issues, and then just point them in that direction. I would actually say, "If I don't hear anything from you, I'll presume that everything is fine." This, I came to learn, was not very fine.

When it came to parishioners, however, I had an open schedule. I would meet with anyone who asked. You had a better chance of sitting down with me if you were someone with whom I had no relationship than if you were part of my team. That approach might work with a minority of people on your team, but it creates a sense of anxiety and disconnect in the vast majority.

Eventually, as we built this servant leadership structure, I invested personally in my Senior Leadership Team members, and they operated the same way with their own team members. They would meet as whole teams, and then they would have individual sessions. We were investing deliberately in the people doing ministry.

Living Jesus' Leadership Model

Ultimately, this is the model of Jesus. My friend Patrick Lencioni says that all the best business books get their content from the ministry of Jesus in the New Testament. We are appropriating that content for use in the Church.

If you look at Jesus' ministry, you will see that he invested his time specifically in certain people. He never did what I used to do. In the early years, if I had eight slots in my schedule, it was first come, first served. I would start meeting with people indiscriminately right after morning Mass and keep it up until 5:00 in the evening. I never had time for my own staff, because I filled my days meeting with anyone about anything.

Jesus, on the other hand, did minister to the crowds, but he invested much of his time in Peter, James, and John. These men were like Jesus' Senior Leadership Team. The Lord also gathered the Twelve around him. He spent time with them, challenged them, taught them, and corrected them. Then he sent them out to minister. The Twelve, then, were like a parish staff.

So as a pastor, you have a Senior Leadership Team and then your staff. If you are a bishop, you have a Senior Leadership Team (of perhaps four or five people), who then support a larger number of other key leaders: perhaps an executive staff or a team made up of department heads within the diocesan structure. The goal here is to invest in your SLT members, meeting with them individually. Then they lead other teams, whose members they invest in.

If we read the New Testament carefully, we also see a group, made up mostly of women, who followed Jesus and the Twelve, caring for their needs. Within a parish, this group would be analogous to certain volunteers: parishioners who give an extraordinary amount of time and energy to various areas of parish life. They function almost as volunteer staff members, and every parish has them. At the diocesan level, this group would be like a council of priests or a diocesan pastoral council whose members work closely with the bishop and his key collaborators.

We see in the Gospels that Jesus also spent time with another group—the seventy-two—and then sent them out. In the context of the parish, these seventy-two are like ministry leaders who coordinate the various areas of pastoral care and outreach. At a diocesan level, these would be pastors of parishes, who need to meet frequently together around their bishop.

Scripture identifies another group that followed Jesus: his disciples. These men and women believed in Jesus and committed their lives to him. This group is like the committed disciples who are present in our parishes.

Finally we have the crowds, those who came to hear Jesus out of curiosity. Members of the crowd possessed varying degrees of commitment to Jesus, but they were not yet disciples. We find the members of the crowd in our parishes: perhaps they come to Mass, whether regularly or occasionally, but they do not have much commitment to either Jesus' mission or the parish. These men and women are in different stages of their spiritual journey. Some may simply be curious; others might be ready to commit themselves to Jesus if someone showed them how.

Although Jesus taught the crowds and ministered to them, he remained focused on his purpose. In the Gospel of Mark, we read that after healing Simon's mother-in-law, Jesus rose in the early morning and went off to pray. Simon found him to let him know that the crowds were looking for him. Jesus said that he and the disciples had to move on to the next town (see Mark 1:29-39). In short, he stayed focused, and he invested strategically in others.

If you start living according to this pattern that we see in the ministry of Jesus, it will challenge your model of priestly or episcopal ministry. For example, you might be overwhelmed by your current schedule, packed tight with meetings. It seems that this model will mean having more meetings and taking on other challenges. You are absolutely correct!

We are all bound by the limitations of time—no one has more than twenty-four hours in a day—so we will not be able to continue doing all we are doing if we adopt this model of leadership. We must ask ourselves hard questions about how we spend our time. Despite our frantic pace and busyness, are we actually making disciples? Are people being transformed in tangible ways by an encounter with the living God? Are we creating parish cultures that celebrate and replicate transformation? Are we moving our parishes and our diocesan organizations from maintenance to mission?

If the answer to these questions is no, then we have to adjust how we spend our time. We must let go of the activities that do not bear fruit so that we have the time and energy to do the things that actually make a difference.

Transforming Priestly Ministry

When we work with priests in our coaching network, we invite them to sit down with their teams and a few key parish leaders to do a ministry assessment. In this assessment, we ask them to chart their workweek in light of the three dimensions of the pastoral office—the ministries of Word (preaching), sacraments, and governance (leadership). For this exercise, we tell them to include time spent celebrating the sacraments as part of the workweek but to exclude personal prayer time. In addition, we distinguish leadership—time spent working with SLT, investing in team members, working at the strategic level with a pastoral council, and making the difficult calls that a pastor must make—from managerial and administrative responsibilities.

The priests in our coaching network are hardworking priests trying to change their parish. What we see from most of them is that in a sixty-plus-hour workweek, they will spend about 10 percent of that time on preaching, including preparing for and giving the weekend homily and daily Mass homilies, as well as preaching for weddings and funerals. They spend about 15 percent of their time celebrating the sacraments. Finally, they spend only 6 percent of their time on leadership. I remember working with a priest about three years ago who said that before he learned about any of this, he spent 0 percent of his time on leadership!

As we help priests make those distinctions, they discover something powerful: they spend the vast majority of their time (about 70 percent) doing things that may be important but are not absolutely essential to priestly ministry. This includes sitting in meetings that do not require their presence, engaging in one-on-one pastoral counseling, visiting the sick or homebound for nonsacramental ministry, and paperwork.

Now imagine a scenario in which a priest reconfigures his schedule, carefully ensuring that gifted parishioners are able to take on the things that are not essential to priestly ministry. Imagine a priest spending

25 percent of his time on preaching. Does that sound like too much time? It really is not. When a priest leads a parish from maintenance to mission, seeking to mobilize parishioners, the homily is one of his biggest assets. In order to proclaim that overarching story of what we are about as God's people on mission, priests must improve the focus and quality of preaching.

When it comes to sacramental ministry, the time spent should remain about the same, if a priest can engage it in the right way. We have discovered that as parishes come alive, there is a greater demand for the Sacrament of Reconciliation. A priest can offset this in his approach to other sacraments—such as offering a weekday Mass once a month that includes the Sacrament of Anointing of the Sick. This can reduce the incidence of individual requests for that sacrament. An associate pastor or deacon can handle most baptisms, weddings, funerals, and committals.

Moving to this kind of structure is not shirking the responsibilities of the pastoral office. Remember that governance is an essential part of this office, which means that leadership is one of the most important areas that a pastor can invest in.

Now imagine a priest moving from 6 percent of time spent on leadership to 40 percent. What an impact that would have both on growth in leadership, for the priest as well as the team members he directly supports.

Regarding the responsibilities that we lumped together as nonessential to the pastoral office, reducing time spent on those to about 20 percent seems like a good number in our experience. After all, some of these nonessential activities are still important, and they may even be personally life giving. A priest with a shepherding charism, for example, will love visiting people in the hospital, even if he is not ministering sacraments. He will also love one-on-one meetings and pastoral counseling.

A priest with a teaching charism will be drawn to leading Bible studies and catechetical classes. Yes, other people could do these things, but God has hardwired you with these charisms. They bring you joy, and they bring great fruit to the people you serve in these areas. So honor how God has made you—and do it. We all need to engage in areas of ministry for which we are gifted—even if they are not essential.

To do that and still prioritize time for the essential areas of pastoring requires that we deliberately change the shape of our priestly ministry.

The same holds true for bishops. It is critical for episcopal leadership to assess their weekly ministry priorities. How much time is spent doing things that are not central to the role of a bishop? How can they move to spend 40 percent of their time on leadership? Determining this is not easy; it requires letting go of so much that is nonessential yet highly valued by the current culture within our parishes and dioceses.

It took several years for us to get this right at Saint Benedict. It was tremendously difficult for people to accept the fact that I did not attend all the meetings of the traditional Catholic men's and women's organizations. I also no longer dropped in on committee meetings. I could not engage in this servant leadership model and do all these things at the same time.

I found myself coming up against the ingrained expectation of parishioners that I be available for everything and everyone. This expectation reflects the basic pastoral strategy in most parishes: no matter the situation, meeting, question, or event, call Father. We shifted away from that at Saint Benedict. That call-Father model might work if a parish is small, say two hundred members, but past that point, the pastor cannot deal with everyone and implement everything. That leads to burnout. You cannot take up the mantle of leadership without letting go of that older model.

Bringing It All Together

Pastors, parish staff members, and key leaders interested in making this change often ask how the leadership approach works in relation to other leadership structures in a parish. How do parish staff members, or entities such as finance and parish or pastoral councils, for example, work in conjunction with a Senior Leadership Team?

Let us break it down.

Most parishes have a regular staff meeting as well as monthly finance and pastoral council meetings. In parishes with traditional models of leadership, parish councils can take many forms. What are the various forms a parish council can take, and how does a council differ from a Senior Leadership Team? I include here a table, which appeared in the *Divine Renovation Guidebook*, to help clarify these questions.

Models of Parish/Pastoral Council

Composition	Focus	Driving Question
Doers	Tasks	What must be done?
Managers	Organizing	Who will do it?
Reporters	Supervision	How is it going?
Representatives	Themselves	What about us?
Passionate dreamers and planners	Strategic/big picture pastoral issues	Where are we going and how will we get there?

As a pastor, I have seen these different models of parish or pastoral councils at work in various parishes. Small parishes tend to have parish councils made up of "doers." In very small places or rural areas, these parishioners are often highly committed, and they do everything. When they meet for parish council, they focus on tasks. The major question that drives them is "What must be done?"

As parishes grow in size, the parish council tends to be made up of managers. These parishioners might oversee a group of doers, and when the council meets, the primary focus is on organizing. The foundational question for this type of council is "Who will do it?" If you ever attended a parish council meeting that spent a great deal of time determining whom they could find to organize an event or facet of parish life, that council probably consisted of managers.

Another type of parish council consists of reporters. They focus primarily on supervision. They may oversee some aspect of parish life, but the primary question they wrestle with is "How is it going?" When Saint Benedict was being formed and the new building was under construction, this became the model out of necessity. Each of the members was supervising different aspects of the construction, and they came together to report what was going on.

A very common type of parish council consists of representatives (often elected) of ministries or stakeholders in the parish community. The focus of their meetings is the people themselves, and the ultimate question they ask is "What about us?" The representative model of parish council, therefore, is the one least likely to help a parish move from maintenance to mission. In fact, the inward focus of this council will most likely hinder a parish's transformation into a community of missionary disciples.

Members of representative councils often come to meetings ready to protect their turf. The factions on the council lead to disunity and distrust between members. The climate in representative councils generally does not support vulnerability-based trust, alignment with vision, and healthy conflict.

Passionate dreamers and planners make up the final model of parish council. This type of council focuses on strategic, big-picture pastoral issues. In this model, the council is best able to be truly "pastoral." Their driving questions are "Where are we going?" and "How do we get there?"

This is the model of pastoral council that integrates well with a Senior Leadership Team, because the Senior Leadership Team handles the tactical issues of implementation, leaving the dreamers and planners to tackle vision and broad strategy. We want the SLT to have a balance of strengths across all the four domains, but it is okay in this model of pastoral council for council members to have strengths heavily weighted toward strategy, as long as there is some representation in the other strengths categories.

Sometimes people ask if a pastoral council could also do the job of a Senior Leadership Team. The answer is no. First, in order to deal with the tactical issues before them, SLTs usually must meet every week, and most pastoral council members cannot commit to such an intense schedule. Second, most pastoral councils have eight to twelve members which is simply too big to sustain an effective weekly meeting focused on tactics. Third, pastoral council members do not sit close enough to the action, especially in larger parishes. They are somewhat removed from the day-to-day realities of parish life and ministry. SLT members, on the other hand, deal with that stuff on a daily basis.

In practice, the Senior Leadership Team needs the pastoral council, and vice versa. SLT members can get easily lost in the details and lose the big picture, while parish council members need the SLT members, who are more hands-on.

No matter what form your pastoral council currently takes, you need to move to a strategically focused council as you begin to mobilize your parish for mission. One of the ways that we shifted to this approach at Saint Benedict was to change the pastoral council meetings from a two-hour monthly format to all-day meetings—9 a.m. to 3 p.m.— four or five times a year, on a Saturday. We discovered that this format allowed us to accomplish more in a given year. Our SLT members were also *ex officio* members of the pastoral council, helping us keep a tight connection between strategy and tactics.

If diocesan leaders want their parish leaders to take on such a model, they will have to move in this direction themselves. Diocesan leaders will then be better able to help train pastoral councils to function as dreamers and planners. So how could this function at the diocesan level? Diocesan leaders have to think about the balance of strengths within the groups that consult the bishop, the difference between Senior Leadership Teams and executive teams that serve the bishop, and the tension between those who work on the big picture versus those who work on implementation.

For example, some dioceses have a diocesan pastoral council. If they do not, they will generally have a council of priests. Understanding the functions of these councils and how they need to interact with the Senior Leadership Team will be critical for helping the diocese move from maintenance to mission.

Flexibility Is Key

Whatever structure you put in place, whether at the parish or diocesan level, you cannot enshrine it in stone. At some point, it will most likely change. Flexibility regarding structure is one of the key elements for parish transformation. Generally you will need to change your structure for two reasons.

One, it does not work. If the structure you have created does not bear fruit, do not suffer under the weight of it. Change whatever needs changing.

The second reason you might need to change your structure is that it is actually working! If you have healthy, functional teams whose purpose is to lead your parish or diocese into growth and change, then you will be changing and growing. Your parish or diocese will transform, and therefore you will have newer and possibly different needs that your current structure can no longer address.

In our experience, healthy, working structures last around two years. To help resist the ossification of structures, we have found it useful to use the language of experimentation: tell yourselves and others that you are experimenting with this current model. This helps keep the culture open to structural change.

To dive deeper into the question of "How does it all work together?" I want to examine one of the team structures that we used at Saint Benedict a number of years ago. You can see it in the image below:

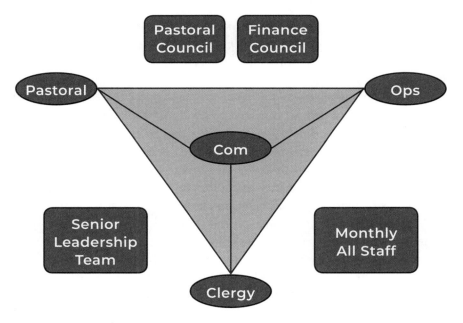

In the lower left-hand corner, you can see our Senior Leadership Team. We then had four staff teams—the pastoral team, the operations team, the communications team, and the clergy team. As mentioned earlier, each of the SLT members led one of those teams. Some parishes may not need a clergy team, because the pastor is the only cleric assigned. If you do have an associate pastor or deacons, remember that they should not automatically become part of the SLT. Regardless, the pastor should meet with them once a week as a group and then regularly one-on-one.

Initially at Saint Benedict, we only had one weekly staff meeting. As the staff grew to about twelve or thirteen people, however, our meeting effectiveness started to break down, and so we broke the staff up into teams. The image above represents a time in our history when we had about nineteen staff members, some part-time, others full-time, and two completely volunteer staff positions. We held a monthly meeting with our entire staff, which focused on building community, fostering teamwork, learning more about leadership, keeping in touch with our parish vision, and praying together. During the other three weeks of the month, the staff met in their respective teams.

When we prayed at the monthly staff meeting, we did not just say a quick Hail Mary. We took time to sing songs of praise, welcome the Holy Spirit, and listen to the word of God. Then we had a time of silence, followed by a sharing of what we sensed the Lord was saying to us.

As pastor, I met weekly with the SLT and the clergy team, and I met monthly with the staff team and the finance council. Four or five times a year, I met with the pastoral council—in addition to my weekly one-on-ones.

I wanted to lay this all out so that you could visualize a working model of servant leadership. In order for this or similar structures to work, you must delegate *authority*, not just responsibility.

We have seen, at Saint Benedict and in our work around the world, that the principles behind this leadership approach enable parishes to experience transformation. They unlock the giftedness of the baptized and allow for individuals and communities to mobilize for mission. Whether you are a part of a parish that is larger or smaller than Saint Benedict, or you work at the diocesan level, once you discover the right way to implement these leadership principles in your situation, they will bear fruit.

CHAPTER 14

Leading When You Are Not in Charge

Many of you reading this book are not in leadership positions or on staff at a parish or diocese. You might be wondering how you could possibly help change anything in your community. "I'm just a parishioner," you might think, or, "I'm just one of a hundred thousand Catholics in this diocese. What can I do?" Remember that leadership is, at heart, about influence. You may not have a leadership position, but you *do* have influence.

When I point this out to people, inevitably they say, "But you don't know my pastor. This won't go anywhere" Even parish priests and chancery staff wrestle with this when we talk about parish and diocesan transformation. They tell me, "This is all good stuff, Fr. James, but you don't know my bishop."

So how can you influence your parish or diocese to move from maintenance to mission when you are not in charge? To help you assess your situation, I would like to offer some background information based on our work with pastors over the years. We have learned that pastors generally fall into one of six categories; knowing which category applies to your pastor will help you discover how best to use the influence you do have to effect change. Keep in mind that when we talk about pastors, we include both parish pastors and diocesan pastors (bishops).

The Six Categories of Pastors

1. Enthusiastically Supportive

We are in a critical moment in history. The Church needs to regain her missionary spirit, remain faithful to revealed truth, and unleash the baptized on the world by making them disciples, equipping them, and sending them out. The enthusiastically supportive pastor wholeheartedly embraces this approach. He loves it. That does not mean that he has a plan for how to do it. Nor does it mean he is currently *acting* in a way that supports this. Nevertheless, he is open to and supports ideas and strategies to move in this direction.

2. Cautiously Supportive

This pastor generally supports change and transformation, but he is not bouncing off the walls with excitement. He is warm rather than on fire, but he is open to moving in the direction of renewal and transformation.

3. Permission Giver

This priest or bishop will not be an obstacle to moving in a more missionary direction, but neither will he encourage it. Generally such pastors give permission to do things as long as these things do not increase the pastor's workload or cause too much disruption.

4. Controller

These pastors may give permission to move in a missionary direction, but it will not be blanket permission. They will be interested in what you would like to do, but they are primarily intent on maintaining control. Controllers tend to micromanage. Eventually they become major bottlenecks rather than bottle openers.

5. Passively Opposed

These pastors resist the notion that the Church must become more missionary. Perhaps their worldview prioritizes feeding the sheep—a focus on holiness to the detriment of mission. Or they have an isolationist worldview: the Church must be isolated from the world to remain doctrinally pure. Maybe a pastor operates out of a clerical mindset, and he distrusts laypeople; he might think only the ordained should do the work of ministry.

No matter the reasons, these pastors never directly voice opposition to missionary-focused ideas. They may say nothing or may even agree to a direction—and then quietly work to sabotage it. Other times, these pastors come up with excuses for why they cannot give permission, and these excuses pile up until they act as roadblocks.

6. Actively Opposed

This category is self-explanatory. These pastors have no qualms about directly resisting, denying, or opposing missionary viewpoints and activity. Often they do everything they can to shut down attempts at missionary renewal.

Take a look at these categories, and think about your parish pastor or bishop. Where does he fall in this framework? If he is enthusiastically supportive, cautiously supportive, or a permission-giver, you will have opportunity to use your influence openly. This is the bottle-opener area.

If your pastor is a controller, passively opposed, or actively opposed, you will need to carefully and prudentially discern how to use your influence and spend your time. This is the bottleneck area.

Ten Things You Can Do When You're Not the Boss

I do not want you to lose heart if you find that your bishop or parish pastor is a controller or even sits in the actively opposed category. You have a vision for how things could be, and you have a passion for missionary transformation. God placed that passion in your heart for a reason, and he wants you to share it and bear fruit.

This does not mean that you will never be frustrated. As Catholics, we experience the tension between how God has called us to live as Church and how we *actually* live as Church. At the end of the day, we are not Congregationalists. We cannot form a vision independent of our bishop.

That being said, here are ten ways that will help you move your parish from maintenance to mission when you are not in charge. Anyone can do most of these, regardless of their pastor's category. In the long run, any of these strategies can help even the passively or actively opposed pastor become a permission giver or even a supportive pastor of some kind.

1. Pray.

Have you noticed how easy it is to examine and criticize the faults and limitations of your priest or bishop? This is human nature. Parishioners love to pick at their priest, and priests love to pick at their bishop. What we should do instead is pray for our leaders.

Most priests feel overwhelmed by the weight of ministry and the unrealistic expectations that people have of them. As we have seen, some of that stems from an earlier model of priesthood, in which priests were expected to be everyone's personal chaplain and counselor twenty-four hours a day, seven days a week. The chancery office and the priest's or bishop's own understanding of what his vocation should look like add more weight. In the end, these expectations tend to crush pastors rather than lift them up.

In addition, many priests and bishops have been hurt. They have tried to lead change, to call their people to renewal—and they have been kicked in the teeth repeatedly. Some of our Church leaders have essentially quit and yet remain on the job. Something vital inside them has died, and though they try very hard, the constant criticism and judgment are too much for them.

Therefore pray every day for your bishop and parish priest. In prayer you will discover a deeper capacity to love them, even with all their faults and failings. The more that love for our leaders takes root in our heart, the more we will find the grace to support and influence them.

Before you do anything else, pray for your pastor or bishop.

2. Encourage.

The word "encourage" comes from the French word, *encourager*, which means "to put heart into" someone. When someone encourages us, it does strengthen our heart. When someone speaks a discouraging word, it deflates us. It weakens the heart and makes whatever we are trying to accomplish more difficult.

Remember: encouragement is free. Parishes and dioceses often spend significant amounts of money on developing strategies, bringing in consulting firms, and purchasing programs, yet they overlook the important role encouragement plays in building a healthy parish and diocese.

When I speak about encouragement to others, I often mention a particular character in the early Church without whom few of us would be Christian today. No, I am not talking about Peter or even Paul. This figure is a man few have heard of: Joseph of Cyprus. Joseph of Cyprus became a follower of Jesus, and moved by God's love, he sold his field and gave the proceeds to the apostles (see Acts 4:36-37).

The apostles called this man Barnabas, which means, in Aramaic, "son of encouragement." You probably recognize that name. No one has really heard of Joseph of Cyprus, yet lots of people know Barnabas. The apostles called this man Barnabas not simply because of the gift he gave them but also because Barnabas went around encouraging others. He saw the potential in others and affirmed their gifts while equipping them and sending them out.

One of the people on whom Barnabas had an impact was Saul of Tarsus, who would become St. Paul. Scripture tells us that Barnabas "took charge" of Saul after his dramatic conversion. The disciples in Jerusalem were afraid of Saul because he had persecuted the followers of Jesus, but Barnabas brought him to the apostles and vouched for him (see Acts 9:26-27). He also accompanied Paul on his first missionary journey (see Acts 13:1-3).

Without the encouragement of Barnabas, Paul might never have made it to the Gentile lands, and without Paul's mission to the Gentiles, what would have become of the Church? What a difference encouragement makes!

Sometimes, though, we act as if there is a hidden vault with a finite amount of encouragement. If we make a withdrawal to encourage someone, there might be less for us. However, the opposite is true. The more we encourage others, the more likely they will be to reach out to encourage others.

We need to pay attention to how we put heart into our leaders. How can you encourage your priest or bishop? Imagine calling up your parish priest to thank him for that homily that moved you or to let him know how much you value his presence at the parish. What a difference that can make!

Consider too how those of us at the parish level can encourage those who work at the diocesan level. A number of years ago, the staff at Saint Benedict decided to go to the diocesan offices as a team, bringing a twenty-gallon container of coffee and plenty of donuts. We arrived unannounced and went around to all the offices in the building, thanking people for the work that they did on behalf of parishes. The diocesan staff was shocked; no one had done anything like this before. A few people even had tears in their eyes.

Imagine how different the dynamics would be within parishes and dioceses if we encouraged each other. Regular encouragement could even cause a bottlenecking pastor to move toward becoming a bottle-opening leader.

3. Buy in.

It is easy to disconnect if you are in a parish or diocese without a clearly articulated vision, where no one exercises authentic leadership, where things are in decline and no one has the slightest sense of urgency about it. People who have the capacity to be agents of change remain uninspired when leadership is poorly exercised. They go to Mass, do the Catholic thing, and then direct their passions elsewhere. They use their time and talents to serve some other organization.

If you really want to influence your pastor and see the parish or diocese move from maintenance to mission, get involved. Do not opt out. Do not withhold your financial contribution out of frustration.

Join a small group, or serve in a particular ministry. When you get involved, eventually you will register on your pastor's radar. As a pastor, I was far more likely to take seriously the input, comments, disagreements, or suggestions from a person who actually participated in the life of the community. Getting involved is one way to grow your influence.

One day, in the parish where I served before Saint Benedict, I had a 4:00 p.m. appointment with a man named Tony, who had recently joined the parish. Those were the days when my schedule was wide open to everyone, and I was run ragged by all the demands. It had been a long day, and honestly, I was not looking forward to this meeting. In general, most of the people who came to see me wanted me to do something for them. They had an agenda. I wondered what this man would want from me.

When Tony arrived, we sat down and made small talk. All the while, I was trying to figure out what his demands were going to be. Finally he said, "Fr. James, we've been here at the parish for a few months."

Cynically I was thinking, *Okay, here it comes! Here it comes!*

He continued, "We really love this parish, and we think that we have found a home here. So I'm wondering, how can we serve you?"

I said, "Excuse me? What did you say?"

Tony replied, "Well, my family and my friends who have joined the parish have been praying, and we wanted to ask you how we can use our gifts to serve the parish. What's on your heart for this parish? How can we help you?"

You could have picked me up off the floor. I was stunned. This had never happened before.

If you want to influence your parish leadership, then go to your parish priest, and ask how you can serve. If you are a priest or layperson who has the capacity to serve at the diocesan level, then buy in there as well. Resist the temptation to withhold financial support—a common temptation when people are frustrated with the bishop and what seems like a lack of leadership. Get involved.

Even priests can become frustrated with the diocese and withdraw by saying no when asked to be on a committee or the priests' council. They choose to isolate themselves in their parish. If you want to see your diocese change, get involved there. Show up for gatherings of clergy. Show up for the Chrism Mass. The chance of influencing your bishop is going to be far greater.

4. Dream.

All of us, pastor or not, can have a dream for our parish or diocese. If you do not have a dream, a picture of the future that makes you passionate, how will you influence the people around you? Remember, passion is one of the key components of influence.

A couple months ago, I met an Anglican bishop who said that the Church suffers from IDD—Imagination Deficit Disorder. This is so true. Our Church has a deep poverty of the imagination, of the capacity to dream—both at the parish and diocesan levels. This in turn inhibits our ability to take bold steps into the future as missionary communities.

5. Scratch the itch.

Another way to say this is "Embrace your discontent." Discontent and passion are two sides of the same coin. If you are passionate about your parish and about your diocese, there are things about them that most likely drive you crazy, things that you wish were different. Scratch that itch.

In other words, do not make peace with the status quo. Do not surrender or give in. If an aspect of the diocese bothers you, do not ignore it. Name it, and work to make it better.

We need to avoid letting our discontent overflow, taking over our thought process. This is spiritually and emotionally unhealthy. I have been down that path.

At Saint Benedict, for many years, I handled my own dissatisfaction in an unhealthy way. I became negative and sarcastic about the diocesan offices to such an extent that eventually I saw my attitude reflected by a staff member. I realized that my dissatisfaction had crossed the line into sin.

So as you attempt to scratch the itch, stay close to the heart of Jesus. Then your discontent can remain holy and life-giving.

6. Be filled with the Holy Spirit.

Only the person, power, and presence of the Holy Spirit can empower the move from maintenance to mission. As you work out your particular call to serve in the parish or diocese, pray to the Holy Spirit. Of course, we pray to the Father and to Jesus, but let us not forget the Third Person of the Trinity, the One who animates the Church's mission of evangelization.

Remember that Jesus instructed his disciples at the ascension to "stay in the city until you are clothed with power from on high" (Luke 24:49). He did not release them for ministry until they received the promised outpouring of the Spirit. We received the Spirit at Baptism, and we must not neglect to cultivate our relationship with him. Pray that ancient prayer of the Church: "Come, Holy Spirit, fill the hearts of your faithful and enkindle in them the fire of your love."

Opening ourselves to the Holy Spirit is especially important as we scratch the itch of our discontent. It will allow us to experience a discontent that is holy.

7. Influence your sphere.

Because you have influence, even though you might not have a particular position in your parish or diocese, you must ask yourself: How am I going to exercise that influence? Am I going to share my discontent in a healthy way? Am I going to share my dream with people? Will

I be an encourager and offer hope? Or will I be a chronic complainer—someone who discourages?

Your pastor or bishop might not ever become enthusiastically supportive. He might only be a permission giver. Despite that, you have an immediate circle, such as an area of ministry, where your influence is not limited at all. Within that sphere, you can live out the principles that we have explored.

You might be a pastor or a parish leader who has influence at the diocesan level. That influence can have a trickle-down effect, helping transform your parish. Or your parish, as it grows and transforms, might impact your diocese in positive ways. In either case, you can exert influence in one sphere that will impact another sphere.

8. Help implement an evangelistic tool.

Anyone who knows the Divine Renovation ministry knows that we highly recommend Alpha as an evangelistic tool. Is it the only tool for evangelization? No, of course not. There are many tools at our disposal today, and God works in all of them. We chose Alpha for a variety of reasons. You can find the details about how we use it in a book that I cowrote with Ron Huntley, *Unlocking Your Parish: Making Disciples and Raising Up Leaders with Alpha.*

We have seen people use Alpha when their pastor was only a permission giver. Over time, as this priest witnessed the transformation of lives through the Alpha process, he changed his attitude. We have also seen bishops' attitudes toward Alpha change as parishes started to come to life.

9. Give your pastor permission to lead.

It is essential that you support your pastor or bishop as he tries to change his fundamental model of priestly or episcopal ministry in the ways we have discussed. This shift will be one of the most difficult things he will undertake.

When a priest or bishop no longer makes himself available to people 24/7, when he begins to invest time and energy in specific people, and when he stops doing things that do not make a difference and starts doing the things that will, he will feel guilty. He will feel as if he is being unfaithful to his vocation—especially if all the other priests around him are not doing what he is doing. Sometimes that judgment will come internally, and sometimes he will experience judgment from brother priests, his bishop, and from parishioners.

So give your priest or bishop permission to not be present at every meeting or event, and support him as he tries to let go of doing things that are nonessential to his ministry. In fact, do not just remind him that it is okay to make these changes; hold him accountable when he regresses to the older model.

There is a particular image that speaks to me about leadership in the Church today: a crowded airplane sitting on the tarmac. The primary purpose of an airplane is to fly, to transport people from one place to another, but the captain obviously has not flown this plane in years. He still wears his captain's uniform, and he spends time mingling with the passengers—listening to them and serving them food and beverages. He does everything but fly the plane, and for years he has not even thought about flying the plane.

In 1982, while I lived in Scotland, there was a commercial for Air Canada that featured a plane arriving at the airport and sitting on the tarmac with its door open. No one got off. Laughter and the sound of clinking glasses emanated from inside, balloons drifted out, and eventually someone put milk bottles outside the door for the milkman to pick up in the morning. The voice-over said, "Air Canada's good old Canadian hospitality. Makes flights so good, you won't want to get off."

Unfortunately, that ad captures something of where the Church has been for a while. Not just stuck on the tarmac but enjoying good food and having a great time in our club. The Church was created to go somewhere: to lead people, form them, send them on mission. God does not call pastors to be captains of a plane going nowhere, who spend their time serving the coffee. The pastor is called to fly the plane. So support your priest and bishop as they take up the mantle of leadership.

10. Be a vision carrier.

Several years after *Divine Renovation* was published, we felt overwhelmed and challenged by the response and the sheer amount of work we were dealing with. Members of our SLT used to joke that our next book would be called *From Mission to Maintenance: What the Hell Were We Thinking?* It always gave us a good laugh.

The truth is that we always need to be reminded about why we are doing what we are doing and where we are going. This is about vision. Vision gets people excited, it provides hope, and it motivates members of a parish to move in the same direction. Vision, to be effective, must be communicated. And the more people there are communicating this vision, the more effectively it will mobilize a parish or a diocese.

How can you lead when you are not in charge? Be passionate about the vision. Communicate it with hope and enthusiasm to those around you, to your fellow parishioners, to your brother priests. Be sensitive to negativity, fear, and discouragement, and help others return to the *why* behind it all.

There will be times on the journey from maintenance to mission when people will ask, "Why are we doing this?" If the passion for renewal burns in your heart and you own the vision of the bishop or of your parish, you will have tremendous influence in helping others own the vision and become vision carriers themselves.

PART 4

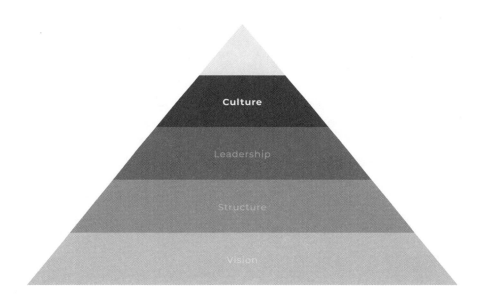

CULTURE

CHAPTER 15

Is Your Culture Fit for Mission?

So far we have explored the concepts of vision, structure, and leadership as they relate to diocesan and parish renewal. Now it is time to dive into the reality of culture.

In the introduction to this book, we discussed the pyramid schematic, which illustrates the elements that must be in place for parish transformation. (It also represents how this book is arranged.) Vision, structure, and leadership build on one another to form the base of the pyramid.

Fundamentally, the diocese is responsible for taking the lead in these areas. After all, a parish cannot create a vision that is independent of the diocesan vision, and although parishes can shape their internal structure, they operate within the structure of the diocese to which they belong. The diocese is also responsible for raising up, forming, and investing in the development and growth of its key leaders, the pastors.

The questions of culture and strategy, however, sit at the intersection of diocesan and parish responsibility. Dioceses must embrace and live out a missionary culture, which will foster the growth of a missionary culture in parishes. Ultimately, both dioceses and parishes must ask themselves, Is our current culture fit for mission?

Culture is extremely powerful. It does not matter how well researched, developed, or organized your latest strategy is; it will not succeed if the current culture does not support it. Many dioceses and parishes have experienced this reality. They brought in consultants, invested considerable time and money in developing plans, and discovered that the new strategy yielded no fruit.

What Is Culture?

Organizational culture is the environment we create by what we allow, celebrate, and value in the life of the diocese or parish. On one level, you can think of culture as "the way things are done around here."[45] In spite of its power, however, organizational culture often does not receive the attention that it should within the Church. In many ways, culture is like an iceberg, 90 percent of which sits below the waterline, invisible to observers. We might not be able to see culture, but it is there, and it influences everything we do.

Therefore we need to actively shape our culture. Mission statements, strategic plans, the things we value—all of these will remain aspirational if we fail to address the realities of our parish or diocesan culture. Our statements and plans will reflect how we would *like* to live rather than the values by which we *currently* live.

The beautiful thing is that we can shape culture through how we lead. If, as I have heard it said, culture eats strategy for breakfast, leadership eats culture for lunch. Authentic leadership can help create a healthy culture through the way it rewards, celebrates, prioritizes, and communicates.

First, however, leaders must have a sense of their baseline culture, the culture they have right now. In particular, they need to determine whether that culture is toxic or healthy.

People who encounter a Divine Renovation Network parish often comment on its vitality and ask about specific practices that transformed the parish. They want to take those practices back to their own community, but they do not understand the cultural values that underpin the transformation. Instead of addressing the realities of culture, they return to their own parish and introduce some of those practices there. Their parish culture is not fit for mission, however, and they become frustrated when they do not experience immediate results.

This is similar to what happens when two gardeners plant the same type of seed, but only one garden comes to life. The unsuccessful gardener wonders, "What's wrong? I bought the same seeds, I planted them in the same way, but there is no fruit!"

There are many reasons why seeds might yield fruit in one garden but not another. In the spiritual life, we can have confidence in the seed, which is the Word of God. Jesus promises us that there is nothing wrong with the seed. Therefore, if we experience problems with fruitfulness in the Church, the problem is not the seed but the soil—the soil of our hearts and the soil of our culture. Healthy soil promotes the growth of healthy plants; toxic soil stunts growth.

Have you ever worked in an organization that had a toxic culture? Bitterness, factionalism, antagonism, distrust, backstabbing, and a host of other ills generate anxiety and distress in those settings. If our baseline parish culture leans toward the toxic, is it any wonder that we do not bear fruit?

Fostering Healthy Culture

In order to build a healthy culture, a parish or diocese has to start at the beginning. To that end, we take dioceses and parishes who partner with Divine Renovation ministry through an exercise to determine health versus toxicity. Our goal is to help a team identify what health and toxicity look like in a culture, agree to aim for health together, and agree to hold each other accountable to living that out.

Having gathered the leadership team or staff, we ask them to think about a time when they were part of an amazing team—whether in business, sports, or wherever—and describe the attributes that made the experience so wonderful. People immediately shout out words like "teamwork," "trust," "fun," "joy," "respect," "communication," and so on. We jot the words down on a whiteboard, and when the feedback slows to a trickle, we read them back to the group to emphasize how good and life-giving these characteristics are. Who would not want to be on a team like that?

Then we ask people to describe the characteristics of a poorly functioning team, based on their own experience. If you thought people would be quick to identify what they loved about a healthy culture, just wait until you ask them for the signs of a toxic culture! Words like "gossip," "lack of trust," "backstabbing," "jealousy," "anger," "passive aggressiveness," and so on come rolling off their tongues. No group has ever had any trouble filling up the whiteboard.

Then we ask who wants to be on that type of team. Of course, no one raises their hand.

In a short period of time, we have helped people identify what health and toxicity look like, and they have expressed a desire for a healthy culture. However, the exercise is not yet complete. The facilitator now asks the group what the obstacle might be to living this healthy culture, and then he quickly acknowledges that the problem is *us*. We all want to be part of a healthy team, but we are all capable of contributing to toxicity.

In fact, we have all been guilty, at one time or another, of acting in toxic ways. The facilitator asks the team for a favor—which sounds something like "When I behave in a way that is not healthy and promotes toxicity, will you love me enough to speak to me about it, rather than just let it pass?" People will generally say yes.

The facilitator will next ask if they can do the same for each other—as members of a team—and again they say yes. So the group has now agreed to take these things up with one another.

This exercise brings a team to a starting place, but this kind of radical honesty with one another is difficult in practice. It might take some time before team members are able to have difficult conversations, but now they can refer to this agreement when they need to address toxic behavior.

After doing this exercise in the diocesan chancery office where I work, I was delighted when two employees came to me and, referencing the agreement we made, talked to me about the negative impact my words and actions had on them. Of course, no one likes being told this sort of thing, but I rejoiced that these staff members had the courage to be honest with me. I had been completely blind to what I was doing, and now I could avoid those behaviors. Slowly but surely, we are changing the chancery's culture and making normal a value that certainly was not normal in the past.

I have had this experience on various teams, and I think it is important to celebrate when these challenging conversations happen. That is what we did at Saint Benedict during our monthly staff meetings.

If, for example, Fr. Simon and I had a conversation in which he needed to hold me accountable for something I said or did, and the conversation went well, we would share that experience with the team. On the surface, it sounds like a strange thing to do. However, we wanted to celebrate that healthy interaction and encourage the entire staff to engage in this kind of behavior. Remember, we form culture by what we celebrate.

In many ways, culture is contagious. The organizational culture of a diocesan chancery impacts the organizational culture at the parish level. If we want our parishes to become healthy, missionary communities, then our chanceries and diocesan leadership must build healthy organizational cultures. Everything flows out of this reality. When you have healthy leadership, you will have healthy teams—and leading from teams is one of the essential shifts we must make in our model of leadership within the Church.

If we want to foster healthy culture, we can no longer tolerate toxicity at any level. When we tolerate toxicity—when we allow negativity, gossip, passive aggressiveness, and any other sign of poor leadership to continue—we actively contribute to the growth of unhealthy culture and toxic teams. As leaders in the diocese and parish, we must acknowledge our part in that and ask forgiveness—from God and from the people we lead. The more repentance we demonstrate, and the greater our commitment to living out healthy behavior in the context of servant leadership, the more we foster the manifestation of the fruits of the Spirit: "love, joy, peace, patience, kindness, generosity, faithfulness, gentleness, self-control" (Galatians 5:22-23).

However, I have encountered parish and diocesan staff who seem to think that the fruits of the Spirit are unattainable ideals or Pollyannaish naivete. Their attitude is that "mature" faith is thick-skinned. Church workers must live in the real world, which of course is not peaceful, loving, and joyful all the time. This attitude is simply a poor excuse for toxic behavior.

Working for the Church, at any level, *should* be different from working for any other organization. The fruits of the Spirit must increase, and jealousy, factions, and division must diminish at every level of leadership. Only then will we begin to develop a healthy organizational culture.

Building a Culture of Leadership

As I noted earlier, Saint Benedict had 865 individuals serving in ministry with a Sunday attendance of 1,400 in my last year as pastor there.

We achieved that rate of commitment in part because of the structural changes we made but also because we shaped the culture over a number of years to foster and unleash leadership.

We recognized that we had to help our parishioners broaden their concept of spiritual leadership. We needed to help them move from a clerical perspective—by which they saw the priest and perhaps his staff as the only leaders—to one that included laypeople who headed up ministries and other persons of influence. There was a notable lack of a leadership culture throughout the almost seventy ministries we had at the parish.

At that time, even some heads of ministries and a few of my staff did not see *themselves* as leaders. Many had no vision for their ministry, and they had not take ownership of it. They saw their role essentially as "doing a favor for Father." They functioned as schedulers rather than leaders. These were wonderful people who worked exceptionally hard, but they were burning themselves out because they were not raising up the next generation of leaders.

The first step in creating a culture of leadership is to define leadership. You cannot be intentional about leadership unless you have a clear definition of what it is.

I saw the need for such clarity several years ago, during a diocesan meeting devoted to evaluating how we were going to use an adult formation program that we had recently put on hold. I asked what the purpose of the program was: to make disciples or to form leaders? I thought it should have been about leadership, but most of the group thought it should focus on making disciples. We went back and forth repeatedly, until I understood that we did not have the same definition of leadership in a Church context. When I talked about forming leaders, they immediately thought I was speaking about forming priests, deacons, or laypeople who would serve as paid staff members.

To avoid similar confusion, we spent many months at Saint Benedict just talking about leadership—until someone challenged us to define it. Here is what we came up with: *Leadership means answering the call to influence, inspire, and equip individuals and teams to form disciples who joyfully live out the mission of Jesus Christ.* Let us break that down a bit.

First, leadership is a response to a call. No one assumes a mantle of leadership simply because he is available, for example, or wants the position or has been in the parish for decades. Rather the Lord calls a person to a role through the local parish or diocesan community.

It took time, but at Saint Benedict we were able to institute a policy that eliminated the option of volunteering for a leadership position. If we thought someone was right for a position, we discerned the possibility together with the individual, and, if the person seemed to be a good fit, we formally invited her to take on the role. As you build a culture of leadership, you will have to say no to volunteerism; it is antithetical to your goal.

Second, authentic leadership consists of influencing, inspiring, and equipping. We have explored the notion of leadership as influence in an earlier chapter. Leaders also exert influence through their ability to powerfully inspire and equip others to live as missionary disciples. They form disciples to do the work of leadership themselves, so that these new leaders go on to influence, inspire, and equip even more parishioners.

It might help to sit with your diocesan or parish leadership team and wrestle with your definition of leadership. How would your team define it? In the end, authentic leadership is broader than the positional, or clerical, model of leadership that currently prevails in the Church. Leadership is ultimately about raising up other leaders.

That is why the ability to delegate is an essential building block in a culture of leadership. Delegation, in its broadest sense, means giving someone the responsibility and authority to accomplish something that falls under your purview. As I have said before, we can only delegate that which is properly our own responsibility. When it comes to delegation in the Church, we must distinguish responsibility for Jesus' mission to the world from tasks or ministries that formally belong to the ordained ministry and are canonically mandated as such.

Our participation in and responsibility for Christ's mission to the world is rooted in the Sacrament of Baptism and is therefore the obligation of all the baptized. A priest or bishop does not need to delegate a layperson to participate in this mission; Jesus himself has given the layperson that right. In general then, when we talk about building a culture of leadership, we are talking about those things within the life of a parish or diocese that fall between these two realities—ministries and areas of service where only informal delegation is needed.

For example, distribution of Communion at Mass and to the sick in hospitals is an ordinary responsibility of the ordained ministry. Laypeople who distribute Communion at Mass are called extraordinary ministers of Holy Communion, precisely because their participation in that act of service is not an ordinary part of their baptismal responsibility and requires formal delegation from the pastor. Heading up the parish bereavement team, on the other hand, is a kind of informal delegation.

The goal of authentic leadership is to move away from simply giving people things to do and asking them to take responsibility for areas of parish life. When we move beyond the delegation of tasks and invite people into leadership, two things occur.

First, doing so allows the parish or diocese to bear more fruit. Leadership in this case acts like a bottle opener. If we relied on the pastor to do everything, this would slow down missionary activity. Raising up leaders, in short, multiplies our effectiveness.

Second, when laypeople take on responsibility for an area of parish life or ministry, they begin to grow spiritually and deepen their commitment to mission. To serve as a leader fosters sustained prayer, discernment, and reflection, all while rooting laypersons in their identity as beloved children through whom God wants to touch and change the world.

To effectively invite people into leadership, we must move beyond simply delegating responsibility and give people authority. This will help deepen a culture of authentic leadership. When you have responsibility for a task but no authority to accomplish that task, your ability to fulfill the responsibility is severely limited. In order to get anything done, you have to present your case to the decision maker. If the leader, pastor or bishop, who is not on the front line, does not understand what you require or disagrees with your approach—even going so far as to countermand a decision or override the direction that you choose—then you have a serious disconnect.

If that happens once, it is strike one. If it happens again, that is strike two. On strike three, the pastor will drive away gifted people who have the ability to accomplish what he needs.

Delegating, by its nature, presents risks. Sometimes people will make decisions that you would not have made. Sometimes people will do things in a manner that you would not have done. The quality of their work might not be as polished as yours. They may even make wrong decisions. That does not mean we should not delegate.

Think of parenting. The central act of parenting is to raise children up to become mature, healthy adults. In the course of that process, there will be times when children make, or will be about to make, wrong decisions. Rather than jumping in and fixing things for them, it may sometimes be wiser to allow them to live out the consequences of those decisions so that they learn and deepen their own capacity to make the right choices.

Of course, there are times when children may make potentially life-threatening or negatively life-altering choices; parents must intervene there. The same is true at the parish or diocesan level. Pastors, bishops, and their staff must intervene when other leaders are about to make decisions that will tank a particular ministry, for example. However, we must strike a balance between too much control and too little control if we want to succeed in building this culture of leadership.

The Principle of Low Control and High Accountability

In order to steer clear of both extremes, we must cultivate the principle of low control and high accountability.

Identifying and releasing the gifts of others means, by definition, that we cannot control everything. High control creates bottlenecks and kills innovation, energy, and commitment. If a diocese wants healthy, growing, missionary parishes, diocesan leaders must recognize that they cannot exert a high degree of control.

In my work with churches around the world, I have heard of dioceses that would not allow parishes to start any kind of program or process without clearing it with the chancery first. That degree of control is crippling. If we want growth, we have to release our control. That being said, you cannot release control unless you create a system to provide high accountability. Low control with low accountability breeds chaos.

At Saint Benedict, we created systems of high accountability within the organizational structure. I supported my Senior Leadership Team members, and these SLT members supported our staff members. These staff members supported ministry leaders, who in turn supported those serving in their particular ministry. I met with my SLT members regularly, the SLT members met with the staff members regularly, and the staff members met regularly with the ministry leaders, who in turn met with their team members.

We also have certain events, like Leadership Summits, that leaders are required to attend. If someone misses several of these summits in a row, the supporting leader has a conversation with that person. This reinforces accountability. In other words, we can act with low control if people know that skirting a commitment will be dealt with. You cannot have low control without high accountability.

Where does your diocese or parish fall in terms of the principle of low control and high accountability? This is a critical question. In our experience around the world, some dioceses and parishes exhibit high control, but most do not. Along with that, unfortunately, we see low accountability. The result is maintenance, ongoing decline, or sometimes a train wreck within a parish, requiring the diocese to step in.

There may be a degree of retroactive accountability; that is, a diocese pays attention to a situation *after* a major blow-up or disaster. Proactive accountability, however, is what is needed in order to foster parish health.

Leadership Summits

At Saint Benedict, we also required ministry leaders to attend Leadership Summits. These are regularly scheduled events that have had a profound effect on Saint Benedict and the various parishes we coach through Divine Renovation ministry. What do they look like?

Three or four times a year, we bring together all our ministry leaders, pastoral council members, and finance committee members for an inspiring and fun Saturday morning focused on reviewing and developing leadership skills. We welcome participants with coffee and breakfast foods and spend time together chatting and catching up with one another. Then we pray, followed by an icebreaker to help mix people up into various groups.

We follow this with a talk: about an upcoming pastoral change at the parish, for example, or a broader dimension of leadership. After the talk, facilitators lead discussion within small groups, and then we take a short break. During the second half of the morning, the pastor talks about an aspect of the parish vision, and we review our performance through the lens of that vision. The goal here is to equip and inspire leaders to become better leaders and vision carriers to the rest of the community.

We end the summit in a time of prayer. We invoke the Holy Spirit through word and song. Then we break into groups and pray over each other.

We want these gatherings to be inspiring, uplifting, and fun. By and large, we have met those goals. It is not unusual to see people hanging around after the summit is over—a testament, I think, to the quality of the experience for our people.

We make a point of sending invitations to these gatherings early, so people can plan to attend. Since we have a high accountability culture, we track attendance. We usually have 110 to 130 participants.

Your Leadership Summits do not have to look exactly like ours, but they should have similar goals and follow similar principles. These gatherings have done a great deal toward moving us culturally forward. They are important in our effort to live out healthy and effective leadership principles at all levels of our parish life.

Ownership and Pipelines

Another core element in establishing a culture of leadership is for leaders to take ownership of their ministry. Too often, long-time ministry leaders come up to the parish priest to let him know that they are moving or otherwise stepping down from their ministry—and only giving two weeks' notice. These departing ministry leaders never owned their ministry; they never saw it as theirs. Maybe they viewed it as a volunteer assignment or a favor they were doing for the pastor.

Leaders working within a culture of leadership, on the other hand, see their ministries as expressions of a personal calling from the Lord. They are not doing a favor for the pastor; they are responding to the call of God, and, because they have that understanding, they invest themselves in their ministry. They build up a network of leaders, create and recruit healthy teams, and commit themselves to the ministry's growth and fruitfulness.

What we witnessed at Saint Benedict were ministry leaders who actively worked to transition out of their ministry when the time came. They gave their supporting staff member enough heads-up that together they could identify potential replacement leaders from the network of people they had raised up.

Using Alpha as a leadership pipeline was one of the key ways we raised up this culture of leadership at Saint Benedict. Guests who begin the Alpha journey as nonbelievers, unchurched individuals, or unawakened parishioners may have a powerful encounter with Jesus through the Alpha process. Alpha team members, who are actively looking for people who demonstrate leadership potential, may invite people to serve in the area of hospitality during the next Alpha. As that course progresses, Alpha team members consider who on the team may have the gifts to cohost a small group for the next Alpha and invite those individuals to serve. Cohosts are then invited to be the main host, and after that, the leaders might invite him or her to be an emcee for the following Alpha or serve in other ways on Alpha.

We limited participation on the Alpha team to two or three years, in order to make room for others. Typically we would invite Alpha team alumni to serve in other ministries according to their gifts. Throughout this process, we looked for people who were faithful, available, contagious, and teachable (FACT).

Faithful. When matching people with an area of leadership, we considered their level of fidelity. In other words, someone still young in the faith, without a deep understanding of the principles of discipleship in the Catholic Church, could handle a basic level of responsibility. We looked for deeper levels of fidelity—to the gospel and the teachings of the Church—in those we asked to assume higher levels of responsibility.

Available. Sometimes people want to serve and lead, but they are unable to follow through on their commitments. We looked for people who, in spite of their busyness, were able and willing to be available without causing undue strain in other areas of their lives.

Contagious. We looked for people who manifested the fruits of the Spirit in such a way that others would be drawn to them. In addition, we looked for people who exhibited healthy behaviors, knowing that their influence would help spread health rather than toxicity throughout our network of leaders.

Teachable. The more we grow as leaders, the more we discover what we do not know. The greatest leaders display a capacity for continuous learning, a quality we looked for when inviting people into leadership at Saint Benedict.

As we formed leaders, we asked them to look for these same characteristics in others, whom they could raise up as leaders in their area of ministry.

Through our Leadership Summits, we also trained ministry leaders to create a leadership pipeline within their ministry. Here is what we did not want: identical "job" descriptions within a ministry—for example, simply giving the eight members of a team one week every eight weeks to do everything related to that ministry. Rather we helped leaders develop their ministries so that there were maybe four different levels of responsibility, beginning with an entry level where people could get their feet wet. They would then progress toward greater responsibility.

We wanted to follow Rick Warren's advice: "Don't use people to raise up your church; rather, use your church to raise up people." We wanted to help our leaders establish people in ministry and help them grow as leaders themselves.

We soon learned, at Saint Benedict, that if we were to grow a culture of leadership, we needed to develop a system of apprenticeship. This is critical for anyone hoping to establish a culture of leadership. We invited every ministry leader to identify an apprentice—someone with the gifts and talents to be a phenomenal leader in his or her own right. We wanted the apprenticing relationship to develop naturally, with a leader identifying someone's gifts and then investing in them. So as leaders performed the duties associated with their particular ministries, they would invite their "apprentices" to come alongside them.

The progression for a leader apprenticing someone might look something like this:

- I do; you watch; we talk.

- I do; you help; we talk.

- You do; I help; we talk.

- You do; I watch; we talk.

We challenged each other in regard to this approach, which is essentially a form of mentoring. People did not hesitate to challenge me, as a parish priest, asking, "Who are you mentoring?" We challenged the members of the SLT: "Which staff members are you mentoring?" We challenged the staff members: "Which parishioners are you mentoring?" And so on.

As a culture of leadership starts to take hold, highlight the work of leaders who exemplify the cultural values you want to encourage. Tell stories about the efforts of an SLT member, staff member, ministry leader, or anyone whose work is bearing fruit and who exercises a positive influence in relation to the mission. At Saint Benedict, we stopped doing a weekly bulletin and created a monthly magazine to help shape the culture that we wanted to develop. We often profile our leaders in the pages of that magazine. This is a powerful way to help broaden people's understanding of leadership beyond the priest, pastor, or bishop.

Finally, if you want to continually deepen the culture of leadership, you need to invest in your leaders—personally, professionally, and spiritually. I have already described some of the ways we did that at Saint Benedict: through one-on-one meetings with the people we supported, monthly staff meetings, and our Leadership Summits. In addition, every other month, we held a leadership lunch after our staff meeting and watched a leadership-related video. We also sent key staff members and lay leaders to leadership conferences—even some held overseas. In fact, one year we sent over sixty staff and parishioners to the Global Leadership Summit put on by the Willow Creek Association.

Investing in leaders not only produces fruit in them; through them, it allows the parish to bear more fruit as a deeper culture of leadership takes root within the community.

Diocesan Implications

When their parishes become healthy, dioceses become healthy and bear fruit. When dioceses become healthy, parishes will become healthy and bear fruit. Leadership investment, therefore, must also happen at the diocesan level. The cultural change at the parish level must be mirrored, lived out, and supported at the diocesan level.

How do we get there? By asking hard questions and making a deliberate effort to change. The bishop and his team should reflect on the following:

- Are diocesan staff members simply doers, or are they leaders?

- Do we delegate authority in addition to responsibility?

- How do we delegate authority in terms of the role and canonical responsibilities of pastors within their parish?

- Is the level of support on offer appropriate to the degree of challenge involved in the role?

- Do pastors have a sense of ownership of their parishes, and do we help or hinder that at the diocesan level?

- Are there low control/high accountability systems within the diocese?

- Do we have a leadership pipeline within the various ministries, departments, and agencies of the diocese?

- Are we raising up the right people, or do we simply accept volunteers?

- How are we apprenticing people? Have I personally identified anyone as an apprentice?

We will cover the relationship between dioceses and their parishes in more depth in the next section of this book, which focuses on strategy. It is crucial to consider these questions, however, when trying to build cultures of leadership at any level in the Church.

CHAPTER 16

Growing Your Key Cultures

Establishing a healthy organizational culture and creating a culture that fosters authentic leadership are not ends in themselves. Christ does not simply call the Church to higher organizational standards or better leadership. Rather he calls the Church to holiness and mission—to "worship in Spirit and truth" (John 4:24) and to "make disciples of all nations" (Matthew 28:19), who will labor for God's kingdom to come more fully into our world. Therefore we must also work to build three primary cultures within the parish and diocese: cultures of evangelization, discipleship, and worship.

Evangelization as a culture and not just a program pushes newly made disciples into other aspects of parish life: into deeper discipleship, community, fruitful sacramental participation, serving in ministry, and dynamic worship. It does this because it does not simply give information, convict, or inform consciences; it changes hearts.

A culture of evangelization should take root primarily at the parish level. Though dioceses should be evangelizing in their outlook and approach, it is not, strictly speaking, the job of the chancery or diocesan staff to evangelize. Dioceses should assist parishes in becoming outposts of the Great Commission.

In order to form a culture of evangelization at the parish level, certain elements must be in place. The first of these is clear communication from the diocese that evangelization is an integral and foundational part of the vision for the local Church. Furthermore, the diocese must make clear their expectation that parishes intentionally focus on evangelizing. Part of that intentionality means choosing a tool for evangelization.

Most parishes, however, do not engage in any formal evangelization process or use an evangelistic tool. They may have adult faith formation or faith enrichment programs, but these are typically catechetical in nature. These programs presume faith and often focus on transferring information or intellectual content. That is why it is critical for diocesan leadership to ask parishes to choose an evangelization tool and hold them accountable for its use.

A parish will never be catechized into doing evangelization, but it can be evangelized into doing catechesis. When parishes begin to do this, dioceses should celebrate that fact and share stories of these parishes, similar to the way we celebrated the stories of leaders and transformed lives in our monthly magazine at Saint Benedict. What we communicate and celebrate shapes the culture around us. If diocesan leadership gets this right, it will impact all parishes within the diocese.

The Right Tool for the Job

As we complete our restructuring in the Archdiocese of Halifax-Yarmouth, we will eventually ask every parish to identify the tool they will use for evangelization. The goal is to have an evangelistic tool that is distinct from catechetical ones and is accessible to people who do not attend church. In actuality, the list of tools that fit those criteria is quite small.

At Saint Benedict we use Alpha, but it is not the only tool. Some parishes that we work with use Discovering Christ, by an organization called ChristLife. Sycamore is a new evangelistic tool coming out of London, England. Organizations like the Augustine Institute are creating new evangelization tools as well. Some parishes and dioceses have opted to use small-group resources, such as those developed by a Canadian Catholic student ministry called CCO (Catholic Christian Outreach).

Once a parish chooses a tool, they must commit to that tool. Many parishes succumb to the temptation to have too many things going at once, under the mistaken assumption that activity equals fruitfulness. When a parish runs multiple programs and processes for evangelization at the same time, it actually inhibits the growth of an evangelizing culture. Each tool or process is seen as one program among many, and the community never goes deep with any of them. The parish's energy and attention become diluted.

One parish we worked with initially used Alpha to reach those on the outside and another tool to evangelize churchgoers. They discovered that their energy was divided and that using two tools made it more difficult for nonchurchgoers who had been evangelized to enter into the life of the parish. Now they use Alpha to evangelize both sets of people.

I had a conversation with a priest who described his ministry in recent years as constantly being asked to do more with less. I said that the goal of transforming our model is not to get priests to do more with less but to do less with more! In other words, we want parishes doing fewer things, with a higher concentration of resources on actions and activities that truly make a difference.

In order to achieve that, we need to move into the pruning mindset we discussed around diocesan restructuring. We know that gardeners trim away extraneous growth to focus the vital energies of the plant. Pruned plants and trees produce healthier fruit. Diocesan leadership can encourage their parishes to trim away the extraneous and focus their efforts on life-giving growth.

From the outset, parishes must use whatever tools they choose with an eye toward those outside the parish. This will help them develop a sensitivity to the needs of the unchurched. They will avoid using "churchy" language and speaking about their faith in a way that those outside the Church find unappealing. If someone's initial experience of parish evangelization is of a group of committed Catholics sitting around talking about their faith using insider language, that person will find it difficult to break out of any preconceived and negative impressions they might have about the Church.

A parish that uses its evangelizing tool as a way to reach those on the outside will learn how to draw them in, share the gospel message with them, and help them see the Lord at work in their lives. For this reason, it is important to constantly track the percentage of nonchurchgoers who participate in our evangelistic process, but more about this later.

Building a Culture of Discipleship

Discipleship is a lifelong process of growing in intimacy with Jesus, learning the ways of his kingdom and the truths of the faith, and maturing, so that our lives conform more perfectly to his. In many parishes, however, there is very little growing, learning, or maturing happening on a regular basis with adults. A select few might be involved in a discipleship process at the parish level, but this is certainly not the norm. In fact, most parishes focus almost exclusively on children's catechesis.

Once parishes begin to bear fruit with an evangelizing tool, however, they will find that evangelization creates new believers or awakens practicing Catholics to a more dynamic, living faith. The parish will need to help these adults to mature as disciples.

In many ways, the process of evangelization is like giving birth. When a woman gives birth, the new parents' job is just beginning. They must raise that child to adulthood. In a similar way, evangelizing parishes will need to raise up those who have been evangelized to mature faith. These parishes, supported by their diocese, will need to have a process in place for forming disciples

In our work at Divine Renovation ministry, we encourage every parish to develop a discipleship process. At Saint Benedict, we call our process the Game Plan. Every parish is unique, however, and one size does not fit all. We tell parish leaders with whom we work to develop their own process, one that will fit their parish.

To better understand how a defined process supports the cultures of evangelization and discipleship, I want to share with you the plan we developed at Saint Benedict, as illustrated below:

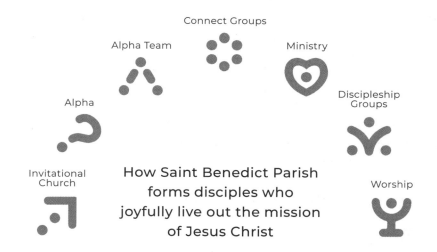

Connect Groups

Alpha Team

Ministry

Alpha

Discipleship Groups

Invitational Church

How Saint Benedict Parish forms disciples who joyfully live out the mission of Jesus Christ

Worship

THE GAME PLAN

This game plan has some critical features. First, it is clearly a process but not a linear one. God works in different ways, so there is no single on-ramp. Despite this, no matter how we connect with people, Alpha is our primary point of invitation to insiders and those on the outside. A tool like Alpha thrives only through normalizing the reality of invitation—of inviting people in. In the Game Plan, this culture of invitation is represented by the "invitational Church" icon.

Although we use Alpha, invitation can happen with any kind of evangelizing tool. The tool itself is not the most important thing. Rather, what is critically important is that you have a place intentionally designed to be evangelistic and a tool that is appropriate for those outside the Church. Think of it this way: the mystery, beauty, and depth of our Catholic faith is like a pool. As Catholics, we should celebrate the existence of and immerse ourselves in this pool regularly. We should also invite others to join us in this pool. Few people will swim in the deep end, however, unless we have a shallow end—a place where they can dip their toe and check out the temperature before immersing themselves. We need a shallow entry point so that we can eventually bring people into the depth of the mystery.

At Saint Benedict, Alpha works as that shallow entry point. At the same time, it helps those in the shallow end begin to move into the deep water.

After people participate in Alpha, we invite many of them to join us on the Alpha team. As we discussed in the last chapter, this is how we begin to build our leadership pipeline and support a culture of leadership. Connect Groups are next: midsize groups of twenty to thirty people who meet every two weeks. The goal of these groups is to foster a sense of belonging and community, and to help members continue to grow spiritually, especially in exercising the gifts of the Holy Spirit. Think of them as permanent "house churches" led by laypeople.

During the Connect Group sessions, participants gather for a meal, a short talk, and a time of prayer. We have seen great fruit develop within these Connect Groups at Saint Benedict and in some of the parishes we coach. We also use Discipleship Groups in our game plan. These smaller groups, of maybe six to eight people, focus on adult faith formation. Often they are more temporary than our Connect Groups.

This is the way Saint Benedict has done it, but in the Divine Renovation model, parishes need simply to create some system of small groups and resist the temptation to enshrine any one way of doing that. As I write this chapter, the Saint Benedict leadership is tweaking the exact way we do small groups as a follow-up to Alpha.

From a diocesan-parish perspective, it is important that the diocese communicates to parishes an expectation around what to do "after Alpha"—ensuring that further opportunities to mature in discipleship take place. An essential part of any discipleship process is to help people identify their unique gifts and discern how God is calling them to serve the mission. This step is represented by the ministry icon in the Game Plan.

Finally, we include worship in our game plan. Worship is not only the celebration of the Eucharist, which is the center of our parish life; it is also the celebration of all the other sacraments. All the major structures and systems within a parish should integrate with the sacramental processes.

When a parish does not have a culture of evangelization or discipleship, the major work of the parish focuses on sacramental preparation. These are the only processes that parishioners generally go through, with most being only for children or youth. We have processes for Baptism, First Reconciliation, First Holy Communion, Confirmation, and RCIA (Rite of Christian Initiation for Adults). Some parishes may have a process for forming parishioners for ministry, but it is generally not very well developed. Most parishes also do not have leadership pipelines or a system of small groups as a normative part of parish life. Dioceses must help move parishes in these directions, in order to support cultures of evangelization and discipleship.

A Culture of Authentic Worship

The central act of worship for Catholics is, of course, the Eucharist. Doing liturgy well, in an orderly and beautiful way, is one of the essential components of living as a missionary Church. We need to cultivate a culture of authentic worship and refuse to tolerate sloppy, messy, irreverent liturgy.

In the Divine Renovation model, we support a diversity of music at liturgies, but our principles are the same regardless of musical style. We give primacy to the hymn of praise, and we aim for a high level of excellence. We do this because authentic worship is not about objective measurements of certain styles of music or certain ways of presiding. Rather the fundamental question in a culture of authentic worship is whether people are uniting themselves to the objective worship of the Eucharist—the eternal, once-and-for-all self-offering of Christ to the Father. Are people simply passive spectators, or are they worshiping in a way that is "fully conscious and active"?[46] Are they living their baptismal priesthood?

St. Paul writes:

> I urge you therefore, brothers, by the mercies of God, to offer your bodies as a living sacrifice, holy and pleasing to God, your spiritual worship. Do not conform yourselves to this age but be transformed by the renewal of your mind. (Romans 12:1-2)

The core act of worship is not standing before God and saying, "Here I am, Lord. Come and do *my* will." Rather we must pray in earnest, "Here I am, Lord. I come to do *your* will." In a culture of authentic worship—during the celebration of the Mass, during Eucharistic adoration, or during an evening of praise and worship—people enter into this kind of surrender, laying down their lives before the Lord.

The more we foster this culture of worship, the more people are able to offer themselves to the Lord, opening their hearts to him. They begin to hear God's call. They step forward to lead. They take ownership of the Church's mission out of an experience of love rather than obligation.

The Role of Supporting Cultures

There are several other related or supporting cultures that can nurture, sustain, and grow the primary cultures of evangelization, discipleship, and worship within a parish. I would like to focus on just two of these supporting cultures: a culture of quality and a culture of invitation.

Culture of Quality

Many parishes and dioceses seem to think that the spiritual nature of our message excuses us from striving for excellence. The world may value quality in messaging, advertising, marketing, and entertainment, but the Church should be above the world. We do not need to produce high-quality work or strive for excellence. It is okay for things to be done sloppily or produced shoddily. It is okay for things to be second-rate, because we have the Eucharist, and that is all that matters.

That current cultural value manifests itself in parishes as low-quality sound systems, low-quality music, and low-quality preaching. We have poorly designed and produced bulletins that use clip art from the early days of desktop publishing. Not only have we accepted low quality seemingly across the board, but we have internalized this culture of mediocrity so well that parishioners are upset when a parish strives for excellence.

When we moved from a weekly bulletin to a monthly magazine at Saint Benedict, we decided to create not only a digital version but also a print version, using high-quality glossy paper. Our dream was to create something that you could put on your coffee table or give to someone. Parishioners who were professional photographers volunteered their services, and we used a professional-level magazine design for the cover and interior.

One morning a parishioner I knew well asked if we could talk. She was a holy woman who prayed the Liturgy of the Hours, went to daily Mass, had read the Bible many times, and loved the Lord. I knew she was very shy, so I was surprised when she approached me and said something was bothering her.

"It's the new magazine, Father," she said. "It's awfully fancy. I'm just not comfortable with it because, you know, we are called to embrace simplicity. I just think it's too fancy for us and must cost a lot of money."

I listened carefully as she shared her thoughts. Truth be told, because of sponsors and the volunteer work, the magazine cost nothing to produce. What really took me by surprise, however, was her next sentence.

"You know, Father, you could print the bulletin on toilet paper, and that would be fine for us."

I am not quite sure what this woman was saying about the quality of our communications. I smiled at her and said, "Thanks so much for your feedback. It's really helpful. And I understand that for you, quality is not important. You know something, though, we are not creating the magazine for you. We're aiming for high quality not for the sake of our committed parishioners but to help us reach people on the outside."

When I said that, a light went on for her. She had never thought about it that way before.

That is my point: if we are going to reach people who have been formed by the world, we cannot rely on any shoddy way of doing things. We have to earn our right to be heard. We have to look at what we produce with new eyes and aim for higher levels of quality.

I am not saying that if we cannot do something that way, then we should not do it. I am saying that in the life of a parish or a diocese, can we aim to do the best that we can do? Can we evaluate what we have done and ways we can improve and then pursue that higher standard?

A culture of quality fosters that mindset. It recognizes that we strive for quality not for our sake but for God's sake. I think of the Jesuit motto coined by St. Ignatius of Loyola, *Ad Majoram Dei Gloriam*—"For the greater glory of God." St. Ignatius did not want to settle merely for the glory of God; he wanted the greater glory of God! I think that is a good ambition—to do things to the highest possible standard for the sake of the kingdom.

Why should what we produce be of lower quality than what the world produces? Who has the more important mission: the Church or Nike?

Culture of Invitation

Having a culture of invitation simply means that parishioners at every level of parish life find it normal to invite people who are outside the parish—non-Catholics, non-Christians, atheists, agnostics, and so on—to an event. At Saint Benedict, as at many parishes, we can always invite people to the Mass. Our parishioners trust that the experience of Mass at the parish will be a positive one. There will be a degree of hospitality that will be warm and welcoming to people outside the Church, the music will be good, and the preaching will be good.

Many people without any Catholic background, however, find Mass intimidating, hard to comprehend, and difficult to participate in. In one sense, the celebration of the Mass is inherently inhospitable because it presumes that a certain level of believing and formation has already happened. The Eucharistic liturgy is not meant to be a frontline evangelistic tool. It is essentially the Church at worship. So a distinguishing feature of the Divine Renovation model is that our primary invitation point for those outside the parish is *not* an invitation to attend Sunday Mass.

At Saint Benedict, we chose Alpha as our main invitation point. Even so, there are times when people might not be ready even for

Alpha. Therefore we have a number of ministries that are evangelistic in nature—such as men's and women's breakfasts that feature testimonies—and we encourage parishioners to invite nonchurchgoers to those. In addition, other ministries—such as our grief and addictions support ministries and our marriage enrichment ministry (The Marriage Course[47])—serve the purpose of pre-evangelization and are open to people outside the Church. We also host musical events, such as praise and worship nights and concerts in which our traditional choir performs polyphony and Gregorian chant. These programs are not explicitly evangelistic, but they help us build relationships that could lead to an invitation to attend Alpha.

We have worked hard at normalizing invitation, because once you normalize something, it becomes part of your culture. We also started celebrating and rewarding invitations, even when they do not translate into attendance, as often happens. If you want to change the culture into one of invitation, you cannot simply reward invitations that result in the invited person actually showing up.

In the early years of Saint Benedict, when Ron Huntley and I ran Alpha together, we would hold a contest at the end of the Alpha season. The person who invited the most people, not just who had the most guests in attendance, would win a meal cooked by Ron and me in their home.

A culture of invitation is necessary in order to support a culture of evangelization, because a parish's outward focus will shrivel up if invitation is not normative. There is a gravitational pull in every parish that draws its members to become inwardly focused. A culture of invitation can overcome that inward pull.

We see that inward focus often in parishes that use a great tool like Alpha but never pursue a culture of invitation. After several years, when 30 to 40 percent of parishioners have experienced Alpha, the Alpha process grinds to a halt because it was only about parish members, and that market has been saturated. When we first started Alpha ten years ago at Saint Benedict, parishioners made up 90 percent of our guests and nonchurchgoers only 10 percent. In recent years, we have seen about 60 to 65 percent of our guests come from the nonchurchgoing demographic.

A culture of invitation helps ensure the ongoing health of your evangelization processes.

CHAPTER 17

The Power of Measurement

Building primary cultures of evangelization, discipleship, and authentic worship, as well as the supporting cultures of quality and invitation, is not an easy task. We also know that if parishes are to live out these realities, dioceses must help them establish clear expectations and accountability. In order to hold parish leaders accountable, those involved must have a sense of their expectations—their objectives—and must measure those objectives as they unfold, both at the parish and diocesan levels.

Most people who undertake a major initiative, task, or great adventure stop at some point and ask themselves how they are doing. Whether formally or informally, there are numerous ways they can keep track of their progress relative to their goals. Think about the dashboard in a car. Have you ever lost track of your progress as you drove down the highway, while your brain was engaged with your thoughts? You might gaze at the speedometer and realize that you are traveling thirty miles over the speed limit! What do you do? You adjust your speed.

Or perhaps you know that your destination is sixty miles from home, and so you check the dashboard for your mileage, to see how much farther you have to go. Or the check-engine light might suddenly come on, and you know you have to pull over to evaluate the problem.

When you want to be intentional about parish renewal, you need a dashboard, a way to measure whether you are on track and how everything is working.

When it comes to organizational movement and transformation, we must make sure that we measure not only what is happening but also the right things. In his book *Keeping Score: How to Know if Your Church Is Winning*, Dave Ferguson mentions a man named Jim Marshall, who played football in the NFL. On October 25, 1965, he picked up a fumbled ball and ran it all the way into the end zone.

The curious thing was that no one cheered. In fact, his teammates had shouted for him to stop. Marshall had somehow become disoriented, and he ran the ball into his own end zone. From that moment on—even after his retirement—people called him Wrong-way Marshall.

That story reminds me of a lot of parishes whose nicknames should be Wrong-way. We fumble balls left and right, we are disoriented, and we run in every direction as we try to keep up. Most of our parishes are very busy, but we are often busy doing things that do not make any difference. We are headed in the wrong direction. We need to know which end zone is ours and measure our progress toward that end zone.

The heart of the mission of the Church is to go out and make disciples who intentionally respond to the call to holiness and mission. We cannot be self-referential and inward focused. We must be missionary disciples who make disciples, and our disciples must, in turn, make disciples who grow in holiness, discover their gifts, and receive formation to go out and make new disciples.

A key question is, how do we measure this? Traditionally, both at the diocesan level and at the Vatican, we request statistics: how many baptisms, how many weddings, and so forth. We are measuring participation. I do not know of any diocese trying to measure the number of missionary disciples they have made.

Before we can measure, or create a dashboard, for how many missionary disciples we have made, we have to agree on what missionary discipleship looks like. How will we recognize a missionary disciple when we see one?

Many years ago at Saint Benedict, we discussed and identified the qualities or attributes of a missionary disciple. It is not an exhaustive list, but you might find it useful as you begin to discern what your parish should measure. A missionary disciple is:

- someone who has a personal relationship with Jesus;

- someone who can share their faith and share what God has done in their life with others;

- someone who is open to the gifts of the Holy Spirit;

- someone who has a knowledge and love of the Scriptures:

   A missionary disciple does not have to have a theology degree from a university, nor do they have to sign up for every Bible study class. In our experience, however, when people come alive in their faith, the Word of God comes alive as well. This kind of person is growing in their knowledge and love of Scripture.

- someone who knows basic Catholic theology:

   I think of a man I met a few years ago who had not attended church in over thirty years. Within weeks of his conversion in Alpha, he started reading the Catechism. This man had never read a book in his life, and within months he read the entire Catechism. When people fall in love with Jesus, they demonstrate a hunger to get to know him and the richness of our Catholic faith. They thirst for knowledge of and encounter with him.

- someone who is working toward a daily prayer life:

   In his encyclical Novo Millennio Ineunte [Into the New Millennium], Pope St. John Paul II said that Christians who have a shallow prayer life become Christians at risk. We want people to mature in prayer and have a daily prayer life.

- someone who experiences real Christian community:

   This means someone involved in a small group of some kind. The task of parish renewal has been described as getting people to move from sitting in rows to sitting in circles, so they can experience real Christian community, where they are accountable to and for one another.

- someone who demonstrates a commitment to weekly Sunday Eucharist;

- someone who celebrates the Sacrament of Reconciliation with some regularity;

- someone who can pray spontaneously out loud when asked without having a heart attack;

- someone who sees their life as a mission field:

  A missionary disciple gets out of bed every morning, makes that morning offering, and sees the whole day ahead as filled with opportunity. The proper mission of the baptized is not life within the parish but rather life out in the world. They see their everyday life—among their coworkers, friends, family, and colleagues—as their mission field.

- someone who serves in some capacity within or outside the parish according to their gifts.

These qualities do not constitute membership requirements. In other words, we do not say that only people with these qualities can become members of our parish. These attributes, however, are consistent with what mature discipleship looks like. They are what we want to see in every person. They are what we aim for.

Traditional Measurements

If we aim for this maturity, what do we measure to tell us if we are on the right track?

Traditionally, parishes measure not only baptisms and such but also attendance, registration, and the Sunday collection. In essence we measure the people who show up, the people who sign up, and the people who cough up! There is nothing wrong with measuring these things. I would say, however, that these measurements are woefully inadequate to the task that is before us—namely, moving parishes from maintenance to mission.

If we use only the traditional measurements, we will not have an adequate dashboard. It will be like driving a car whose speedometer, odometer, and engine temperature gauge do not work.

Giving

There is one traditional measurement that can reflect a general sense of health or indicate a change in health for the parish—and that is the level of financial giving, particularly the per capita collection. For example, if one hundred new people come to your parish and the collection goes up, that is not necessarily a sign of health. You simply drew a larger crowd. When per capita giving goes up, on the other hand, that is a significant metric. A shift towards health can also be indicated when the number of committed registered givers rises in proportion to Sunday attendance or when there is a shift towards automated giving.

Jesus said that our heart follows our treasure (see Matthew 6:21). Such increased commitment to giving leads to, and is a sign of, greater spiritual commitment. People are literally buying in more to the vision and direction of the parish. Greater financial commitment can be a sign of spiritual maturity or an indication that something has happened in the hearts of your people.

Attendance

Attendance in and of itself is not really a measurement of health. If the making of disciples is a key indicator of health, for example, then there are many large parishes that are not healthy. Likewise, there are many small parishes that demonstrate great health.

Even shifts in attendance do not always paint an accurate picture of a parish's health. For example, if you are a parish of two hundred people and you grow to 250 people in one year, that is a significant shift in attendance. The question is whether it is due to healthy growth.

There are places where population shifts and immigration cause parish populations to swell. These areas are even building new churches. However, the growth is not organic from evangelization or mission. It is, in a sense, artificial.

When some parishes begin to mobilize for mission, they attract people from other parishes. This can look great, but it is not the fruit of mission. If all we have accomplished is to offer a better "product" than neighboring parishes, this growth can be misleading. Rick Warren used to say that this kind of transfer growth is not real growth but swelling, and swelling is always a sign that something is wrong.

Nevertheless, attendance is a useful metric to track. Just be cautious what conclusions you draw from it.

In the work of Divine Renovation ministry, we encourage all our parishes to track attendance weekly. At Saint Benedict, the Knights of Columbus are in charge of the attendance count for every Mass. We devised a method that allows them to count the different sections of the church without being noticed. They track the total number of individuals at Mass on a chart, as well as the number of children in our children's ministry. We put that information into a spreadsheet that collates the weekly attendance and weekly collection. It is great data to have on hand.

Many parishes do not have any idea what their weekly attendance is, or they estimate that it is 20 to 30 percent higher than it actually is. We want real numbers, so that our dashboard gives us an authentic measurement.

Registration

Parish registration is probably the least valuable of all the traditional measurements. The number of people who register has no bearing on anything; it merely tells you the number of people who filled out a card or online form. Registration does not even give you insight as to whether people attend Mass, and it cannot reveal whether people are growing spiritually and in their commitment to mission.

When I speak to parishes in the United States, I often ask pastors about the size of their parish. Almost every pastor will give me the total number of registered families. The fact is that families register in parishes for many reasons—to attend a sacramental program, for example. It could have been five years ago, and they have not been back since.

We have found little correlation between registration and participation. In fact, there are active parishioners in our parishes who have never registered at all. This is especially true for younger families, many of whom do not even know that you are supposed to register in a parish; it is not on their radar.

If you have five thousand families in your parish, but only about twelve hundred people attend Mass somewhat regularly, which is the more meaningful number? Of course, it is the twelve hundred who come on a mostly regular basis. We should use that number as the starting point as we measure parish participation.

Sacraments

Dioceses generally ask parishes to send the chancery two kinds of measurements: participation in sacramental celebrations and financial data. Detailed sacramental data goes to the diocese because Rome asks each diocese for that data in preparation for the ad limina visits of bishops every five years or more. We measure the number of infant Baptisms, the number of Confirmations, first Holy Communions, marriages, and funerals. We are, for the most part, counting sacraments.

In a Christendom Church—in which faith and secular culture overlapped, the vast majority of people went to church, the core charisms of parish leaders were shepherd/teachers, and all that was required of pastoral ministry was to catechize and sacramentalize people. The number of sacraments celebrated was a fairly important measurement. It gave a sense of the basic vitality of the Church.

In this new era, however, we are called to make missionary disciples. Simply measuring sacraments is not going to work anymore. We know this for a fact: many Catholics have been sacramentalized and catechized, but they have never been evangelized, and they are not being discipled. Offering sacraments and catechesis does not necessarily make a difference in people's lives. Obviously it is important work, and we know that when people are evangelized and catechized, they hunger for the grace of the sacraments. We should not ignore this data, but we should not use it as our primary measurement, either at the parish or diocesan level.

There is one area within the category of sacramental participation that might be a useful metric: the numbers of adult Baptisms and Confirmations. They can be an indicator of adult conversion and the effectiveness of evangelization.

A number of years ago, a priest from Montreal did a six-month internship at Saint Benedict. After the Easter Vigil, at which we baptized a number of adults, Fr. Mike called his parish secretary to ask her to look up when the last adult was baptized at his parish. Her answer was 1978. Since then Fr. Mike has baptized adults every single Easter Vigil.

Funerals

Another traditional measurement we have in parishes is the number of funerals. Now, it is an interesting metric, but what does it really tell us?

All it tells us is how fast we are dying relative to our Sunday attendance. In many places across the Western world, the number of funerals outpaces the number of infant Baptisms by a vast margin.

Critical Metrics

Given the limitations of the traditional metrics of the past, what measurements can we use that will truly help us mark our progress? What are the vital areas we should examine?

We have established that evangelization, leadership, discipleship, and authentic worship are core cultures necessary for any parish that hopes to move from maintenance to mission. Further, parishes must have a discipleship process if they hope to form those cultures. What we need to measure then is how well our core strategy for making disciples is helping raise up those cultures.

I would like to highlight some of the metrics we developed at Saint Benedict in order to give you a sense of how you might develop metrics that work in relation to your own parish's strategy.

Alpha

Since Alpha is central to our Game Plan, it was critical that we develop metrics to help us gauge Alpha's impact. The first metric was to calculate the number of guests we had for each Alpha. The second, related, metric was to calculate the percentage of guests who completed the whole Alpha process. That has been a very interesting measurement.

We often see a 20 to 30 percent drop-off from the number of guests who begin Alpha and the number who stick with it. Over time we determined this to be a general baseline percentage drop-off. Monitoring deviations from that baseline—whether positive or negative—helps us evaluate how well we executed a particular Alpha and where we might need to improve.

The number of guests who participate in the Holy Spirit Weekend or the Holy Spirit Day—a key experience that takes place at the midpoint of Alpha—is also an important measurement. The vast majority of people who experience conversion during Alpha attribute it to the encounter they had with God during the weekend away. Therefore, if you are running Alphas in which only 40 percent of the guests attend this retreat, you have a bit of a problem. That metric will flash like a warning signal on your dashboard, and you will need to address it. Rarely do more than 80 percent of your Alpha guests attend the weekend away, however, so do not hold yourself to an unreachable standard here.

The next important metric is determining the percentage of your Alpha guests who are unchurched—those individuals who do not have any significant church connection. Lots of folks roll up into this category, including fallen-away Catholics (some of whom consider themselves atheist or agnostic); Catholics who come to Mass maybe once or twice a year; Christians who are not a part of their faith communities; people from other faith traditions, such as Hindus, Muslims, and Jews; as well as agnostics and atheists.

The biggest challenge here is how to gather this data from our guests without becoming intrusive. We solved this problem by putting the following question on our registration form: Would you describe yourself as a committed churchgoer, a frequent churchgoer, or someone who does not attend church?

The answers helped us place people in small groups: there is nothing worse than putting an unchurched person in a group that is overwhelmingly filled with "churchy" people. This metric also gave us a sense of how well we were reaching beyond the confines of the parish to invite outsiders. An advantage of using unchurched as a category is that it is an objective measurement; it does not rely on asking people if they identify as a believer.

We also capture the percentage of our Alpha guests who are under thirty-five, for the simple reason that if we do not reach the next generation, we are not going to exist as a Church. When we first began Alpha, the average age of our team and guests was sixty-five. Nine years later, the average age of our Alpha team and guests is roughly twenty-eight. One of the ways you can try to drive down the age is to choose younger Alpha guests to join the Alpha team for the next round.

Another measurement we took was related to our Alpha team: what percentage was made up of first-time team members? This helped us take stock of how well we were developing our leadership pipeline. We wanted 50 percent of our Alpha team to be first-time members.

If you are not deliberate about moving people on from the Alpha team, individuals can confuse their conversion experience with the tool that helped bring them to conversion. They become "Alpha-holics," people who want to camp out on team and never leave. When that happens, it thwarts the ability of Alpha to raise up leaders and change the culture of your parish.

Connect Groups and Small Groups

Connect Groups, Discipleship Groups, and other small groups represent our effort to foster community and adult discipleship within the larger parish structure. We track the number of groups we have and how many of our people have joined them—a simple but key measurement. We have found that it is also important to track how many people show up for their group meetings on average. For example, for a midsize group of thirty-five people, you might have an average attendance of twenty-five. For a small group of twelve members, there may be an average attendance of eight.

Other important elements to track are the number of group leaders you have, the number of leaders you need, and the number of leaders who are being mentored. Our leadership pipeline does not end with Alpha. Helping individuals grow into Connect Group or small group leaders is an important facet of raising up a culture of leadership within our parish.

Ministry and Sunday Attendance

While it is important to measure the total number of parishioners who serve in ministry, by itself it tells us nothing about the objective health of your parish. It is better to look at the percentage of your parishioners who serve in ministries relative to your Sunday attendance. This metric is quite useful for measuring the health and life of a parish.

Take, for example, a parish that has 20 percent of its parishioners involved in ministry. That is probably a little higher than average for a Catholic parish, but let us keep that number for simplicity. Now, imagine if, within two years, the percentage of parishioners involved in ministry doubled, going from 20 percent to 40 percent. While there is no way to objectively measure spiritual growth, such a significant shift represents a real movement in the hearts of people.

A number of years ago, the staff team developed some metrics around serving in ministry at Saint Benedict. We created a dashboard and placed it in the staff room. That dashboard measured a number of things:

- the total percentage of parishioners serving in ministry relative to Sunday attendance

- the number of new people stepping up to serve in ministry during that year

- the number of people currently serving in ministry who took a significant step up in their leadership—moving from leading a small project to a larger project, for example.

- the number of people under the age of thirty-five serving in ministry

By the end of this initiative, we had 865 individual parishioners serving in ministry out of an average weekend attendance of 1400 (62 percent). Since I stepped aside as pastor, this has grown to about 1,000 out of an average attendance of 1500 (67 percent). Being able to measure this has helped us manage it, plan around it, and grow it.

I spoke with a parish priest from an exceptionally large parish in the United States. If I recall correctly, they had something like five thousand people attending Mass over a weekend. I asked him how things were going, and he told me that they were going very well. I thought that was great and followed up with a question regarding the percentage of his people who were involved in adult faith formation. He said lots of people, so I pressed in and asked him how many. He replied with a general number—around three hundred. I remember thinking that three hundred people in a parish that has a Sunday attendance of five thousand is not very good at all.

The truth is that a large population can disguise the health problems of a parish, and small parishes can hide the presence of health. Years ago I led a parish mission for a small rural parish, with a Sunday attendance of about 250 people. When the mission evenings started, roughly 100 to 150 people showed up. The pastor was clearly disappointed and kept apologizing to me, but I told him that proportionately, this was the greatest turnout I had ever experienced with a parish mission.

It is very easy for small parishes who have fewer members overall to lose sight of actual health. Again, this is why it is important to track involvement in groups and ministry in proportion to Sunday attendance. The goal of parish renewal is not to attain a particular size but to move to a place of health.

All the metrics listed above are important to track at the parish level. The question for diocesan leadership is how to help parishes value and capture that kind of data. Imagine a diocesan report that requested measurements like these from parishes: the bishop would like to know what evangelistic tool you have chosen and what percentage of participants were nonchurchgoers this year. Lots of parishes would have to answer the second half of that question with the number zero.

However, if diocesan leadership starts asking those kinds of questions, I think it will affect the numbers. What we measure communicates what is important. What we communicate to be important creates and shapes the culture of our diocese and our parishes.

Measuring Engagement

Gallup's ME[25] Member Engagement Survey is a measurement tool that we have used over the years at Saint Benedict and that we encourage our Divine Renovation Network parishes to use. We spoke of this tool earlier in this book. I wanted to mention it again here because it measures organizational health relative to member engagement. Therefore it can be very useful in measuring progress and buy-in by the community.

Remember that by "engaged" Gallup does not mean involved or active. The word refers to members who are onboard and excited about what is going on. Neither is engagement the end game. Instead it drives spiritual commitment, which in turn produces fruit. If you are trying to mobilize your parish for mission, and you are successfully communicating that vision, your engaged parishioners will demonstrate the most excitement.

Recall the Rogers Innovation Adoption Curve (chapter four). Your engaged parishioners will likely be made up of the 16 percent who are innovators and early adopters, and they will eventually also comprise a good chunk of the 34 percent who make up the early majority. These parishioners tend to give more to the parish, serve in ministry, engage in the discipleship process, and thus grow spiritually. They are fun to be around.

Unengaged parishioners are quite different. If you ask an unengaged parishioner if they are happy with their parish, they will most likely answer yes. They are not jumping up and down with excitement, nor are they wearing "I love my parish" pins. They have not bought into the vision yet, but they are not opposed.

Actively Disengaged parishioners, on the other hand, represent the laggards—the final 16 percent in the Rogers Innovation Adoption Curve. They are grumpy and disgruntled. When you start to move the parish from maintenance to mission, some of these unhappy folks will leave and be unhappy somewhere else. A number of them, however, will feel called by God to stay in your parish and spread the unhappiness.

We talk about leadership as influence. The Actively Disengaged have a lot of influence. In fact, Gallup says that the point an organization moves into health occurs when the proportion of engaged parishioners to actively disengaged parishioners is four to one. You need four engaged parishioners to detoxify the effects of one actively disengaged person.

The very first year we tried to move from maintenance to mission at Saint Benedict was frightening precisely because of this reality. We were very far from that four-to-one ratio. In fact, the ratio was 0.83 to one. We had more actively disengaged parishioners than engaged parishioners.

However, in the five years that followed, we saw a substantial shift in that proportion. Roughly 40 to 42 percent of our parishioners became actively engaged. We eventually arrived at the point where someone walking through our door was about two-and-a-half times more likely to encounter an engaged person than an actively disengaged one. That changed the basic health of the culture and the feel of the parish.

We used Gallup's ME[25] metric in the early years to measure organizational health. It requires a financial investment, but I would say it is worth it. It is not a "required" part of the Divine Renovation model, but we encourage the parishes that we work with to use it every eighteen to twenty-four months. After you complete the survey, Gallup creates a report that shows your results, as well as the average Catholic numbers in the Gallup database and the average numbers for all Christian churches. These reports make it easy to compare your growth relative to your own community as well as to other churches in Gallup's database.

As you drill into the data, you begin to see how small changes can make a big difference in terms of engagement. You also can identify and celebrate growth in areas where you have improved as a community. In addition, the survey asks for basic demographic data, and we discovered that about 95 percent of participants answered those questions, giving us information that has been invaluable.

For example, the survey asks for the number of years a participant has been in the parish. This data provides a great way to track turnover of parishioners—something of particular interest to us, because if you try to move from maintenance to mission, you will experience turnover. When you clarify your vision and mobilize for mission, you will attract and repel. Some people will leave your parish and go where they know they will not be called out of their comfort zones. Others will come to your parish specifically because of what you are trying to do.

In addition, if you are building a culture of evangelization, people will join your parish because they encounter Christ there and are falling in love with him. That is exactly what we saw at Saint Benedict. And in the early years, we saw a high degree of turnover.

The data from the ME[25] Survey can, over time, also help you identify problems. For example, the data helped us understand that, despite the fruitfulness of Alpha and the number of conversions in our community, there were lots of people we were not keeping. We had a well-functioning front door, but we had a back-door problem. People came to our community and had positive experiences, but lots of people were not moving on to the next stage.

This is a common problem in evangelizing churches, but that should not prevent us from asking how we can improve. The data helped us flag the issue and work on solutions. When Fr. Simon Lobo became pastor of Saint Benedict after I left, he wanted to address this issue. Jesus made us fishers of people, Fr. Simon said, but he was pretty sure that Jesus did not mean "catch and release."

Other Important Metrics

At this point, you might be thinking, "Good grief! You guys measure so much!"

Remember, the purpose of these metrics is to help us get a sense of what is actually happening. We are not interested in what we *think* is happening. We want to know the reality. If we want to grow in fruit-fulness, data can be extremely helpful. Here are a few final suggestions for what you can measure.

New Parishioner Events

Every Sunday we started to invite people—those who had been attending our parish and who were looking for a spiritual home—to touch base with us at our welcome center in the foyer of the church. There they could fill out a connection card. If they were serious about becoming members of the parish, we would invite them to a new parishioner event, which would take place every two or three months.

These wine-and-cheese events lasted for about an hour and included time to socialize, a word of greeting from the pastor, and brief comments from staff regarding the missionary identity of the parish and the belief that everyone has a role to play in that mission. Each event was an opportunity to get to know people interested in joining the parish and help them understand that being a member of the parish did not mean being a bystander but rather supporting the parish financially, sharing their gifts through service in ministry, connecting with the community, and joining us for Sunday worship. We shared these points as our five expectations for our parishioners, in a low-key, nonthreatening way.

To help us track how well we were doing, we measured how many parishioners attended these events. We also took a group photograph and used it to recall which parishioners attended these events but have since dropped off the face of the earth. It was a way of measuring how well these events helped "onboard" new parishioners.

The Return of the Fatted Calf

One development at Saint Benedict, which is beginning to spread among Divine Renovation parishes throughout the world, focuses on a significant metric and challenges parishes to step out and also celebrate it. In chapter five, we considered the father of the prodigal son ordering the fatted calf to be killed and what that would mean for a parish.

A number of years ago, Ron Huntley, who was on our parish team at the time, came to me and he said, "Fr. James, so many people here have experienced transformation, whether their faith was renewed after many years or they were outside the Church and gave their lives to Christ for the first time. There is always a sacramental moment to their journey, and for many it was adult Baptism or Confirmation. However, many people experienced a more private moment in the Sacrament of Reconciliation, and we don't really celebrate that sacrament publicly. Is there something we can do to acknowledge their journey and celebrate it as a community?"

We wrestled with that as a leadership team, and eventually someone proposed what we called the Pentecost challenge. On the Feast of Pentecost, we would preach about this feast being the celebration of the birthday of the Church. We would point out that the Church is called to be reborn in every single generation—reborn through faith, through the waters of Baptism, and through people being activated in living out their Baptism. This rebirth is the process of making disciples, which the Church is called to do.

After pointing that out, we would invite anyone who, in the previous twelve months, had had a life-changing encounter with Jesus Christ to come forward. We would not be talking about someone who was "enriched" by taking a Bible study or faith formation class. We meant full-on, transformative encounter with Jesus.

A couple of weeks previous, this idea sounded very exciting, but to be honest, as the days went by and the Feast of Pentecost drew near, I started getting nervous. I worried whether anyone would come forward. It was a risk for sure, especially since the first weekend Mass took place on Saturday afternoon. Although a wonderful group of people attend that Mass at Saint Benedict Parish, many of those who attended this liturgy were not necessarily excited about our missionary vision and tended more to tolerate what was happening.

When the day came, I gave the homily and made the invitation— and there was a very awkward silence. No one moved in the whole church. Five seconds went by, and then ten seconds. I broke into a sweat. Around the fifteen-second mark, someone started to laugh, but then a young man in his twenties got up and came to the front. There was an audible gasp in the congregation as he came forward. Then a lady in her seventies came forward, and before you knew it, fourteen people were standing in the front of the church. We thanked God for their witness as we prayed a blessing over them. Over that weekend, a total of 118 people (out of 1400 to 1500 people) came forward.

Now, did we interview each and every one of them to determine the legitimacy of their claim? No, we did not, but for someone to stand up in front of the parish is a sign that something significant happened to them!

We have been doing this Pentecost Challenge every single year, and we continue to see lots of people coming forward. Indeed, the parishes in our coaching network are starting to do this, and they are seeing lots of people come forward as well. Parishes around the world are sending us some astonishing stories of people self-identifying as new disciples.

The fundamental point is not about the numbers, which we do count. It is about the celebration itself. We are living from the heart of the Father when we kill the fatted calf for those who were lost but have been found!

One of our dreams at Divine Renovation ministry is to directly or indirectly equip and inspire thirty-five thousand parishes around the world by 2028. Those thirty-five thousand parishes represent 16 percent of all Catholic parishes in the world. Remember the early adopters? If all those thirty-five thousand parishes make fifty-seven disciples a year, that will be two million new disciples per year. What a dream! What a goal! The only way we will know if we have achieved it is to somehow measure the number of disciples we are making.

Some people push back and say that this seems to be all about the numbers. It is absolutely *not* about numbers. It is about people. My friend and colleague Rob McDowell often says that "we count people, because people count." We do not simply want to measure attendance, registration, collections, or sacraments. We want to find the key indicators of spiritual growth and measure those.

The more diocesan leadership can assist parishes in developing and capturing these metrics, and the more they celebrate those results, the more intentional parishes can be about moving from maintenance to mission. This in turn will have a powerful effect on changing the overall culture in a diocese.

PART 5

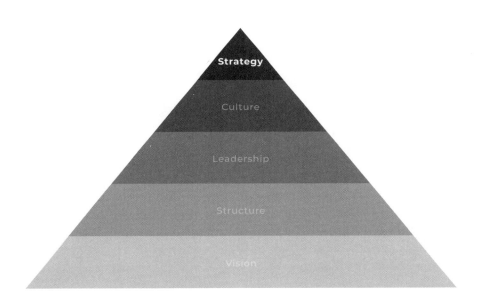

STRATEGY

CHAPTER 18

Healthy Relationships

Our journey through this book has been an exploration of linked realities. Diocesan and parish renewal require vision to ignite passion and clarify mission. Even the clearest, most inspiring vision requires a structure that will enable the mission to be lived out by supporting the role of authentic leadership. Leadership, in turn, shapes culture, and culture is the soil in which strategy flourishes or withers.

As we dive into the area of strategy, we should keep in mind that this is a cooperative endeavor between the diocese and its parishes. A parish cannot develop a missionary culture without the support of the diocese, and it should not develop a strategy that does not reference the diocese in some way.

When we talk about strategy, we need to make a distinction between broad strategy and lower-end strategy. As with vision, which flows from the mission of the universal Church and should be contextualized by the bishop's vision in the local Church, dioceses should create a broad strategy, or general road map, for accomplishing the vision. Parishes then bring that vision to their neighborhoods by developing localized, lower-end strategies.

Problems can occur, however, when a diocese moves from the level of broad strategy and gets involved with developing the strategy within specific parishes. One reason for problems are the different socio-economic and cultural realities among parishes within a particular diocese. There is a tendency for dioceses to expect a uniformity that is detrimental to renewal and transformation. Diocesan leadership that tries to involve itself in more than a broad strategy across these different parish realities cannot respond effectively to the unique needs, gifts, and histories of its varied parishes and their leaders.

The principle of subsidiarity—that decisions should be made as much as possible by the people who are impacted by those decisions—plays a critical role here. Within the framework of subsidiarity, parish strategies are not less important than broad diocesan strategies. They take into account the lived realities of the local community.

For this approach to bear fruit, the parish and diocese must interact and listen attentively to each other. Throughout my seventeen years as a pastor, passionately working and leading renewal in three parishes of different types—rural, urban, and suburban—I have experienced a lot of "interesting" tension between what we try to accomplish at the parish level and what happens at the diocesan level. I have learned what not to do as well as what one should do in relationship with the diocese.

For almost three years now, I have worked half-time for the Archdiocese of Halifax-Yarmouth. I have discovered, to my horror, that now I am "the other guy." Accompanying parish leaders from this perspective, as well as in my role at Divine Renovation ministry, I have discovered a whole new set of skills and approaches that can foster the movement of parishes from maintenance to mission.

Ultimately the goal of diocesan leadership is not to create detailed strategies for each of our parishes. Rather our job is to facilitate the work of parish leaders in the creation of their own parish strategy. When we can do that well, without micromanaging or drilling too far into areas that rightly belong to the parish, we can call it a win.

Resistance to Strategy

Earlier in this book, we mentioned the adage "Culture eats strategy for breakfast." Though it is important to acknowledge the power of culture, we must not understate the importance of strategy. If we want to realize our vision, if we want to arrive at our destination, we need a plan.

In order to explore the intersection of diocesan and parish strategy, we must acknowledge the fact that many people in the Church view strategy with suspicion. I recently read an article by Dale Sellers, an evangelical author, entitled "5 Reasons Churches Avoid Developing a Strategy."[48] It appeared on the website of The Unstuck Group, a ministry that offers consulting services to Protestant churches, but it holds a great deal of truth for Catholic parishes. I have adapted his points as follows:

1. Strategy is opposed to the work of the Holy Spirit.

Many Catholics think that strategic thinking and planning is opposed to the work of the Holy Spirit. Of course, that is not true. This way of thinking is more than a failure to recognize that grace builds on nature; it is more than a mistaken belief that we must be purely spiritual. Rather it involves a fundamental misunderstanding of the nature of the Holy Spirit.

This misunderstanding manifests in two major ways. One is the idea that if we plan too much, we will "squeeze out" the Holy Spirit. Conversely, the other is the idea that if we are truly guided by the Holy Spirit, everything we do will be spontaneous. This is just not the way it is

Planning and the Holy Spirit are not opposed. Is it possible to put so much emphasis on our own thinking that we do not leave room for the Holy Spirit? Of course. However, that has nothing to do with the nature of planning and everything to do with the attentiveness and openness of those doing the planning.

2. Planning and strategy employ "unspiritual" business practices.

This point of view develops from a misunderstanding of Christian anthropology. Remember that grace does build on nature and perfects it; it does not replace it. Therefore any secular discipline that can help authentically heal, grow, free, and transform the human person has a role and place within the Christian life.

In addition, there is no room for a dualistic understanding of the human realm in Christian theology and practice. There is nothing that is purely spiritual or unspiritual. Of course, these secular disciplines cannot replace our theology, Tradition, or the spiritual patrimony of the Church. Rather, if we place these disciplines within the context of the Catholic faith and see them through the lens of our Tradition, we can use them to help us cooperate with the grace of God.[49]

3. Developing a strategy requires honest evaluation of our current condition and effectiveness.

This relates to the previous chapter on measurement. Many Church leaders refuse to develop strategy because they do not want to seriously confront the reality in which we find ourselves. This is a difficult time for churches of all stripes, let alone Catholic parishes. We are losing ground and losing people because we are using an operating system from a bygone culture. This is an essential part of our problem, but our leaders often refuse to evaluate our situation honestly. A cultural predisposition to avoid evaluating effectiveness fosters this way of thinking. We tend to believe that if we are *doing* things, we are vital. Yet there is a difference between an output and an outcome.

In parishes and dioceses, we measure output—all the things we are doing. We often talk positively about the activities and work in which we engage. Unfortunately, we rarely stop to ask ourselves if we are effective. What are the outcomes? Does what we do make a difference? Are we moving the ball down the field when it comes to our fundamental mission—making missionary disciples? These are critical questions, and they highlight the difference between an output and an outcome.

4. Developing a strategy will rock the boat and challenge our comfort zones.

How is it that a Church following Jesus of Nazareth can be so intimidated by the idea of rocking the boat? Jesus is the ultimate rocker of boats. Look at his life and ministry. He provoked reactions all the time. He ate with sinners and tax collectors and spent time with Samaritans. Jesus raised the dead, cast out demons, cleansed lepers, and healed the sick.

We believe in an amazing God who wants to do amazing things, so why are we unable to envision doing something amazing in his name and plan accordingly?

I think of the feeding of the multitude from the Gospel of Luke. Faced with the needs of the crowds who gathered to hear Jesus, the apostles say to the Lord, "You have to do something. Send them away so that they can buy food." Jesus, however, turns to his disciples and says, "Give them some food yourselves" (Luke 9:13).

I believe that the Lord is saying the same thing to us today: "You do something, and as you do it, rely on me. I'm not just going to do it for you; I am going to do it with you, and I'm going to work miracles through you. But you have to be willing to step out and do it."

We must not merely create a vision for doing amazing things, as important as that is. We must also create plans that deliberately cooperate with the power of God in Jesus Christ to accomplish them.

5. A written strategic plan brings accountability.

As we mentioned in the section of this book on leadership, we struggle in the Church today because, while we might have low control, we often lack high accountability. A written strategic plan allows us to ensure accountability. When we create plans with clear timelines, visible critical milestones, and measurable objectives, we can evaluate how we are doing relative to that plan.

Fostering Parish and Diocesan Interaction in Planning

Sometimes a diocese will recognize the importance of strategy and call on parishes to produce strategic plans within a defined timeframe. Often though, there is no communication of vision or investment by the diocese in raising up and developing parish leaders. Strategic plans, by themselves, are not silver bullets, and they will probably collect dust if they are not undergirded by an inspiring vision, a supportive structure, authentic leadership, and a nurturing culture. Given this, I would like to look at the key elements that we will encounter at the intersection of parishes and dioceses.

First, however, we must remember that vision is essential to strategy. Vision focuses on the destination. A clear and inspiring vision makes the construction of a solid strategy easier. Parishes, as we have mentioned several times, are not free to create their own vision apart from the bishop's vision: they need to live out of the Church's ecclesial communion. Ideally, a parish's vision flows from that of the bishop.

In addition, parishes cannot create strategies independent of a relationship with their bishop, because the bishop is the chief shepherd and leader of the local church. If a pastor tries to mobilize his parish to move from maintenance to mission without a healthy relationship with his bishop, there will be a host of problems. Relationships, of course, go both ways. Developing a loving, mutually supportive relationship between the parish and the bishop is essential in bearing the fruit we are called to bear.

Let us examine three possibilities that can exist relative to a parish's relationship with the diocesan vision and its relationship with the bishop himself:

Relationship with Diocesan Vision

1. It makes you excited.

Ten years ago, while I was at a conference overseas, my bishop released a pastoral letter on the occasion of the Feast of Pentecost. This letter was essentially a vision statement for the diocese. I was astounded, as I read that letter, because my bishop's dream for the diocese matched what I had so long desired for the Church. This letter inspired a passion within me. I was excited and eager to move forward. Truly, it was a gift to me.

2. It does not excite you.

In this scenario, the bishop has communicated the diocesan vision, and it does not elicit any excitement or passion in you at all. I am in touch with a number of priests in different parts of the world who have missionary hearts and are sadly uninspired by their diocesan vision.

3. It does not exist.

There are many dioceses in the world that flounder, without any clear vision or rallying cry from their bishop at all.

The best-case scenario, of course, is the one in which your bishop lays out a vision that inspires you and fills you with passion. Believe it or not, I would rather have a bishop who has no vision than a bishop who has a bad vision. If your bishop does not have a vision but you have a good relationship with him, you can at least rely on magisterial documentation from beyond the diocese.

For example, if your bishop does not have any vision, and you come to him with the vision put forth by Pope Francis in *Evangelii Gaudium*, what is he going to say? That it's not Catholic? We have other places to go if the bishop has no vision.

If the bishop communicates an overall vision that does not excite you, there will most likely be parts of the vision that you can get excited about. Spend time focusing on those parts of the vision, and then draw on other magisterial documents that call the Church to mission.

Relationship with the Bishop

1. He gives you enthusiastic support.

This is the ideal. You sit down with the bishop and share your vision for the parish, and he is so passionate about it that he throws his full support behind you. He lets you know that he will have your back and help any way that he can.

2. He gives permission.

In this scenario, the bishop does not show much active support for what you want to accomplish, but he does not stand in the way. This may not be a matter of your particular bishop's ideology, theological stance, or missionary passion. It may be related to his personality and leadership style.

3. He opposes your vision.

This is a challenging situation: the bishop does not want you to proceed in the direction your parish wants to go. He may even throw roadblocks in your way. Navigating this relationship takes a great deal of prayer and discernment.

The truth is, before we can lead others, we have to allow ourselves to be led. If we are going to call others to obey the gospel, we have to live that obedience ourselves. It is never good for diocesan leaders to work around pastors by going directly to lay leaders. Likewise, it is never a good move for priests to try to bypass or work around their bishop.

If your bishop opposes your vision, I encourage you to make time to sit down and speak with him. You might find that most of the opposition stems from a misunderstanding or from an interpersonal issue that can be resolved.

Pray for your bishop and invest in him, as discussed in chapter fourteen. Buy in at the diocesan level, serve, do not isolate yourself, and work to build trust. Through God's grace and a lot of personal investment, you might help move your bishop out of opposition, at least to the point of giving permission for your vision.

Ten Essentials to Help Parishes Keep a Healthy Relationship with the Diocese

We have spent some time highlighting the importance of a mutual, loving, supportive relationship between the diocese and the parish. I want to share with you ten key strategies that will help parishes nurture such a healthy relationship. I have learned these the hard way!

1. Expect tension.

Do not be surprised if from time to time you become frustrated with the diocese and they become frustrated with you. Parishes and dioceses exist in an essential unity. One of the primary callings for bishops is to be a source of unity in the diocese. Every one of the parishes in a diocese must be in communion with him, and he is the bishop of everyone— regardless of where a parish might be relative to the Church's mission.

Recall once again the Rogers Innovation Adoption Curve (chapter four). When it comes to new initiatives, you have innovators, early adopters, the early majority, the late majority, and laggards. The priests and pastoral leaders of the diocese will fall into those categories, and your bishop must shepherd all of them at once. You will have laggard parishes led by laggard pastors—and the bishop must care for them just as much as he does for the innovators. You might be an innovator and therefore become frustrated because you are way out ahead of the curve. It might seem that your bishop is far behind you. Be patient.

Likewise, the whole diocesan engine is not trying to oppose, sabotage, or frustrate you. That is exactly what it may feel like, however. Your bishop may be getting feedback from other parishes that see your community moving ahead, and he is trying to keep it all together. There is a lot going on behind the scenes that will create tension. Do not be surprised; expect it, and see it as a sign that things are actually on the move.

2. Monitor the discontent.

We have spoken about how a healthy level of discontent is important, especially within a parish and diocese. Remember, a key part of leading and influencing is experiencing an appropriate level of discontent. You need to monitor it, however. There is a fine line between discontent that moves you to action and unhealthy discontent that makes you sour.

For many years, when I worked at the parish level, it seemed that the diocese did not have a clear vision or strong plan to deal with the decline that we faced. No one seemed to be addressing the issues, and I had not been invited around the table. I was becoming increasingly frustrated with the situation and spent time at diocesan meetings venting all that passion in not so constructive ways. I would stand up and say, "All we ever do is talk, talk, talk, and we never actually accomplish anything."

I was certainly correct in my assessment, but standing up and saying it that way was not exactly wise. My brother priests, and perhaps even the bishop, experienced it as my passing judgment on them. I was acting like a jerk. It was that simple, and it was the obvious reason for why I was not invited around the table.

So you can have a healthy discontent and, like me, express it in unhelpful ways. I was not wrong in what I was saying, but I said it in ways that decreased trust. If all you do is point out the problem and never offer a solution, you will eventually find yourself in an unhealthy place.

That happened to me. My discontent moved to a toxic level. I started to withdraw. I told myself that I would just go to my own corner, do my own thing, and forget about anything at the diocesan level. It was too painful to keep caring.

3. Take care when venting.

This connects to the previous strategy. I vented unhelpfully at diocesan gatherings, but I also vented in a nonconstructive way to my brother priests at our priestly gatherings—completely blind to the fact that my rants came across as judgments on them and their ministries. I also vented quite a bit to the staff in my parishes. When I started to see my negativity regarding "downtown" reflected back to me by my staff, I realized I do not have the luxury to complain whenever I want and to whomever happens to be nearby. I had become toxic, and I needed to repent. As leaders with influence, we can enliven people or weigh them down with negativity.

Now, we all need to vent. When you are leading change, you are going to experience opposition, frustration, and tension. You have to release your feelings about that somewhere, or else you will explode.

A healthy way to do that is to vent before the Lord. Go to him with your anger and frustration. Take more time in prayer. Also bring your frustrations to your spiritual director, close friends, and other leaders outside your parish who are walking the same path. Be careful about where, when, and with whom you release these emotions.

4. Guard your heart.

Again, this touches on the realm of discontent. If we do not monitor our discontent and if we vent unhelpfully, our frustration can turn to anger and then bitterness. These end up hardening our hearts. We become overwhelmed by the negativity, and in order to survive, we shut down. Closing our hearts to other people is never going to help us manifest the kingdom of God in the world.

Our hearts can also become hardened by the criticisms of others. Not everyone in a diocese, including brother priests, will line up to congratulate you as you start moving from maintenance to mission. Sad to say, sometimes jealousy, insecurities, and gossip appear. People will say things about you that are not true.

Over the years, I have been shocked to discover all the things that I purportedly said and did at Saint Benedict Parish. People can distort stories, forget important details, and try to paint you in the most negative light possible as you move a parish from maintenance to mission. When people leave your parish because they disagree with your approach, they take with them a narrative that often justifies their choice to leave. Ultimately that narrative boils down to the "fact" that you are a jerk.

Sometimes people complain about you and your parish to the diocesan office, and then the diocese reaches out to you only when they have something negative to discuss with you. That negativity coming from downtown can also harden our hearts. We must be vigilant!

5. Pray for the bishop and his team.

Prayer is a great antidote to the hardening of the heart. Prayer does not change God's heart; it changes ours. If we regularly practice prayer for the bishop and his team, naming them specifically in our prayer, God will open our heart to them. Invite your staff members to pray specifically for the diocesan staff with whom they directly work. This way you cultivate within your team the habit of praying for them.

6. Make appointments to share good news.

When I look back on my ministry, I realize that even though my bishop gave me permission to execute the vision that he himself wrote, my relationship with him was not in a healthy place. There was limited trust between us, and I think that was at the root of much of the tension that I felt. I allowed my frustration at the slow rate of change to sour our relationship.

At one point I decided that I had to do something, so I made an appointment with the bishop. When a priest makes an appointment to see his bishop, it is generally because there is a problem. Bishops are already overworked and overloaded. So I can imagine what my bishop was thinking when that appointment appeared on his calendar.

When the time came, the bishop met me at the door of his office. I could see in his eyes that he was saying to himself, "Crap! What problem is he bringing and expecting me to deal with?"

I went in and said, "Bishop, I'm just here to give you an update on what's happening in the parish." I brought some copies of our magazine, which included parishioner testimonies, and I shared with him what was happening in our most recent Alpha. As I spoke, I could tell that he was very moved. I saw him begin to relax as he realized that I was not going to dump a single problem on him. In fact, quite the opposite. I brought him life-giving stories and told him that we were praying for him. I also asked him if he would pray for us. That was it.

Three months later, I had another appointment. The bishop met me at the door, and I could see that same wariness in his eyes, trying to figure out the issues I would lay at his feet. However, I just brought him an update on the parish: more copies of our latest magazine and more stories of transformation. He relaxed once again and clearly enjoyed this interaction, which seemed to build him up.

The third time I met with the bishop, he was a little bit hesitant but not as much as the previous times. I gave him another problem-free update on our parish. By our fourth meeting, he was completely relaxed. Investing in that relationship changed everything, and it drove home for me the reality that I truly had been part of the problem.

If you are a pastor or parish leader, invest in your relationship with your bishop. Do not wait for him to call you, and do not wait for your annual or biannual meeting. Make an appointment, and speak to him about the life-giving things happening at your parish. Take the initiative, even if you are just at the beginning of your journey. Speak with him about the dream in your heart, and watch what happens.

7. Visit.

If you are in the general area of the chancery, drop in and say hello. Stick your head in the door, and maybe visit some of the staff. If you have a scheduled meeting in the building, take a few minutes either before or after that appointment to walk around, greet the staff, and thank them for what they do.

Earlier I shared how we at Saint Benedict brought a "coffee bomb," a twenty-gallon container of coffee, and a lot of donuts to the chancery. Imagine if we took the words of Scripture seriously, that we would seek to outdo each other in the honor we give to our brothers and sisters (see Romans 12:10).

8. Get support for major changes.

When you are considering making a major change, get permission upfront to go on this journey. This is critical.

When parishes apply to our leadership coaching network, one of our conditions for acceptance is that they have the support of their bishop. He has to know what they are doing. Investing in parish renewal is not a quick fix; it takes a long time. There is no point in our going down this road together if the bishop is going to move you to another position in two years. Talk with the bishop, and see if he can at least give his support for your long-term leadership. Moving forward, solicit his support for major changes as you journey from maintenance to mission

We have discovered over the years that some changes are a bit more controversial than others. We experienced some controversy at Saint Benedict when we shifted our catechetical programs from a classroom model to a family-centric model that was more flexible. Prepare for fireworks when you want to change a sacramental preparation program, such as the ones I highlighted in *Divine Renovation*—including detaching sacraments for children from ages or grade levels and making them about readiness to receive them. You will need your bishop's support in this area.

We worked with a parish in our coaching network that tackled the sacramental issue a bit too early and did not communicate their plans fully to the bishop. When the inevitable letters and phone calls of complaints came in, the bishop backed down and did not support the parish leaders. It was a difficult, painful experience for the amazing men and women of that parish.

Therefore make sure you secure the bishop's support for major changes, but do not bother him or his staff every time you want to make a lesser change. If you are on board with his vision, and he supports your leadership, you can presume you have his support for lesser changes.

9. Serve at the diocesan level.
We have already discussed this in the section on leading when you are not in charge, but it is an essential point that bears repeating. Whether you are a pastor or staff member, serve the diocese by participating in things at the diocesan level, especially as you move from maintenance to mission. It is a part of Christian generosity to become a blessing to others, even at the diocesan level.

As a pastor seeks to serve at the diocesan level, he should encourage his staff to be generous with their time at the diocesan level as well. Also, pastors and staff should be ready to help other parishes when they ask for help. That assistance might not be directly connected to the chancery, but it is an opportunity to offer your gifts to the local Church.

10. Go to diocesan events.
Most dioceses have an annual formation day or conference for parish leaders. At Saint Benedict, our goal was to get as many parishioners as possible to attend those events. Sometimes that strategy backfired on us. Several years ago, 30 to 40 percent of attendees at a diocesan event came from our parish. People were a bit overwhelmed by us.

Nevertheless, mobilize your parishioners to show their support. Do not let your parish become isolated from the rest of the diocese. I think we may have fallen prey to that tendency in the early years as things began to change in our parish, and we became busy with the work we were accomplishing. Resist that temptation, promote diocesan events in your parish, and invite your people to attend.

Ten Essentials for Dioceses in Keeping a Healthy Relationship with Missionary Parishes

Relationships run both ways. Just as mission-focused parishes can do specific things to invest in relationships with their dioceses, a diocese can work in specific ways to build and sustain healthy relationships with parishes on a journey from maintenance to mission. These next ten strategies deal with mission-focused parishes, not with all the parishes in a diocese. Your local Church might have relatively few of these types of parishes—though I hope most of our parishes will ultimately move in this direction. The underlying principle is that a diocese must treat these parishes differently, a reality that leads into our first point.

1. Do not treat every parish the same.

Treating every parish the same—regardless of size, location (rural or urban), cultural makeup, and so forth—is one of the fundamental sources of tension between a diocese and its parishes, especially those who are moving in a missionary direction. Many dioceses operate under the assumption that treating parishes differently is at best unfair and, at worst, wrong. It is not wrong, however, to treat different realities differently.

In terms of missionary parishes, dioceses have to recognize that a different dynamic is at play, requiring a different approach. The diocese must create strategies for those particular parishes. We will explore what that looks like in the next chapter.

2. Identify your 16 percent.

We must go back once more to the Rogers Innovation Adoption Curve. The first 16 percent of people who adopt a new approach are comprised of innovators (2.5 percent) and early adopters (13.5 percent). These people will become leaders in organizational change. Trying to convince everyone of an idea or expect that 100 percent of your diocese will buy into a new vision will only lead to disappointment. Strategic plans that begin with the principle that we are all going to do this together will always fail, because that kind of buy-in will never happen. Identifying the approximately 16 percent of priests and parish leaders who have the heart and capacity to lead in this new direction allows dioceses to invest limited resources in leadership that will make a difference.

Heart and capacity are important characteristics for leaders. Heart refers to desire or openness, while capacity deals with the natural leadership abilities and competence of a pastor. Finding priests and other parish leaders with high capacity and high openness should be your first priority. They will be your best leaders.

There are other possibilities, however. What about a high-capacity leader with low openness? Or a low-capacity leader with high openness? As a diocesan leader, I would rather work with a priest who has less leadership ability but an open and passionate heart. Leaders like that tend to have humility, and they often recognize their need to grow in the art of leadership.

Priests with a high capacity for leadership and low openness tend to be frustrated, cynical, and negative. In addition, they are influential with their peers but fail to appreciate what they still need to learn regarding leadership.

3. Match leaders strategically.

Once we identify our 16 percent of leaders with heart and capacity to lead in the new direction, dioceses must match them with particular parishes in a strategic manner. For example, if you have forty priests in your diocese, identifying the 16 percent would give you six or seven priest leaders with the requisite openness and leadership skills to lead parishes in a missionary direction. You must look at your parishes and identify those that have the greatest resources and potential to become missionary outposts and have an impact on the world around them. Then connect those six or seven priest leaders with those parishes. The goal is to create missionary parishes that can model the missionary life.

Most dioceses are a mixture of urban, rural, and suburban parishes. Suburban parishes tend to be larger and have more resources than other parishes, particularly those in rural areas. It is important, however, that dioceses avoid the trap of identifying only suburban or urban parishes as high-potential communities. If we move forward in this way, we end up with models of parish life that ignore the rural parish experience—which actually makes up the vast majority of Catholic parishes in North America and throughout the world.

4. Commit to long-term leadership and support.

Once you identify and match a pastor to a high-potential community, you must commit to his leadership of that parish for the long term. Parish renewal takes time. It is not a sprint but a marathon. Tweaking things and making small changes do not bring the transformation that we need.

The initial phase of parish renewal can take anywhere from two to four years. The goal of this phase is to gain momentum in the cultural shifts that need to take place in the areas of leadership, evangelization, discipleship, and authentic worship. This does not happen overnight.

When a new pastor with missionary vision moves into a new parish, that community does not immediately start growing. Most likely it has experienced decline for some time. Even if a new pastor moves in and does everything right, that parish will still move in the direction of decline.

Dealing with parish decline is like trying to slow down an oil tanker. There was a man in one of my parishes who captained oil tankers, and I asked him how many miles outside of port he started "applying the brakes" in order to dock successfully. He said that you have to start slowing down eighteen miles out of port in order to come to a safe stop at the dock. It takes some time to stop decline and then begin to move in a positive direction.

It took three years at Saint Benedict before we had some momentum in the right direction. In Divine Renovation ministry, we have seen parishes we coach break through the initial phase in about two years. The second phase of renewal deals with creating your major systems, crafting a discipleship process, and getting it to function well. While you are creating these systems, you have to keep your foot on the gas in terms of the cultural shift, and you also need to keep communicating your vision.

In phase 1, your goal is to get a critical mass of parishioners to own the vision. You want about 40 percent of your parishioners engaged. You will not convince every single parishioner to buy in to the vision, but once you get a critical mass, things will begin to shift.

In phase 2, you must continue to communicate the vision, but the goal here is to get a critical mass of parishioners to own the strategy. These are parishioners who do not just support where you are going but also support how you are getting there. Completion of phase 2 took us about another four years at Saint Benedict.

Think about that for a moment. We are talking about a period of between six and eight years before a parish can move into phase 3, a phase that will last until the Lord returns. This phase begins when you have put all your major systems in place and they function well. Continually communicating the vision, enforcing the cultural values you have chosen, sustaining the various primary and supporting cultures necessary for renewal—all these things continue to occur in phase 3.

Parish renewal is like renovating a house. It takes years to renovate, and by the time you finish, you have to start all over again because the kitchen does not look so great. The culture of quality we embrace as parishes prompts us to constantly ask the question, "How can we improve?"

As I mentioned, there are two reasons to change how you do things: it is not working well, or it works very well. If it is not working well, you have to change it in order to improve it. If it is working well, the fact that it was successful will change your parish and so will require adjustment so that it continues to work in this new reality. We have to constantly evaluate our systems and embrace the possibility that we will have to tweak or really change our models in phase 3.

All of this takes time—and giving pastors time to lead cultural change is not one of our strengths in the Catholic Church. We opened this book relaying the story of a French priest who had begun to mobilize his parish. He was probably in the middle of phase 2. The bishop moved him anyway, because that is the way things are done. That story shows why it is important to not treat all parishes the same. If a diocese has a policy of moving priests around after a set number of years, it should make exception for parishes that are deliberately moving from maintenance to mission, allowing that parish the time and space it needs to take the journey.

Bishops and diocesan teams should not only commit to long-term leadership in a missionary parish but also commit to long-term support—offering these parishes more resources because of the critical nature of missionary transformation. If one parish in the diocese reaches a place of missionary fruitfulness and health, it enriches the entire diocese and makes it easier for the next parish to succeed on that journey.

Think of the parable of the sower of the seed (see Matthew 13:1-23). It is a powerful story to help us understand what the Lord is calling us to do. When I reflect on this parable, the first thing I think about is how wasteful the sower of seed was. He threw seed everywhere: on the path, on the rocks, in the weeds, and on good soil. I think this is an important principle.

Even though I have said that dioceses should not expect everyone to embrace the journey from maintenance to mission, it is important that diocesan leadership invite everyone to ponder it and not prejudge who may embrace the vision. Cast that vision seed to everyone. Let them examine it and see if it captures their hearts or imaginations.

In the parable of the sower, we know that nothing happened with the seed that fell on the path; it was all eaten by birds. However, things happened with the seed that landed on rocky ground, the weeds, and good soil. The seed was received but with different results.

Similar things will happen when you sow the seed of vision at the diocesan level. Some leaders will immediately reject it. Others will support it. Some will start down the path of renewal with their parishes, but the desire for renewal and new life will wither and die when the burning sun of resistance appears.

The seed that falls in the weeds is like a parish that remains at the level of best practices but is not willing to deal with underlying cultures. They are focused on pleasing their current members, and they cannot look at the best means of moving forward. They end up being spread too thin, and vital initiatives that would make a difference are choked out.

What is the final quadrant? It is the good soil, and just as the parable tells us, it is the good soil that produces fruit forty, sixty, and a hundredfold. These are parishes in your diocese that will bear fruit in the long run. They have an abundance of people willing to serve and give, so they enable the diocese to have the resources that it needs.

Rather than increasing its support of these parishes, however, dioceses often take more resources from them and distribute them to the parishes who resemble the rocks and weeds.

5. Have a different approach for the 84 percent.

If you have a particular plan for the 16 percent, you should also examine how you deal with the remaining 84 percent. Perhaps you have two strategic plans for them: one for the early majority and another for the late majority. When it comes to the laggards, I do not recommend that you invest a lot of time and energy in them, beyond the level of regular maintenance.

A diversity of plans allows a diocese to meet and accompany parishes where they are in their journey. This does not mean a chaotic, free-for-all process. Making exceptions in diocesan policies for missionary parishes does not mean changing or removing diocesan policies across the board.

6. Do not try to do it all together.

You cannot take everybody with you on this journey and assume that they will all follow along. When dioceses try to do this, bishops and diocesan leaders end up spending most of their time and energy on those who resist and complain. The 68 percent of folks in the middle of the road, those who are ready to be influenced one way or the other, see that the bishop mostly pays attention to the laggards. This acts as a reward for complaining. The 16 percent, the open and capable leaders, end up feeling shortchanged and unsupported.

Make it very clear to parishes in your diocese that you have different plans for different parishes. When it comes to diocesan-wide restructuring, however, it is generally not possible to do it with some parishes and not others. In the Archdiocese of Halifax-Yarmouth, we are restructuring with all the parishes, because there is structural and administrative integrity at the diocesan level. This restructuring though is simply the first step in a longer journey from maintenance to mission.

After you accomplish a diocesan-wide restructuring, you must realize that not every parish is going to be able to grow into the new reality. For some parishes, all you will be able to do is help them manage their decline, but this does not mean that we should not bring as many parishes along the journey toward mission as possible.

7. Set vision and broad strategy.

If you are in a diocese with a bishop who does not have a strong vision, you can try to help the bishop discover that vision. Sit down with him, and help him get in touch with what makes him excited. Have the bishop speak to some of his key priests—especially those more mission minded—and help him develop the vision. In doing so, remember to distinguish between vision and strategy. Be clear about the vision, and leave specific strategy for parish leadership.

8. Practice low control, high accountability.

This principle can help mobilize a parish, but it is also critical in the relationship between a diocese and its parishes. Put simply, "low control and high accountability" means "do not micromanage." Do not step into areas that properly belong to parish leaders. You must, however, set up structures that hold parish leadership accountable for the fulfillment of your broad strategy.

Diocesan application of this principle can help hold parishes accountable for

- the development of a foundationally healthy organizational culture;

- the fostering of primary cultures of evangelization, leadership, discipleship, and authentic worship;

- the creation of supporting cultures of quality and invitation

  by

- helping parish leadership develop and articulate their particular expression of the diocesan vision;

- making sure parishes progress in the development of a strategic plan;

- ensuring that parishes identify tools for evangelization, discipleship, and small groups;

- helping parishes develop a leadership pipeline;

- investing in the development of pastoral leaders;

- providing resources and guidance for the creation of sacramental programs that fit within a culture of evangelization and discipleship;

- making sure that parishes have an onboarding process to allow people to serve in ministry.

These things can be done by dioceses that accompany their parishes in gentle but firm ways.

9. Communicate in a timely fashion.

It is easy for us to get caught up in our own concerns, agendas, and timelines. When I worked at the parish level, one of the biggest frustrations came from not receiving enough notice for diocesan events—especially when there was a diocesan expectation of parish attendance. These events always seemed to conflict with a major initiative we had going on at the parish.

Parishes moving from maintenance to mission invest in their leadership, which often means that mission-focused parishes have more long-term planning happening than maintenance-dwelling parishes. Sometimes this planning occurs eight, twelve, and even sixteen months in advance. When a diocese does not work on that same kind of long-term planning principle, it creates problems. Even a one-month notification for an event can be a problem for a mission-focused parish.

As a service to the whole diocese, diocesan leaders should try to plan ahead and put dates for major events on the calendar a year or a year and a half in advance. They should notify parishes of important diocesan meetings as early as possible, at least two months in advance. I recognize that things sometimes change, but diocesan leaders must get better at this. In my role at the diocese, I have not been entirely successful in living this out, but we must prioritize timely communication.

10. Send communications to the right person.

In small parishes living in maintenance mode, communications tend to go through the parish secretary or even directly to the pastor. In growing parishes that mobilize for mission, the staff structure becomes more specialized. Diocesan leaders must pay attention to that.

If a parish hires a director of communications, the diocese should be informed. The diocese should then send diocesan communications to that person. Likewise, information about insurance and building policies should go to the facilities manager. In a mission-focused parish, if everything continues to go to the pastor or to the secretary, there is a greater chance that the communication will not reach its intended target. Dioceses should diversify their communication recipients.

Doing this will demonstrate to the parishes that the diocesan office is there to support the life of the parish—and not the other way around. By expecting all parishes to somehow adopt to diocesan communication practices and do all the legwork to ensure that messages and information get to the right person, the diocese signals to the parishes that we believe they exist to serve us, to make our lives easier. The goal of authentic leadership is to make others great. Diocesan offices exist for the sake of the life and fruitfulness of parishes.

CHAPTER 19

Living as a Missionary Diocese[50]

We have looked at ten strategic principles that will help parish leaders maintain a healthy relationship with the diocese, and we have also explored ten principles that will help diocesan leaders launch parishes in a missionary direction and help maintain a healthy relationship with them. In the earliest chapters of this book, we acknowledged that the biggest obstacle to the flourishing of a missionary parish is a maintenance-focused diocese.

Now it is time to take several steps back and examine the characteristics of a missionary diocese. Just as we might call a parish where 40 to 60 percent of parishioners embrace mission a missionary parish, we can say that a missionary diocese exists when 40 to 60 percent of parishes within that diocese embrace mission. We may not have encountered such a diocese yet, but based on our experience, we can deduce the principles by which a diocese can reach that goal.

Ten Principles for Living as a Missionary Diocese

1. Submit infrastructure to mission.

The fundamental reality is this: structure exists to support the mission. As my friend Alan Hirsch points out, one of the greatest tragedies in the history of the Church is the emphasis of model over mission. The very structures that we create to advance the mission eventually became the mission itself. There is a choice before us today: we can cling to structures that no longer advance the mission, or we can release them for the sake of the mission.

This raises the question of diocesan restructuring. At the diocesan level, we must keep the call to pursue mission over maintenance front and center at all times as we work our way through restructuring. We are not restructuring for the sake of maintaining our buildings and churches but rather for the sake of advancing Christ's mission of love to the world.

2. Kill the benefice mentality.

I intentionally use the word "kill" here to signify an important truth. In his Letter to the Colossians, Paul writes that we should "put to death . . . the parts of you that are earthly" (Colossians 3:5). I think that St. Paul intends this instruction not just for individual believers but for the Church at every level. The Church is in the world and it has always been in the world, but it is not of the world, not rooted in it. Nevertheless, we have often let the values and understanding of the world into the heart of the Church's life.

During one of those times, in the Middle Ages, the concept of a priestly benefice arose—a church position that came with property or revenue or often both. (The word "benefit" and the word "benefice" come from the same root word.) Back then, when most Europeans were Christian, the life of a parish priest could be quite cushy—especially if your parish was well-off or you found a position as a chaplain or tutor with a wealthy family. Likewise, to be a bishop in those days was like being president of a small country. You were essentially a feudal lord—and that came with financial benefits. Wealthy parishes and dioceses would be given to priests and bishops as rewards.

In essence, parishes existed for the comfort and prestige of the cleric; they were not seen as parts of the Church that required servant leadership. A system began whereby younger priests were sent to poor parishes in the boondocks—the equivalent of Siberia—and had to work their way up. In the ensuing centuries, seniority became an important component of parish and diocesan assignments. When it came to assigning a priest to a parish, Church leadership asked, "Whose turn is it?"

Dioceses did not search for priests with a missionary heart and leadership capacity, nor did they attempt to match such priests to parishes with strong potential. No reference to mission, no prayerful analysis of the signs of the times, no evaluation of the particular gifts of a particular person. Just simply "Who is next in line to receive the reward?"

Until the 1970s, the way priests received remuneration made matters worse. Previous to the Second Vatican Council, most priests did not receive a salary. Rather they received stipends from their ministry. Generally people paid the priest a small sum for his service in particular ministries—such as when he performed a Baptism or officiated at a wedding. He could also keep the proceeds from one or two of the collections during the year. If you ministered in a very small or poor parish, you were lucky if you did not starve to death. Similarly, if you were assigned to a wealthy parish, you managed very well; you had a lot of helpers, did very little work, and made a lot of money. In this system, you had to put in your time before you moved up to a decent benefice.

This mindset is not as dominant within the universal Church today, but it still exists. When I talk with bishops about aligning priests with heart and capacity to parishes with the greatest potential, they often say something like "Wow, I'm not sure I could ever do that, because my most senior priests would be very upset." In other words, it is not yet time for these younger, more missionary-focused priests to get their reward; you are going out of order.

I was part of a discussion in my diocese a number of years ago, when the bishop invited a community of younger priests to minister in the local Church. He wanted to bring priests with missionary zeal to parishes with potential. In particular, he wanted to send them to a parish close to the universities, where they could reach out to students. From a missionary standpoint, this made a great deal of sense. This particular parish, however, was the jewel in the diocese's crown. It was in a wealthy area of town and had lots of resources. The bishop's potential decision to place these younger priests at that parish violated the benefice mentality. This assignment had traditionally been given to the vicar general of the diocese.

One of the senior priests grew very upset about this. He said to the bishop, "I can't believe that you're giving this parish to a bunch of . . ." As a naïve young priest, I waited in suspense for what he was going to say. I thought maybe "guys from a religious order," or "guys from outside the diocese," Or "a bunch of conservatives." I was not sure where he was going with this. What he finally said took me by surprise. He said, "I can't believe you're giving this parish to a bunch of young guys!"

At first I could not figure out his objection. Why did their age matter? Then it struck me that many priests still saw plum parishes as rewards for the older guys in ministry. This was our system for centuries, and remnants of that mindset still seriously hamper attempts to move parishes and dioceses toward mission.

We must kill the benefice mentality. Parishes are not rewards. Priests, and indeed all the baptized, exist to serve the kingdom and not to build our own little kingdoms and sit comfortably on thrones of our own construction.

3. Avoid long-term clustering.

We explored this topic in the structure section of this book, when we examined the difference between amalgamating parishes and clustering parishes. Amalgamation literally means that multiple separate parishes canonically, legally, and administratively become one new parish. Amalgamated parishes may still have multiple locations, becoming a community of communities, but the new parish functions with one pastoral council and one finance council.

Clustering means that one priest now pastors multiple parishes. When we cluster, we take the structures that are dragging us down and put all their weight on a single priest. If three parishes cluster, for example, a pastor must deal with three pastoral councils, finance councils, and staff or leadership teams. This will kill priests and minimize chances of moving in a missionary direction.

A situation being what it is, you may need to cluster parishes in the short term. However, avoid clustering as a long-term strategy! It is a dead end.

4. Beware of the policy trap.

This is true for any organization. We create policies because we live in an imperfect world with imperfect people. The Church knows this more than anyone; that is why canon law emerged. In a perfect Church, you would not need policy, and you would not need law. There is no such thing as a perfect Church, however, and if you managed to find such a Church, the moment you joined it, it would no longer be perfect.

Policies provide a safety net for us, and they are not of themselves bad. When the diocesan answer to every problem is to create a policy though, we have a major problem. Want to find out if you have fallen into the policy trap? Just take a look at your policy manual. How many pages is it?

Here is how policies tend to spin out of control. Let us say you have a small number of priests, or perhaps even a single priest or pastoral leader, doing something they should not be doing. Rather than going to that person and having the critical (and possibly uncomfortable) conversation, we create a policy and send it out to everyone. The crazy thing is that most people who receive that new policy will know the exact person you are trying to address (and the person whose behavior you are trying to address will not even read the policy). By sending out that policy, diocesan leadership has signaled to other parish leaders that the diocese does not have the courage or conviction to deal directly with that person.

Use common sense when creating policy. Policy reinforces the primacy of positional leadership. Policy is not only about enforcing the rules but also about following the rules to avoid being punished. That feeds into an unhealthy culture.

Wherever possible, keep your policy manuals short, and do not respond to problems by issuing more policies. The more parishes you have within a diocese, the more tempted you will be to respond to every problem with a policy. Just do not do it!

5. Evaluate the assessment policy.

I do not know what you call it in your diocese, but in mine, the assessment is the tax a parish pays to the diocese. Just as in the secular world, where we pay a federal tax based on income, parishes pay a portion of their income to the diocese in order to support the functioning of the diocesan center, including the salaries of diocesan staff. The diocese also uses a portion of that money to help support under-resourced parishes.

Every diocese has a different approach to how they calculate the amount of the assessment. Some have a fixed percentage: maybe 10 percent or 15 percent of a parish's ordinary income goes to the diocese. Some dioceses, like my own, until very recently, had a flexible percentage, just as with secular income tax. The higher your income bracket was, the more money went to the diocese. I believe that many of our diocesan assessment policies, like many of our other policies, come out of a maintenance mindset rooted in a Christendom model of Church.

Here is where such maintenance-minded policies create obstacles for missionary parishes. Turning to my diocese, you might think that its flexible, rather than fixed, assessment would have resolved any issues. The assessment that you would pay in the coming year, however, was based on the income that you brought in the year before. Essentially there was a two-year gap on the assessment.

If you were a parish mobilizing for mission and focused on evangelization, you could have been starting to grow, and therefore your income would have risen. As your income rose, you would begin to think about hiring a new staff member to help with the increasing responsibilities that come with renewal and transformation.

In general, missionary-minded parishes barely meet their budgets for the year. Every single year that I served as pastor, we ended up spending 99.99999 percent of the budget. We never had lots of money to spare because we invested for mission. When the end of the year would come, we would receive notice of the increase in assessment for the next year because our income had risen and we would feel the pinch.

I learned this as a young priest in a small country parish. When I first moved into that parish, we were not bringing in enough money to pay my salary. The previous priest was living off his pension. So we worked hard to raise enough money to pay my salary. A year later, we worked hard to raise enough money to create a half-time pastoral associate position for a layperson, to work with me to mobilize the parish.

Then the diocese hit us with our increased assessment, because we had managed to increase our income. It took me completely by surprise; I was blindsided. Of course, that was my fault for not paying attention, but in order to meet the new assessment, I would have to terminate the position I had worked so hard to pay for. It felt like the diocesan policy essentially pulled the rug from underneath my feet.

I went downtown and presented my case to the archdiocese. The response was fantastic: the diocese waived the increase. Thanks be to God!

Now consider this. In general, governments recognize that overtaxing small, entrepreneurial, growing businesses can destroy the health of dynamic companies. If, however, government taxes a small business at the right level, if that small business is allowed to grow, say, over a period of ten years, it pays more taxes to the government than it would if it was initially overtaxed and unable to grow to its capacity. That same principle applies to diocesan assessments and parish life. If a diocese overtaxes a parish so that it cannot support its growth, it limits the parish's ability to grow into a mission-minded, flourishing community.

Bottom line: Lowering the assessment will facilitate growth and allow the diocese to receive far more financial support from that parish in the long term. Think of it this way: when you plant a vine, you need to build a trellis to support it as it grows. The same principle is at work in a mission-minded parish. In order to facilitate growth, parishes need to invest in staff members and resources to support new members, small groups, spiritual growth, and expanded ministries. These parishes need the resources that will allow them to build the "trellis" that will support new growth.

As many of my readers might know, I am originally from Scotland. The Highlanders in Scotland were farmers trying to eke out a living in a very bleak landscape. If the crops did not yield enough food, the survival of the family would be at risk as winter wore on. In the Highlands, it was not uncommon for farmers to bleed a cow a little bit. They would mix that blood with oatmeal and cook something called black pudding (blood sausage). It was a way of stretching their food in order to survive. The fundamental question for those farmers was "How do you bleed the cow in such a way that you can keep feeding your family without killing the cow?"

Dioceses are often faced with a similar question. They may have parishes that are mobilizing, growing, helping nearby parishes, and serving at the diocesan level. Too often though, dioceses are hampered by maintenance-minded policies that are rooted in a different cultural era. These policies, combined with a one-size-fits-all approach, can end up inhibiting the growth of this missionary parish and potentially "kill the cow."

In fact, some dioceses take a higher percentage of resources from missionary parishes than they do other parishes. For example, parishes in maintenance mode might pay a 10 percent assessment, while parishes mobilizing for mission, the ones who most need income to invest in supporting that growth, pay 20 percent.

You might think, based on what I have just written, that I am against assessments. Nothing could be further from the truth. The basic concept of an assessment is rock solid. In fact, I dream of a time when a parish can give 30 percent of its income to the diocese and still sustain healthy growth. But in the crucial early years of a parish's journey out of maintenance, dioceses need to pay attention and adopt assessment policies that strategically support the growth of that parish.

Why do we have these policies? A financially secure, maintenance-focused parish in the Christendom era did not have any pastoral staff to speak of. The "staff" consisted of the pastor, the pastor's dog, the associate pastor, a housekeeper, and perhaps a secretary or janitor. That was it.

As we moved into the 1970s, parishes started hiring directors of catechesis. Even in the 80s, 90s, and into our current time, however, the idea of a larger paid pastoral staff is often not the norm in most places in the world. Parish income covered salaries for the very small staff surrounding the priest and basic administrative costs, such as keeping the buildings open and paying the light bill. Any money brought in over and above those needs was not invested in making and forming missionary disciples; it was deposited in the bank. The Church rightfully developed a policy to address this: a diocese would take upward of 20 to 30 percent of surplus money and use it to help other parishes.

This made sense in the Christendom world, but we are no longer in that world, and the system is now working against us. Remember, we shape culture by what we reward and tolerate. In the secular taxation system, governments offer rewards through tax breaks for activities that they perceive will benefit the common good. This incentivizes positive behaviors and punishes negative behaviors. We need to ask a key question as we examine our assessment policy within a diocese: what does our policy reward, and what does it punish?

As a parish priest I have often tried to rob Peter to pay Paul, pouring a lot of energy into finding loopholes within the assessment policy. My archdiocese, for example, offers a break if you channel your income into new building construction. So if you want to pay less money to the diocese, you invest in buildings and infrastructure. If you want to invest in evangelization and discipleship, and the salaries needed to support this focus—that money is fully taxable. Is it any surprise therefore that in many parts of the Church, building new buildings takes precedence over investing in people and missionary growth?

In a very real sense, we punish parishes for investing in people. What if dioceses gave only moderate tax breaks for infrastructure and generous tax cuts to investments in evangelization and discipleship?

Do you think that might make a difference? What if a diocese wanted to encourage such investment by applying a higher tax rate to parish money sitting in the bank?

First of all, money in the bank is not a sign of vitality. There are many declining and dying parishes with nice bank accounts. Second, parishes that mobilize for mission, that are growing, tend to reinvest their money into that growth. They do not have much money in the bank, because they are too busy investing it in the kingdom of God.

One last thought on assessments, and this has to do with dioceses that are in the process of amalgamating: if you combine three parishes into one, and your assessment policy scales with parish income, you essentially cripple these new amalgamated structures. Often the income from these combined structures doubles or even triples, but they have the same level of activity and the same number of people to serve. When that adjusted assessment hits, these parishes will have even less money to invest in future growth.

6. Change financial policies that disconnect giving from mission.

I have seen, over my years of working toward parish renewal, that people increase their giving as they buy into the mission. The more a parish focuses on the mission of making disciples, the more people experience conversion. The more people experience conversion, the more they will buy into the mission. The more they buy in, the more they give. The more people give, the more a parish can focus on the mission.

In addition, the more people give, the more connected they feel to the parish. It creates a kind of virtuous cycle. Focusing on evangelization and discipleship, therefore, is one of the greatest things we can do to increase giving. There is a direct correlation between the evangelization and discipleship formation that happens in your parish and the income you receive.

That is why it is important to change financial policies that disconnect giving from mission. This is not so much an issue in North America, but as I have traveled around the world with Divine Renovation ministry, I have witnessed the Church's diverse financial policies at work. In some dioceses, financial giving at the parish level does not go to the parish. Rather it goes straight to the diocese, and the diocese allots the percentage of money each parish receives based upon the number of registered families or the Mass attendance in those parishes.

I first discovered this kind of policy in Latin America. I spoke to a group of priests in Bogota, Colombia, about the connection between evangelization, discipleship, and increased giving, but they could not grasp the concept. I finally understood why when I discovered the diocesan financial policy: there was no direct connection between parish giving and available parish resources.

Dioceses in Europe, particularly in Spain and Italy, have similar policies. The Church in Germany receives money from taxes levied against Catholics by the government. Switzerland and Austria have similar systems, but these are not as centralized. If you identify yourself as a Catholic, a portion of your income goes to the diocese you belong to. It does not matter whether you are active or inactive; if you identify as a Catholic, you are taxed.

The system in Germany represents probably the greatest obstacle to developing missionary dioceses and parishes, because it creates a complete disconnect between giving and mobilizing for mission. For example, giving that normally occurs at the collection during the celebration of the Eucharist is minimal, even for the 10 percent of people who actually go to Mass. Church giving in Germany takes place at a distance from parishes and largely outside the conscious awareness of those who choose to give through their taxes.

What kind of giving actually changes the heart? Conscious, intentional, proportional, and generous giving. The German Church taxation system may have some degree of proportionality baked in, but most people are not consciously aware or intentionally desiring to give.

In addition, something happens when we place our gift into the collection basket during the celebration of the Eucharist: it is brought to the altar and connected to Jesus' self-offering to the Father. In other words, our giving becomes part of worship. Part of our sacrifice then is our financial giving for the sake of the mission. It is critical therefore that those of us in diocesan and parish leadership make that connection clear. The Lord does not call us to give our leftovers but to give of our first fruits as an act of worship. How better can we accomplish that than at the Eucharist?

When giving becomes disconnected from this reality, as in places like Germany and Latin America, the link between the spiritual transformation of people within a parish and the resources that parish may have as a result of that transformation is broken. Unintended consequences occur. For one thing, the system ends up rewarding complacency. Your income remains the same whether you create missionary disciples or not. Moving in a missionary direction requires hard work and brings with it a great deal of stress and difficulty. Why would a priest bother when he can just coast into retirement?

Another unintended consequence of a taxation system such as the one we see in Germany is that it dilutes the influence of leadership. Due to the State's financial support, church buildings in Germany are beautifully maintained, and very few close. The number of priests continues to decline, however, and so each priest must now look after multiple parishes that are financially controlled by boards made up of parishioners.

Two years ago, I met with a young priest who told me he was unable to do something as simple as buy vestments, because the lay board controlling the parish's budget was in protective mode. In order to assert control over the parish, the board members refused to spend a dime. This priest's parish had enough resources, but it was essentially immobilized in terms of mission. The priest had six parishes, each with a board of trustees. Needless to say, he was frustrated.

Again, if we want to mobilize ourselves for mission, we must connect giving directly with mission. In order to foster the kind of buy-in we need, the pastor or bishop must have a compelling vision. Raising money to pay a bill does not really inspire anyone, while a big dream can inspire many. When people begin to see movement toward the fulfillment of a dream, it solidifies their commitment.

In addition, when you preach and teach on giving, and you ask people to step forward and give proportionally, intentionally, and sacrificially, they will step forward and do it.

If you want to lay the foundation of a giving mindset, however, one thing is more important than even transparency and accountability: you have to practice what you preach. As a pastor or parish leader, you have to give.

When I was in the seminary, I gave nothing. I figured that the sacrifice of my life for this vocation took care of everything. I was giving my life to this outfit, why should I also give what meager money I had?

I went from not giving anything to giving regularly after I was ordained, gradually increasing the amount. In fact, I discovered that anytime I preached on giving, I was moved to give more. Then a layperson challenged me to start tithing, which I did based on my tax return. Then I was challenged to tithe according to my equivalent income.

Priests receive a number of benefits that can be roughly converted into a cash equivalent (remember benefices?). Giving proportionately of my equivalent income liberated me to preach, teach, and call others to give in the same way. It is critical to do this, because we still have a mindset in the Church that says, "When I give to the parish, I am giving it to the priest."

Fundamentally that is not true. Giving is for the mission of the Church. When priests and pastors give, it frees us from any sense that the collection is for us. It is another way to kill the benefice mentality.

7. Support difficult decisions.

Moving from maintenance to mission requires many difficult decisions at the parish level. If you are in a leadership role, you have to take the heat. It is the pioneers, those forging ahead in a new direction, who often receive arrows in the back. If you lift your head above the trench, people will shoot at you—both from outside and inside the organization.

Sometimes bishops and diocesan leaders who craft a grand vision and call for a missionary response from pastors and parish leaders do not support the 16 percent who actually embrace that vision and begin to lead. When problems arise, whether from the resistance and complaints of others or from the fact that no missionary leader will do everything perfectly, these diocesan leaders sometimes either discipline the groundbreaking parish or put the brakes on their efforts.

At the end of the day, if dioceses want missionary leaders, they absolutely must back them up—especially during difficult moments.

If diocesan leadership has placed a pastor in a particular parish, presumably they have done so because they trust and support him. They must follow through on that trust. Many priests and parish leaders feel a bit betrayed and undermined when diocesan officials give credence and power to the complainers.

One element of owning difficult decisions is finding a balance between doing justice to people's concerns and supporting parish leadership. When trusted and accountable parish leaders make the tough calls, in line with the diocesan vision and strategy, and resistance or negative reactions occur, the bishop must support the front line leaders. Diocesan leadership cannot blame parish leaders or minimize the reality that a difficult call had to be made. Diocesan leaders need to communicate the fact that a decision was made because our vision is *this*, and pastors are leading accordingly.

8. Plan succession for key parishes.

Even when a diocese decides to invest in the long-term leadership of parishes mobilizing for mission, they may need to shift leadership resources and move pastors. It is important to do this kind of shifting strategically. Right now our pastor placement processes are essentially based on plugging holes rather than on matching the gifts of a priest with the needs of a community.

Even where dioceses take a very deliberate approach to pastor placements, there is more involved for a missionary parish. It is critical to identify the right candidate to take over the reins of a parish mobilizing for mission. Even when you do, you cannot just drop him in a slot and expect that everything will continue at the same speed and trajectory. When leadership changes in an organization, some backpedaling inevitably occurs. Things might slow down.

Dioceses must ask, "How do we maximize the chance that a new leader will be successful?" The answer generally lies in succession planning. This is a mentoring and apprenticing process especially designed for moving a priest into a missionary parish that has multiple staff, a culture of leadership, and a culture of evangelization.

Someone once asked me how healthy a parish must be in order to survive bad leadership. My answer was that parishes cannot survive bad leadership—no matter how healthy they are. You can put a bad leader (or an unequipped one) into the healthiest parish in the world, and in six months that parish will start to fall apart. No parish is immune to poor leadership.

If there is a mission-focused parish, or one that is clearly moving in that direction, the diocese must do everything possible to support that parish in moving forward. Therefore dioceses must invest in succession planning.

At Saint Benedict, we inadvertently stumbled onto the benefits of apprenticing in relation to succession planning. As mentioned in chapter eight, Fr. Simon Lobo came to work at the parish for a two- or three-year apprenticeship, after which we intended to "mission" him to a neighboring parish along with a group of twenty or thirty parishioners.

(Fr. Simon's book, *Divine Renovation Apprentice*, describes his experience of this mentoring process.) In the end, however, God surprised us all. Fr. Simon became the pastor of Saint Benedict as I moved on to work for the archdiocese and Divine Renovation ministry.

At the time, we were not planning for the next pastor at Saint Benedict. The apprenticeship was a good way of setting Fr. Simon up for success. In many ways, the parish is doing better under his leadership than it did under mine, because we took the time to prepare him for that role.

It is critical for dioceses to begin this process of succession planning—especially for the 16 percent of parishes that are moving in a missionary direction. Again, due to resource restriction, we must develop different succession policies for different parishes and not be afraid to treat different parishes differently.

9. Place every pastor in a team.

Many priests function in isolation. It is a tragedy that these men are often left on their own, without other priests or deacons to support them. Many do not have lay leadership or staff around them either. Dioceses in the West, including my own, have treated international priests terribly in this regard. We are so desperate for priests who can serve that we welcome these men, give them perhaps a week's orientation, and then drive them to the middle of nowhere. We drop them off at the parish, slap them on the back, and say, "Good luck. Praying for you. See you at the Chrism Mass."

That is an extreme example, but you could almost conclude that we were deliberately setting them up to fail. This must change.

Over the years of working toward parish renewal, I have discovered that it makes a substantial difference when a pastor leads out of a team, inviting others to share in his pastoral office. When pastors do this, they no longer feel that the weight of leadership is on their shoulders alone, and they multiply their fruitfulness. At Divine Renovation ministry, our dream is for every pastor to lead out of a team and not be isolated.

That was the goal of our restructuring in the Archdiocese of Halifax-Yarmouth—even if it meant restructuring a parish so that it had multiple sites. Each parish would have at least two priests and possibly deacons and lay staff. Furthermore, each parish would have the resources to invest in their staff and create a Senior Leadership Team.

10. Provide coaching and support to pastors.

Earlier we spoke about how best to set up our pastors for fruitfulness in leadership and in ministry. In this chapter, we have examined some ways to do that from the diocesan perspective. As the Archdiocese of Halifax-Yarmouth's Episcopal Vicar for Leadership Support and Parish Renewal (I know, that is a mouthful), I have a dual task: to help pastors and parishes on the parish level (who are open to it) and to work with the bishop and diocesan staff on the diocesan level as we pursue a mission-focused approach. We are at the beginning of our journey as we restructure to get to a healthy starting point.

As mentioned in chapter seven, our new structure will allow parishes in our diocese to spend no more than 30 percent of their ordinary income to support its buildings. This way, the bulk of income will be available for the sake of mission. Part of that mission support will be invested in leadership formation of pastors. This will include the monthly formation days also spoken about in chapter seven. Those monthly morning sessions will allow pastors to hear what is on the bishop's heart, and the bishop to hear what is on his pastors' hearts. It will be a time to share what we are learning and discovering as we take this journey together.

Too often at diocesan gatherings, we do not adequately recognize that being a pastor, bearing the mantle of leadership, is a particularly challenging exercise of priestly ministry. It is indeed valuable to bring all the priests together and gather uniquely as priests, but we also need to gather uniquely as pastors. The bimonthly afternoon sessions will bring pastors and their Senior Leadership Teams together to work on team dynamics, learn about their own gifts, and discover how to work together as teams—in particular, how to have healthy conflict. We also want to equip them with the skills to engage in strategic planning and to work through difficult issues together.

Finally, we want leaders to be able to build strategic pastoral councils and mission-minded finance councils. We aim to offer an unprecedented level of support to our pastors and our lay leadership teams.

On the alternate months, when we gather all the priests, we will talk about our spiritual lives, explore how we can work together and strengthen our relationships as priests. As we have mentioned, one of the greatest threats to this journey is our isolation. Most priests are not used to working with other priests. We need to form them and help them overcome the obstacles and struggles that moving from maintenance to mission will present.

Accompanying priests in the field and supporting them is exactly what my archdiocese has asked me to do. Often my office is a coffee shop. I spend time on the road, going to meet with the priests and pastors of the diocese, sitting with them, and listening to them. Diocesan staff members are assigned in a support role to each of the twenty parishes in the archdiocese. They serve the growth and transformation of the parishes to which they have been assigned.

Imagine if every diocese in the world sought to support its priests and lay leaders in this way. We offer coaching to achieve this level of support when we work with dioceses and parishes in Divine Renovation ministry. Other dioceses are recognizing the vitality in those places, and they want to support their more mission-minded parishes and absorb some of the costs of that coaching.

Of course, dioceses do not have the resources to give that level of support to every parish—nor should they even try to. However, if each diocese can identify the 16 percent cutting edge who are ready for this journey and throw support behind them, it would maximize the chance that they would experience lasting growth and transformation.

I wanted to say a final word in this section regarding bishops. Many years ago, I was leading a retreat for a group of bishops. I was a little intimidated and very nervous—until a bishop I love and respect took me aside. He said, "James, we're flesh and blood, and, we really are just priests. So, don't be intimidated." I have never forgotten that. Just as most priests have not received any training in leadership, bishops do not emerge from ordination fully equipped to lead. In many ways, in terms of growing as leaders it's harder for bishops than for their priests. Why? Just as priests are the last ones to be told how their words and actions have impacted others, it is even worse for bishops. Just as priests experience isolation, it is even worse for bishops. My hope would be that just as priests move towards this new model of leadership, so would bishops.

Joining the Dance

A few years ago, I went on vacation with a priest friend of mine to an ancient Mediterranean city (which will remain unnamed). Throughout history, this city was a bastion of Christianity. We saw churches everywhere we turned, often with crumbling facades dating back to the sixteenth and seventeenth centuries. I noticed, however, that the doors to these historic buildings were never open.

One Sunday morning, my companion and I decided to go to Mass at a church in a residential area near our hotel. It ended up being a memorable experience—for all the wrong reasons.

When I am on vacation, I like to go undercover, so I did not vest or concelebrate the Mass, nor did my friend. Neither of us identified ourselves as priests as we joined the fourteen other people in the church that day. Though the celebrating priest was younger than we were, my friend and I were the youngest members of the assembly by far. No one welcomed us, spoke to us, handed us hymn books, or acknowledged our presence in any way, except for a few distrustful glances thrown us when we walked in, as if to ask, "What are you doing here?" When Mass concluded, there was a coffee social, but no one came up to us, introduced themselves, or interacted with us in any way, despite the fact that we were obviously tourists.

Now, when I have this kind of experience (and it is, unfortunately, not unique), I get a little upset, not because my feelings are hurt but rather because I have discovered yet another cold, inhospitable parish. It was later on, however, that the missed opportunity really hit home for me.

We went out for a walk that evening, and as we returned to the hotel, we passed by that church building again. Like many of the churches in this city, this building was built on a piazza. As we entered the square that Sunday night, we saw that there were hundreds of people all around us, the average age of whom was probably between thirty-five and forty. Some were playing music, some were in restaurants and cafes, some were gathered in small groups, and some were socializing while literally sitting on the steps of the church.

All around us were signs of life, but the church building, with its crumbling facade, remained locked. This seemed to me to be an apt metaphor for the Church in our present age. I wondered if someday soon people would walk past those crumbling facades with the same curious indifference I felt walking past Roman ruins—antiquated buildings from a far-off culture that have little meaning for my life.

As stark as that metaphor is, and as real the threat that the Church will become irrelevant to the people we are called to reach, I began this book by making a case for hope. In spite of all our struggles, all the difficulties, pain, uncertainties, and dying that the Lord is calling us to undergo, I am firmly rooted in hope—even after the experience of seeing an unwelcoming and dying church squander its incredible missionary potential. If the people in that parish, or the leaders of that diocese, could embrace a missionary vision and look outward, the Lord would multiply the work of their hands.

I have hope for many reasons, and one of them comes from St. Paul: "Hope does not disappoint, because the love of God has been poured out into our hearts through the holy Spirit that has been given to us" (Romans 5:5). Our hope will not be in vain as long as God continues to pour his love into the hearts of believers through the power, presence, and Person of the Holy Spirit. This indwelling of the Holy Spirit occurs for us at our Baptism—and God will continue to fulfill the promise he made to place his Spirit within his people (see Ezekiel 36:26). This is the reason I will always have hope.

It is also the reason why experiencing the power of the Holy Spirit is one of the three fundamental keys to the Divine Renovation model of parish renewal. The other two are the primacy of evangelization and the best of leadership. We make a distinction between these *keys* for renewal and what is *essential*.

For example, you will notice that we do not include prayer or the Eucharist in our keys, yet both are essential to fruitful parish life. We do not consider them keys because a key is designed to open a door, and in our ministry, the door we want to unlock is the one that leads from maintenance to mission. If celebrating the Eucharist and praying moved a parish into a missionary posture automatically, every parish in the world would be missionary. The parishes in that Mediterranean city, the ones with few attendees and crumbling facades, prayed and celebrated the Eucharist and yet did not seem to have a single missionary bone in their bodies.

As to the primacy of evangelization, an evangelistic culture drives all the other facets of parish life—including helping people have life-changing encounters with Jesus that lead to conversion and lives of discipleship. That kind of culture drives people into community, into discipleship processes, into serving in ministry, into a vibrant experience of the Church's sacramental life.

When we teach, we appeal to the head or the conscience: we deliver information, or we burden people with an extra helping of guilt. These have limited impact. But when we evangelize, we speak to the heart, and it is in the heart that conversion occurs.

As to the Church's urgent need for authentic leadership, I will not delve into this any further, because it has been the subject of much of this book. However, that third key—experiencing the power of the Holy Spirit—deserves attention as I conclude this book.

An Inside View

When we talk about experiencing the power of the Holy Spirit, here is what we are talking about: experiencing the power of the Holy Spirit in such a way that it leads to a tangible encounter with God that changes us. We are not talking about a reliance on the Holy Spirit or an appeal to the Holy Spirit; we are essentially talking about a lived experience—a religious experience, if you will.

When we use the language of experience in the Church, however, people get nervous. For nearly her entire existence, the Church has existed in the culture of Christendom, and in that culture, the focus has been on the Church as a proclaimer of truth. We perceive truth through the use of our intellect, and so the intellectual dimension of faith has been primary. We were and still are suspicious of religious experience. In fact, a desire for religious experience has long been seen as a sign of spiritual immaturity, something that people should grow out of as they mature.

Certainly, mature relationships, such as those in marriage, cannot be grounded solely on an *experience* of love. Love is an act of the will. Nevertheless, no matter how mature your marriage might be, it has to have an experiential component from time to time, or it will not last.

We still operate out of the Christendom mindset in this regard, proposing universal truth and remaining suspicious of religious experience. Here lies the challenge, for people have become suspicious of universal truth claims but yearn for religious experience. Scripture, Church history and teaching, and the witness of Christians through the ages, however, confirm that God is always ready to draw us to himself in an experiential way. In effect, the Church has precisely what people are looking for.

The experience of being filled with the Holy Spirit is critical for three reasons. One, to open us more fully to the life of grace. Only when baptized believers are fully mobilized and living the life of grace will parishes, dioceses, and the Church truly be the hands and feet of Jesus in the world. Second, the indwelling of the Holy Spirit is essential for the Church's unity, and third, the indwelling of the Holy Spirit is essential for her mission. As Jesus prayed to his Father,

> I pray not only for them, but also for those who will believe in me through their word, so that they may all be one, as you, Father, are in me and I in you, that they also may be in us, that the world may believe that you sent me. (John 17:20-21)

Our ability to impact the world through our mission is grounded in our experience of unity. The Christian community is called to live out the same unity that exists within the Trinity.

That might sound like a heady statement, so let us break it down a bit. The theologians of the early Church were fascinated by the questions of how the Persons of the Trinity were distinct from one another and how God was actually experienced in the life of believers and in salvation history. In the third and fourth centuries, theologians began to shift their focus to explore the inner workings of the Trinity and the interrelation between Father, Son, and Holy Spirit. As a result, theologians today speak about the Trinity by using two distinct terms: "the immanent Trinity" and "the economic Trinity."

"The immanent Trinity" is a phrase used to talk about God's inner life. When we talk about the immanent Trinity, we are discussing the being and essence of God. The economic Trinity is, in simplified terms, the external work of the Trinity in history.

As many of the early Church Fathers reflected on the interaction of the three Persons of the Trinity, moving from the economic to the immanent Trinity, they wanted to explain the essential union and distinction between Father, Son, and Holy Spirit. To do that, they started to use the term *perichoresis*, which comes from two Greek words, *peri* (meaning "around") and *chorein* ("to contain," "go forward," or "make room for").

To better understand this word, we can look at a word in English that comes from the same root as *chorein*, such as "choreography." *Choreo* means "the dance," and *graphein* means "to write." Choreography is the writing or construction of a dance. *Perichoresis*, therefore, at its roots, means "the dance around."

The Church Fathers spoke of the relationship between the Trinitarian Persons not as static or fixed but rather as a dynamic dance in which Father, Son, and Holy Spirit constantly move (or dance) around one another in absolute harmony. As the Church's focus became increasingly fixed on the immanent life of God and away from the question of how believers experience God, a conceptual distance grew between God and his people. The life of the Trinity might, at best, be perceived as a dance, but Christians were simply observers of the dance, far removed from the beauty and power of Trinitarian life. This shift had an impact on Christian spirituality and, I believe, on Christian mission.

Glory

We see this shift in the shape of the doxology that has dominated Western Christianity. "What is a doxology?" you might be asking. A "doxology" means simply a "word of praise" or "word of glory." The Glory Be prayer is a doxology: "Glory be to the Father, and to the Son, and to the Holy Spirit, as it was in the beginning, is now, and ever shall be, world without end." Many hymns in the Christian tradition reflect this doxology, sung to each of the Persons of the Trinity. One of my all-time favorites is the hymn "Praise God from Whom All Blessings Flow." Singing this hymn—a cappella or accompanied by pipe organ, guitar, or keyboard—always makes the hair on the back of my head stand up.

Such doxologies are absolutely beautiful expressions of prayer. Think, however, of the core dynamic that we have just explored, where the believer stands outside the dance and gives praise to the three Persons of the Trinity. Contrast that dynamic, represented by this form of doxology, with the most ancient doxology used by the Church: "Through him, with him, and in him, in the unity of the Holy Spirit, all glory and honor is yours, almighty Father, forever and ever. Amen."

Both doxologies are familiar to us—though we may never have noticed the difference between the two. This last doxology, preserved in the Church's Eucharistic Prayer, does not simply give glory to the Father, to the Son, and to the Holy Spirit. Rather we give glory to the Father through the Son, with the Son, and in the Son, all within the unity of the Holy Spirit. This doxology is not about standing outside the immanent Trinity in awe and praising God for the divine and eternal dance. This is a song, or a cry, of praise that could only be sounded from within the dance.

In other words, as sons and daughters of God, we are not called to stand at a distance and observe, praise, and contemplate. Rather God invites us into the Dance of Divine Life. In the midst of that dance— through the Son, and with the Son, and in the Son—we give glory to God the Father in the unity of the Holy Spirit. We are part of the dance!

This doxology reflects the intimacy with God that Paul writes about in his Letter to the Romans: through the Holy Spirit, our spirit cries out, "Abba, Father" (see Romans 8:15-16). It is within the Dance of God that we experience the fullness of the life of grace. It is from within this dance that we experience unity among ourselves. Finally, it is from within this Dance of the Trinity that we receive power to accomplish our mission.

It is not a coincidence that the doxology of the immanent Trinity, whereby we gaze upon God from a distance, became the doxology of Christendom. The doxology of the economic Trinity, which expresses how God is experienced by the believer and is at work in the world, is the doxology of the original, apostolic missionary age of the Church, sung from the divine dance floor.

Too often we have reduced the lived experience of Christianity to be about *God with us*. However, the point of God's being with us was that he could be *in us*. When we experience God in us, we are led to the doxology of the economic Trinity. Jesus says to his disciples, "I tell you the truth, it is better for you that I go. For if I do not go, the Advocate will not come to you. But if I go, I will send him to you" (John 16:7). This is counterintuitive; it sounds almost heretical. Why would Jesus stop being with us—unless it led to his being in us?

Many Christians have experienced Christian life as only being about the *proximity* of God. Sometimes it feels as if God is close to us, and other times distant. When this becomes our entire experience, I am afraid that we have missed the point. Jesus first came to be with us so that he could be in us. The fulfillment of Christmas, therefore, is not Easter but Pentecost.

Think about that!

The birth of the Church did not happen at Christmas. It did not happen on Holy Thursday, when Christ gave us the Eucharist. It did not happen on Good Friday, when blood and water flowed from the broken, lifeless body of Jesus. It did not happen on Easter, when he rose from the dead. The birth of the Church occurred at Pentecost, when the Spirit came in power and poured himself out to dwell within believers.

We know that the first followers of Jesus "devoted themselves with one accord to prayer" in the upper room (Acts 1:14), but something beyond prayer happened on the Day of Pentecost, and the Church was born. We know too that the Church must be reborn in every generation. We have always been only one generation from extinction, and today we experience this more acutely than perhaps at any other time.

If we wish to see the evangelization of the nations, if we wish to fulfill the Great Commission that the Lord has given the Church, then we need to experience a continual renewal of Pentecost. The Church is only driven from the upper room by the power of the Holy Spirit; without this animating movement of the Spirit, we lock our doors in fear and stay focused on ourselves. Celebrating the Eucharist and praying in our church buildings is not enough. Those things, as essential as they are, will never mobilize us. We must emerge from our comfortable resting places, driven by the Spirit's power.

A Church that is sent by the Holy Spirit but does not continually cooperate with the Holy Spirit will eventually return to the upper room and lock the doors. Inwardly focused communities, afraid to venture forth out of fear, need the fire of Pentecost, the experience of *dunamis*: the explosive, dynamic, life-changing power of God promised by Jesus: "You are witnesses of these things. And [behold] I am sending the promise of my Father upon you; but stay in the city until you are clothed with power from on high" (Luke 24:48-49). We experience this power when we allow ourselves to be caught up in the great Dance of the Trinity.

We might be tempted to think that good strategy, good organizational structure, and the topics we explored in this book are all that we need. As necessary as they are, they will never be enough. Jesus commanded his disciples not to leave the city until they received the power of the Holy Spirit, because he knew that fruitfulness in mission can only be accomplished through the power of God.

St. Paul, in what scholars consider to be his first extant letter and the oldest book of the New Testament, reminded the Church of Thessalonika that "our gospel did not come to you in word alone, but also in power [*dunamis*] and in the holy Spirit and [with] much conviction" (1 Thessalonians 1:5).

I have used this image of dancing to talk about Trinitarian theology, but I have to be honest: I have never been much of a dancer. In fact, mention the word "dance," and I recall memories of awkward high school dances and 80s dance moves. I generally avoid dance floors for fear of being pulled off my chair by some well-meaning woman. One of the great and lasting advantages of celibacy is that I have avoided dancing for much of my life.

When we dance, however, especially with a partner, on some level we surrender. There must be a yielding of the will and an openness to let the music carry us. To dance with authenticity and presence in the moment, we must let go of self-consciousness and surrender ourselves, allowing the song to touch our whole person: body, mind, and heart.

This surrender is also essential if we are to respond to the Lord's invitation to the Divine Dance at this critical moment in our history. Right now the Lord is asking us, his bride, what we will choose. Will we choose our model or his mission?

Entering the dance means surrendering our worry about what preferences, customs, and human traditions we might lose. Only when we make that surrender can we authentically live out the essential nature of our faith for the sake of our world today. We must allow the Holy Spirit to touch our minds, hearts, and bodies, so that we may be filled with God's love and enter into the eternal dance of the Trinity, ready to help others experience the same thing.

This surrender is essential if we are to respond to the Lord's invitation to the Divine Dance at this critical moment in our history. The doxology of the Dance of God is also the doxology of the Eucharist. It is through living out the eternal mystery of the Eucharist—the death and resurrection of Jesus Christ—that the Church will find this path to new life in the power of the Holy Spirit. This means the Eucharist is not just something we do, participate in, or unite ourselves to. We must become a true Eucharistic Church: a Church that ceases to cling to particular ways of doing things; a Church that is broken and given up for the sake of the salvation of the world.

The bride belongs on the dance floor.

"The Spirit and the bride say, 'Come.' Let the hearer say, 'Come.'" (Revelation 22:17).

Notes

1. Abraham Heschel, *The Prophets* (New York: Harper Perennial Modern Classics, 2001), xxiv.

2. cf. Pope Francis, *Evangelii Gaudium* [The Joy of the Gospel], 26, 31, 32, http://www.vatican.va/content/francesco/en/apost_exhortations/documents/papa-francesco_esortazione-ap_20131124_evangelii-gaudium.html.

3. In the original Spanish, the document reads, "y toda estructura eclesial se convierta," which can be translated "and all ecclesial structure convert." This term is a direct reference to the 2007 Aparecida Document of the Latin American Bishops.

4. *Evangelii Gaudium*, 27.

5. Lydia Saad, "Catholics' Church Attendance Resumes Downward Slide," Gallup, April 9, 2018, news.gallup.com/poll/232226/church-attendance-among-catholics-resumes-downward-slide.aspx.

6. Pew Research Center, Survey of US Catholics in America's Changing Religious Landscape, 2015, https://www.pewforum.org/2015/09/02/u-s-catholics-open-to-non-traditional-families/.

7. Pew Research Center, "7 Facts About American Catholics," October 10, 2018, https://www.pewresearch.org/fact-tank/2018/10/10/7-facts-about-american-catholics/.

8. Michael Swan, "Mass Attendance in Canada More Than Doubles on Christmas Day, Survey Finds," *The Catholic Register*, December 20, 2016, https://www.catholicregister.org/faith/item/23875-mass-attendance-in-canada-more-than-doubles-on-christmas-day-survey-finds.

9. Harvard Divinity School, "Catholicism in France," rlp.hds.harvard.edu/faq/catholicism-france, examining "Le Catholicisme en France en 2010," by the Institut d'Études Opinion et Marketing en France et à l'International.

10. "Six Things to Know about Catholicism in Germany," May 11, 2018, The Local, thelocal.de/20180511/6-things-to-know-about-catholicism-in-germany.

11. Matthew Gambino, "Half of Catholics Attending Mass 28 Years Ago No Longer Do, Figures Show," September 5, 2019, catholicphilly.com/2019/09/our-changing-church/half-of-catholics-attending-mass-28-years-ago-no-longer-do-figures-show-2/.

12. Diocese of Orange Strategic Plan 2018-2023, 5, rcbo.org/wp-content/uploads/Diocese-of-Orange-Diocesan-Strategic-Plan-Executive-Summary-Update.pdf.

13. Rev. Dr. Neil Elliot, Statistics Report for the House of Bishops, https://www.anglicansamizdat.net/wordpress/wp-content/uploads/2019/10/Report-to-HoB-2017-stats.docx.

14. Pope Francis, *Evangelii Gaudium*, 85.

15. Joshua J. McElwee, "Catholicism can and must change, Francis forcefully tells Italian church gathering," *National Catholic Reporter*, November 10, 2015, https://www.ncronline.org/news/vatican/catholicism-can-and-must-change-francis-forcefully-tells-italian-church-gathering

16. J. R. R. Tolkien, *The Fellowship of the Ring,* bk. 1, chap. 2, "The Shadow of the Past."

17. Thom S. Rainer, "Six Stages of a Dying Church," June 12, 2017, https:// https:// thomrainer.com/2017/06/six-stages-dying-church/.

18. Carey Nieuwhof, "15 Characteristics of Today's Unchurched Person," https:// careynieuwhof.com/15-characteristics-of-todays-unchurched-person/.

19. Fulton J. Sheen, *Old Errors and New Labels* (New York, NY: The Century Company, 1931), 79.

20. Pope Francis, Address to the Leaders of CELAM, July 18, 2013, 4, http://www. vatican.va/content/francesco/en/speeches/2013/july/documents/papa-frances-co_20130728_gmg-celam-rio.html.

21. see *Catechism,* 863

22. see *Catechism,* 858

23. 5th CELAM General Conference, Aparecida Document, 6.2.1e, https://www. celam.org/aparecida/Ingles.pdf.

24. In fact, Jesus is described as "sent" in the New Testament fifty-one times.

25. Pope Paul VI, *Evangelii Nuntiandi* [Evangelization in the Modern World], 75, http://www.vatican.va/content/paul-vi/en/apost_exhortations/documents/hf_p-vi_exh_19751208_evangelii-nuntiandi.html.

26. Pope Francis, *Evangelii Gaudium,* 27.

27. Pope St. Paul VI, *Evangelii Nuntiandi,* 63.

28. John Ortberg, *Who Is This Man? The Unpredictable Impact of the Inescapable Jesus* (Grand Rapids, MI: Zondervan, 2012), https://www.goodreads.com/ quotes/680427-leadership-is-the-art-of-disappointing-people-at-a-rate.

29. I have been influenced here by a talk I heard Carey Nieuwhof give several years ago that helped bring clarity to may own experience and thinking at the time.

30. Martin Luther King Jr., "A Proper Sense of Priorities," February 6, 1968, Washington, D.C., https://pnhp.org/news/martin-luther-king-jr-a-proper-sense-of-priorities/.

31. Liturgy of the Hours, English translation by the International Consultation on English Texts.

32. A variation of this quote has been attributed to several people including engineer, statistician, professor, author, lecturer, and management consultant W. Edwards Deming; Paul Batalden, a pediatrician, medical director, author, and professor who teaches on health care systems; and Donald Berwick, author and former president and CEO of the Institute for Healthcare Improvement.

33. Smithsonian, *The Civil War, A Visual History* (New York, NY: DK Publishing, 2015), 334.

34. John Maynard Keynes, *The General Theory of Employment, Interest, and Money* (Amherst, NY: Prometheus Books, 1997), xii.

35. Gideon Walter , Mike Shanahan , Martin Reeves, and Kaelin Goulet, "Why Transformation Needs a Second Chapter," Boston Consulting Group, October 21, 2013, https://www.bcg.com/publications/2013/transformation-growth-why-transformation-needs-second-chapter-lean-not-yet-mean.aspx.

36. This data comes from Peter Jesserer Smith, "Pittsburgh Diocese Reorganizes Parishes for Future Evangelization," *National Catholic Register*, September 29, 2017, https://www.ncregister.com/daily-news/pittsburgh-diocese-reorganizes-parishes-for-future-evangelization.

37. Email from Alana Draus, Senior Gallup Consultant, February 3, 2020.

38. This is the sense of the translation of Ephesians 4:11-12 used for Evening Prayer in the *Breviary* for the Common of Apostles. It uses the original 1970 version of the *New American Bible*. This mistranslation has since been corrected in a completely new translation published in 1986, but still remains in the *Breviary* used in North America and in many other English-speaking countries.

39. Tony Morgan, "10 Signs That You're 'the Boss' . . . but Not the Leader," November 5, 2018, https://tonymorganlive.com/2018/11/05/boss-not-leader-team-health/.

40. Kenneth H. Blanchard, https://www.goodreads.com/quotes/129514-the-key-to-successful-leadership-is-influence-not-authority.

41. John C. Maxwell, *Becoming a Person of Influence: How to Positively Impact the Lives of Others* (New York: HarperCollins Leadership, 1997), 107.

42. Rick Warren, Twitter, November 11, 2013.

43. Patrick Lencioni, https://www.youtube.com/watch?v=6pKKYDoHxLs.

44. Image by Eileen Moore, who was chair of the Saint Benedict Parish Pastoral Council during this restructuring process.

45. T. E. Deal and A. A. Kennedy, *Corporate Cultures: The Rites and Rituals of Corporate Life* (Harmondsworth, UK: Penguin Books, 1982; Cambridge, MA: Perseus Books, 2000), cited in C. Cancialosi, "What Is Organizational Culture," July 17, 2017, https://gothamculture.com/what-is-organizational-culture-definition/.

46. Vatican Council II, *Sacrosanctum Concilium* [Constitution on the Sacred Liturgy], 14, https://www.vatican.va/archive/hist_councils/ii_vatican_council/documents/vat-ii_const_19631204_sacrosanctum-concilium_en.html.

47. The Marriage Course, developed by Nicky and Sila Lee, is not only a great tool for enriching marriages but also a great pre-evangelization program. Find out more about this high quality (and free) resource at themarriagecourse.org

48. Dale Sellers, "5 Reasons Churches Avoid Developing a Strategy," The Unstuck Group, September 19, 2017, https://theunstuckgroup.com/2017/09/reasons-churches-avoid-strategy/.

49. For more on the necessity of pastoral planning from Canon Law and Church documents, I highly recommend John A. Renken, "Pastoral Councils: "Pastoral Planning and Dialogue Among the People of God," The Jurist 53 (1993), 132-154

50. This chapter was developed in cooperation with my colleague John Stevens at the Archdiocese of Halifax-Yarmouth.

Acknowledgments

This book has made a case for the necessity of teamwork for the greater glory of God. I am pleased to confess that this is also true of the book that sought to make said case. This book may bear my name, but it truly is the work of a team. First of all, I wish to thank the members of those teams who helped teach and form me over the last ten years. I would like to thank the parish staff, ministry leaders, and parishioners of Saint Benedict Parish who helped to teach me about leadership and parish renewal. Thank you for your patience with me and, as was frequently necessary, your forgiveness. I wish to thank the staff of Divine Renovation ministry and all the pastors and lay leaders throughout the world we have been blessed to learn from. I wish to thank the members of the diocesan staff of the Archdiocese of Halifax-Yarmouth, and my bishop over these last thirteen years, Archbishop Anthony Mancini. Thank you for your vision, permission, and support. I would like to thank my brother priests in my diocese who have put up with me over the years and with whom I am journeying on this great adventure of diocesan renewal.

More immediately, I wish to thank the team from The Word Among Us. To Jeff Smith, president of The Word Among Us, thank you for your gentle and discerning wisdom. To Beth McNamara, thank you for always having time to speak with me, and for your gentle and persistent encouragement. To Deacon Keith Strohm who did most of the leg work in the first edit of the original brain dump, and kept on working on subsequent drafts. I will miss our frequent chats and good laughs about the typos. I hope my voice no longer haunts you at night. Thank you to Cindy Cavnar who took a good manuscript and made it great. William Ockham has nothing on you! To Jessica Montgomery, for your attention to detail and infinite patience with last-minute changes, and to all the other team members with whom I had no direct contact.

I wish to thank my colleagues who reviewed the almost final manuscript and were able to help me say what I really meant: Dr. David Deane from Atlantic School of Theology, my colleague John Stevens from the Archdiocese of Halifax-Yarmouth, Fr. Simon Lobo from Saint

Benedict Parish, and Ron Huntley and Fiona O'Reilly from Divine Renovation Ministry. Thank you to all who offered an endorsement for this book and suffered through the unedited version. Your reward will be great in heaven. Finally, to my almost new bishop, Archbishop Brian Dunn, who has testified to the fact that, as irritating as I may be, I am not a heretic.

Finally, I thank the Lord for his gracious mercy, for his infinite patience, and for his amazing love. He is the proto-missionary and the greatest servant leader.

Fr. James Mallon

Divine Renovation Ministry

At Divine Renovation ministry, we come alongside leaders in their work to bring their parish or diocese on mission. Whether you're new to the journey or if you've been on it for years, our team is ready to join with you in bringing your diocese or parish from maintenance to mission. Reach out to connect, and learn more at divinerenovation.org.

www.divinerenovation.org